Human Development in Iraq 1950–1990

This systematic evaluation of Iraq's political economy and human development offers a complex and sophisticated analysis of Iraq's recent history. Focussing on the period from 1950 up to the Gulf War in 1990, the book brings an understanding of how development has been shaped or constrained in this much misunderstood country.

The author employs the human development paradigm to link human development and human rights to the analysis of political economy. The resulting scholarship, on income and investment, education and health, the status of women, and human rights, presents a nuanced, balanced – but critical – appraisal of the complex interrelationships between economic growth and development, and illustrates the fragility of that development, especially when political institutions fail to keep up with the rapid expansion in human capabilities.

Providing the historical analysis needed to understand Iraq's current political situation, this book will be of great interest to scholars of development studies, Iraq, and political economy.

Bassam Yousif is an associate professor of economics at Indiana State University. He has written extensively on and advised about the economic development and political economy of Iraq.

Human Development in Iraq
1950–1990

Bassam Yousif

 Routledge
Taylor & Francis Group

LONDON AND NEW YORK

First published 2012 by Routledge

2 Park Square, Milton Park, Abingdon, Oxfordshire OX14 4RN
52 Vanderbilt Avenue, New York, NY 10017

Routledge is an imprint of the Taylor & Francis Group, an Informa business

First issued in paperback 2019

Typeset in Sabon by PDQ Typesetting Ltd.

British Library Cataloguing in Publication Data
A catalogue record for this book is available from the British Library

Library of Congress Cataloging-in-Publication Data
Yousif, Bassam.

Human development in Iraq: 1950–1990/Bassam Yousif.

p.cm. – (Routledge studies in Middle Eastern economies)

Includes bibliographical references and index.

ISBN 978-0-415-78263-0 (hardback) – ISBN 978-0-203-63194-2 (eBook) 1. Iraq–Social conditions–20th century. 2. Iraq–Economic conditions–20th century. 3. Iraq–Politics and government–20th century. I. Title.

HN670.A8Y68 2011

306.09567–dc23

2011023140

ISBN: 978-0-415-78263-0 (hbk)
ISBN: 978-0-367-86619-8 (pbk)

Contents

Acknowledgments

With great pleasure, I acknowledge the support that I have received in the research and writing of this book.

Thanks are due to Professor Keith Griffin who supervised the project in its earliest forms at the University of California, Riverside. His encouragement and guidance were invaluable. I would also like to thank Professors Paul Burkett and Donald Richards for their feedback on portions of the book. I am indebted to The American Academic Research Institute in Iraq and Indiana State University for funding portions of this research. Several (mostly anonymous) manuscript reviewers gave useful feedback. Outstanding among these was Professor Karen Pfeifer, who deserves special thanks for her careful, meticulous reading and discerning suggestions.

I am forever appreciative of the moral and practical support of my family, notably my wife who read numerous drafts of the book. Finally, Ms. Leslie Brown's assistance in editing and research proved invaluable. Any remaining errors or omissions are, of course, my own.

1 Human development theory and Iraq's developmental story

Introduction

This book presents the story of development in Iraq from 1950 to 1990, viewed through the lens of human development theory. The beginning date is chosen because most economic and social data first become available around that time, and the last date is selected because it corresponds to Iraq's invasion of Kuwait and the imposition of crippling economic sanctions, followed by a devastating war in 1991. The interval thus represents a period of relative stability in which the development experience of the country can be evaluated.

The human development paradigm is used because, as I argue below, it represents the best way to assess development in a country such as Iraq and also because I seek to explore the linkages between the various aspects of development that only an evaluation of human development can provide. This is the first systematic study of human development in Iraq and it aims to complement the existing literature on Iraq's political economy. At the same time, this book re-evaluates some of the conclusions of that literature. The ultimate objective is to present a careful and nuanced view of Iraq's development story.

The point of departure of the work is the notion that development (broadly defined) is fundamentally about expanding "what people are capable of doing or being."[1] That is, do people live long, well-nourished lives? Do they have the education to become full members of society? Do they have access to paid employment? Do they control their political lives?

Although these concerns of what people can and are permitted to do may seem obvious (even banal), they stand in contrast to the historically overriding theme in development economics, that of the growth of money-metric indicators, such as per capita income or GDP – which as we shall see has characterized most of the scholarship of the economic development of Iraq to date. Amartya Sen has called this growth-centric outlook, which has dominated development thinking since World War II, the "hard-nosed" or "fierce" view of development.[2] According to this "fierce" outlook, "soft" concerns such as low levels of literacy, high infant mortality, and the denial of political rights and freedoms in poor countries are secondary to the first priority of capital accumulation and economic growth. For according to growth-centric thinking, it is only through growth that poverty and low living standards are defeated.

The emphasis on growth was not unique to a particular school within development economics but pervaded the entire discipline. Differences in politics or methods certainly existed, but practically no one questioned the centrality of economic growth to development. As a case in point, while the analytically distinct theories of Hirschman, Nurkse, and Rostow were all concerned to some extent with social and economic transformation, prominence was given to problems of investment and economic growth as obstacles to such transformation.[3] The logic is understandable: high savings finance greater investment, which, in turn, increases income in the future; alternatively high growths in incomes generate more savings and investment, which fuel economic growth in the future.

Indeed, any move outside the cycle of income, savings, and investment are seen to impede growth and development. Excessive spending on consumption or, for example, on education and health are deemed to be undesirable – even though they promote equality and social welfare in the short run. This is because such expenditures were considered to hinder capital accumulation and long-term growth in income, retarding the social development that was thought to issue – almost automatically – from higher income.[4] As a result, economic growth and social welfare (or equity) were often viewed as fundamentally incompatible goals, at least for developing nations. In contrast, developed countries, because they are rich, could "afford" to sacrifice growth to obtain greater equity. More recent scholarship has emphasized the positive effects on economic growth from the egalitarian redistribution of income or assets, although the emphasis is still placed on income and output.[5]

Not only was higher income a main objective of development, it was also considered to be its foremost marker. Wealth signified arrival to the advanced state among nations. Countries that were developed socially and politically were also rich; poor countries, in contrast, were backward and underdeveloped. This was reflected in the practice of ranking of countries by income and their corresponding classification into developed or developing nation, as exemplified by the annual *World Development Report* published by the World Bank since 1978.

Even so, it would be a mistake to view the relegation of soft interests to the aim of economic growth as necessarily unsympathetic to the poverty and distress of people in developing countries. Rather, the privileging of growth came from a "sad acceptance" that growth was necessary for improved welfare, not an "admiration" of the harsh road to development as such.[6] Thus when the importance of "human capital" was beginning to be recognized, the concern was not primarily with how better education and health could improve human lives but rather how enhanced health and education, as inputs into the production process, could accelerate the rate of growth of output.[7]

Yet it was soon recognized, as Keith Griffin and John Knight state, that the supply of "goods may provide the basis for a high standard of living, but they are not in themselves constituents of it."[8] In fact, while a general correlation between income per capita and outcomes in social development, *vis-à-vis* life expectancy or infant mortality, is easy to establish, departures from this pattern were quite common. Poor countries often did as well or better than their rich counterparts in terms of reducing malnourishment, promoting literacy and extending life – that is, in enlarging what human beings can do and be. Writing in the early 1980s, Amartya Sen observed that, in terms of social development, Sri Lanka and China performed as well as Brazil, Mexico, and South Korea, much richer economies.[9]

Income and wellbeing

The use of money-metric indicators of development has its attractions. First, it is plausible to suppose that a person whose income is rising experiences higher wellbeing or welfare, which on a societal level, translates into development. Second, the method is relatively easy to apply in practice: national income statistics are established economic variables and (usually) widely available. Nevertheless, using the approach to assess development suffers from some theoretical limitations.

The underlying assumption of this method is that growth in per capita income enables the purchase of commodities, which in turn results in higher levels of utility or wellbeing, typically defined in term of "pleasure" or "desire-fulfillment."[10] Higher levels of income increase the command over commodities, which enhance welfare; or, alternatively, higher levels of income allow one to fulfill more of one's desires. Yet, there is no way to objectively assess the utility that different people derive from consumption (even from an identical consumption bundle) because utility is a subjective (theoretical) construct that cannot be measured or used for interpersonal comparisons.

Moreover, desires are not independent of one's economic or social condition but are formed in the context of that condition. The curbing of desires to realistic levels is one way for a deprived person to cope with miserable living conditions and derive satisfaction from small comforts. As a result, a highly deprived person might not consider himself "badly off in terms of the mental metric of utility, if the hardship is accepted with non-grumbling resignation."[11] According to the desire fulfillment calculus, an objectively less deprived person may derive less pleasure from life and have fewer of their high desires and expectations fulfilled than the impoverished individual who has learned to restrict their wants. Perversely, the rundown person would be classified as better off. These issues concerning pleasure and desire fulfillment arise in part because of the inability of utility theory to accommodate interpersonal comparisons of utility. Wellbeing comparisons between distinct persons or classes are thus not possible.

There are practical difficulties as well associated with using money-metric measures to assess development. Aggregate income variables, such as GDP per capita, fail to reflect social divisions or inequalities. There is then no guarantee that an expansion in per capita income would benefit the majority of the population, let alone the poorest segments. Also, an expansion in income cannot satisfy some wants, namely those that cannot be purchased. An increase in per capita income may enhance the command over what can be bought and sold in the market, but does nothing, by itself, to reduce pollution, improve governance, or promote human rights.

Human development

Although it first received attention in the 1980s, the "human development" or "capabilities" paradigm has deep intellectual roots. Aristotle noted that "wealth is evidently not the good we are seeking, for it is merely useful for something else."[12] Likewise, the concern with fulfilling human capabilities is found in the writings of Adam Smith[13] and Karl Marx.[14]

As noted, the focus of the human development paradigm is on what a person is capable of "doing and being."[15] These doings and beings (also called "functionings") reflect the wellbeing of the person, but are distinct from the commodities that may (or may not) be utilized to achieve the functionings. The set of doings and beings (also called the "capability set") represents the individual's freedom (or capability) to achieve various functionings.

This freedom may be viewed in two ways. First, to the extent that it is important in itself, the entire capability set is relevant in assessing a person's position, even though only a particular alternative will be chosen and its outcome observed. Alternatives that are not chosen are consequently relevant in evaluating one's freedom. In this formulation, if a person does not attend university, knowledge about whether they had the opportunity (or capability) to attend is nonetheless relevant.

Second, freedom may also be viewed as an instrument in the sense that it affords one the ability to attain various functionings. In that sense, the capability set is valued, mainly because it contains the valued alternative.[16] The attainment of certain functionings may also work to expand freedom in related dimensions. For example, freedom to read and write is surely valuable in its own terms (intrinsically), but may also enhance one's capability to participate in the political life of the community, acting (instrumentally) to expand one's freedom to participate in political life.

In practice, the intrinsic view of freedom is more difficult to apply, since data about alternatives that are not chosen are difficult to obtain. Statistics on secondary education enrollment, for example, reflect whether or not parents send their children to secondary school, but do not tell us whether or not secondary education is an alternative for those who do not attend school. The instrumental view of freedom is easier to apply in practice.

We run into a question here over who decides whether or not an alternative is "valued." This is an important issue on at least two levels. First, to a large extent, desires or expectations are not exogenous but are socially determined. People who live in more basic conditions are likely, correspondingly, to value more basic functionings. As noted, a thoroughly reduced and impoverished person may value material survival only, not education or rights against arbitrary arrest, even though these would undoubtedly expand their capabilities and better they and their family's living condition. In counting as valuable the higher functionings of education and health, would not the researcher be projecting their (own) valued functionings?

This question is not unique to human development. Money-metric measures of development implicitly assume that people care about only what they can purchase. In another respect, however, the hypothetical underscores the distinction between the human development approach and the desire-fulfillment variant of utility theory. The human development metric, namely the expansion (or contraction) of human freedom, and the psychological metric of utility need not be correlated. Human development considers freedom from illiteracy and disease to be intrinsically desirable; even if the reduced person's pressing commitments in their daily life repress these desires. The restriction of desires to attainable levels and the consequent acceptance of one's reduced condition do not nullify the presence of objective deprivation.[17]

Second, the global corollary to this is the notion that the freedoms and values espoused by human development are alien to developing countries. This view holds that human development sustains liberal (or Western) and even neoliberal concerns, which amount to a cultural or ideological imposition on developing countries. The promotion of political freedoms and rights, implied in human development, is sometimes criticized as an artificial and illegitimate import from the liberal West – alien to cultures that place greater emphasis of the values of loyalty and discipline.[18] This claim is discussed in detail later. The claim that human development promotes neoliberal concerns is odd, however, given that the method would view the social development that has occurred in socialist Cuba or the Indian state of Kerala with approval. In mitigation though, the view of human development as a tool for the promotion of the neoliberal agenda was a comment on the *Arab Human Development Report*, not the paradigm as such.[19]

Sharath Srinavasan criticizes the human development paradigm (or rather Amartya Sen's presentation of it) for its failure to specify the capabilities that should matter more than others.[20] Others point to the possible tension in the promotion of some freedoms and the exercise of other rights: on these occasions suppression or surrender of rights rather than their exercise may be required to avoid conflict.[21]

Returning to the issue of putting into practice the human development paradigm, it is possible to imagine instances in which the observed functioning fails to reflect the various alternatives contained in the capability set. For example, a wealthy person who fasts and a poor person who cannot afford to buy food will express identical functionings, even though the former starves out of choice while the latter starves out of poverty.[22] In such a case, the observed functioning may need to be supplemented by other data so as to give a more accurate impression of the alternatives that are available. Or it may be beneficial to distinguish between different classes of functionings. For example, fasting may be considered a "refined" functioning, whereas being adequately nourished is a basic functioning.[23] Such situations are perhaps rare, but to the extent that the attainment of some functionings affects one's position with respect to other freedoms, the informational content of the observed functioning will still be valuable. Fasting and famine, although quite distinct, may nonetheless have important implications on health outcomes.

There is of course no guarantee that freedoms will be utilized in the same way by different people, or even used at all. One person might express their education by becoming involved in community life; another might not. And some functionings are difficult to evaluate, even when they are observed. For example, whether an individual is adequately nourished or not depends not only on nutritional intake but also on their capacity to transform calories into nourishment. Consequently, caloric intake will reflect the level of nourishment only imperfectly, even though the study of caloric intake through time is useful to indicate changed food entitlement.

This ambiguity over outcomes is not unique to the capabilities approach and has its parallel in utility theory. Two people with identical preferences may not derive equal utilities from the same consumption bundle because they may have different utility functions. That is, their rates of transformation from commodities to utility may be different.[24] In general, therefore, the study of achieved functionings has its advantages, even though it may be based on data that are insufficient to attach an intrinsic importance to a specific freedom, as the example above in reference to food intake illustrates.

Of course, were there something resembling a tight one-to-one correspondence between per capita incomes and capabilities, the measurement of income would be (although distinct in theory) indistinguishable in practice from the measurement of capabilities. But that close correlation between income and capabilities does not exist, and there are many instances of wide disparities between the level of per capita income and the corresponding richness of human lives, as expressed in various functionings.[25]

In sum, the capabilities approach offers some advantages in comparison with a traditional concentration on income. Conceptually, the approach permits the study of a person's wellbeing through time and is able to accommodate interpersonal comparisons. Also, the main difficulties encountered in the human development approach are present in the traditional method, which says more about our inability as researchers to quantify human behavior than the viability of either method.

The human development model and Iraq

The human development approach is both theoretically convincing and provides the best way to evaluate development in Iraq: an oil-exporting country with a traditionally unbalanced and inequitable economy; a history of social cleavages; and a repressive polity. In oil economies, a rise in the price or export volume of oil translates at once into an increase in national income, regardless of any change in wellbeing. That is, the use of money-metric indicators alone might give a misleading impression of development. And, such an analysis would have little to say about outcomes in education, health, developments concerning women, or changes regarding political freedoms. Yet these issues are especially pertinent to understanding Iraq's development experience, given the historically unbalanced and inequitable nature of the economy, extant social cleavages and autocratic governance. It is human development theory that can provide a more complete and nuanced picture of Iraq's development.

In filling in this picture, this work seeks to complement and extend the work of Abbas Alnasrawi, Hanna Batatu, and Marion Farouk-Sluglett and Peter Sluglett on Iraq's development and political economy. Alnasrawi's *The Economy of Iraq* and his follow-up *Iraq's Burdens* are outstanding works about Iraq's economy for the period before the 1990s.[26] They provide a detailed study of Iraq's development using the traditional modes of assessment: economic aggregates such as gross domestic product, physical capital formation, and growth in consumption as well as analysis of Iraq's oil sector and debt burden. Alnasrawi's work is meticulous and authoritative, and concerned primarily with money-metric measures, not human development – the study of which I contend is essential to understanding Iraq's rich development tapestry. Moreover, Alnasrawi's analysis says little about the intricate interaction of the different aspects of development and is mainly unconcerned with the attainment of health or the acquisition of skills. His conclusions concerning the failure of the economic policies in Iraq will be reassessed in the present work according to the broader concept of human development and in the context of Iraq's attempts to escape the "Dutch Disease," which is explained later. Like Alnasrawi's work, this study seeks to evaluate development, yet it does so from an entirely different frame of reference.

Hanna Batatu's *The Old Social Classes and Revolutionary Movements of Iraq* is the most exhaustive study of Iraq's modern social and political history.[27] While the period covered ends in the 1970s, it is invaluable in providing social and political background as well as some source material. Marion Farouk-Sluglett and Peter Sluglett's updated edition of *Iraq since 1958* likewise provides an informative history.[28] Both present subtle arguments concerning Iraq's development and political economy, but do not use the tools of human development and rights analysis that this book uses.

Before beginning the analysis of Iraq's human development, one must first establish which capabilities are more important and why. Few would argue that the freedom to use a particular brand of laundry detergent is as important as the freedom from morbidity or undernourishment, but in many other instances the distinctions are less clear-cut and need to be explained or justified. Deciding which freedoms are most important is necessarily selective.[29] The need for selection is not a difficulty that is unique to the human development approach, however, as arguably any descriptive exercise involves discrimination and selection. The question is whether the selection process is relevant to the object of analysis.[30] Indeed, it may be that the selection and discrimination involved in choosing the valuable functionings are an advantage, as they bring forth the underlying social concerns and values.

Chapter 2 explores the political and historical dimension, and reveals a traditionally unbalanced and inequitable oil-exporting economy with a history of social divisions and repressive government.

Chapter 3 studies economic growth, capital accumulation and the distribution of income. This may appear odd as I have thus far argued that income, by itself, is often an imperfect tool to measure welfare and development. There is not necessarily a contradiction between the pursuit of human development as a strategy and economic growth. In fact the reverse may be true: a healthier, better educated population is more productive and likely, therefore, to achieve a high rate of economic growth. Yet economic growth is not the ultimate objective of human development; augmenting capabilities is.

Nevertheless there are four reasons to study income. First, it may be that a sustained growth in income is necessary for continued enhancement of capabilities.[31] Second, the study of capital accumulation is relevant to Iraq, because, as an oil-exporting economy, it is vulnerable to what has come to be known as the "natural resource curse," which is discussed later. The level and sectoral allocation of investment as well as sectoral growth rates are explored in this chapter. Third, as there is no guarantee that the incomes of the poor grow commensurately with average incomes, the distribution of income is studied. Finally, the study of economic growth will uncover how there can emerge sizable disparities between personal incomes (and consumption) and national output in oil economies, and how state policies might promote such disequilibria.

Fundamental to any discussion of capabilities, Chapters 4 and 5 assess human development in education, health, and nutrition – outcomes that have both intrinsic and instrumental significance as regards human development. For example, adequate nutrition is intrinsically significant as no one likes to be hungry. It also improves labor productivity (and hence command over purchasable resources) and promotes better health. Analysis of these is relevant for any country, but especially so for Iraq, where levels of education and health have been historically comparatively low and because, as in other developing countries, the provision of education and health has been characterized by a pronounced urban bias.

Education and health are associated with significant positive externalities: the benefits of education and skills are not (and cannot be easily) restricted to people who hold that education, but overflow to others in the economy. However, were existing incentives, as reflected in the prevailing set of market prices, relied upon to allocate education resources, too few people would receive instruction. This is so even though the private yield on education (or health) spending over a lifetime is generally high – that is, despite the fact that the private rate of return (the private gain or return on investment relative to private cost) is high. The benefits accrue throughout the lifetime. But without government intervention, individuals need to pay the costs of education up front. Fewer people would receive education and health and human development outcomes would be reduced and, consequently, so would the level of output and income. State subsidization of education and health avoids this inefficiency by reducing costs to individuals.

The same economic logic applies to the provision of "public goods" – goods that are non-rival (if one person's consumption does not lower another's) and non-excludable (as it is difficult or costly to exclude someone from using the goods). As producers are unable to appropriate all the benefits that are generated from the production of public goods, provision of the goods is typically insufficient when left to market mechanisms. Unlike public goods such as national defense, education and health are quasi-public goods, meaning that they are to some extent rival and excludable. But education and health have such pervasive positive externalities that it is socially more efficient for government to either provide them itself or to subsidize their universal provision and consumption.

The subsidization of education is all the more desirable in developing countries because the social rate of return to education – societal return on investment relative to social (private plus government) cost – is typically high, sometimes exceeding the rate of return on physical capital.[32] Moreover, there is a great degree of complementarity between expenditures on education and health. For example, primary health care improves the health of the population especially the poor, thereby improving capacities to transform calories into nourishment, which, in turn, improves the ability of children to learn. And improved education and health also tend to raise the rate of return on physical capital.[33]

Yet not all investments in education are equally profitable. Broadly speaking, social rates of return are highest for primary education, lower for secondary, and lower still for higher education, which is the most expensive per student. Thus, expenditures on primary and secondary education tend to raise national income by more than equivalent expenditures on university training. And, emphasis on primary and secondary education, rather than higher education – necessarily for the few – implies a more equitable spread of educational resources. To the extent that education is a major determinant of future income, this results in a more egalitarian distribution of income. University education expands capabilities, but this has to be balanced against the expanded capabilities for many more people associated with primary or secondary education.

The above discussion illustrates how the objectives of efficiency (or economic growth) and equity are not necessarily in tension. Expenditures on primary health care and basic education are likely to yield the highest rates of growth in income and are expected to generate a more egalitarian distribution of resources. This conclusion stands in contrast to the fierce version of development, which viewed spending on education as a drag on economic growth. Even so, there has usually been a pronounced bias in the provision of public expenditure in most developing countries in favor of urban districts and against rural areas. As the supply of education and health services (or the stock of human capital) is normally higher in urban areas, the social rate of return to (the larger) expenditures on health and education in urban regions tends to be lower than in rural areas. This works to exacerbate existing rural–urban inequities.

The extent and evolution of this bias is evaluated with reference to Iraq in Chapters 4 and 5. Also studied is how the state has shaped development outcomes and how state policies and priorities themselves have been influenced by changed international circumstances, notably the Iran–Iraq war. As such, this study highlights the argument of Charles Tripp, in his *A History of Iraq*, who emphasizes the historically central role of the state, predating the rise of oil as a main factor of economic activity.[34] This work also extends the approach of Edith Penrose and E. F. Penrose, in *Iraq: International Relations and National Development*, who in their study of economic development in the period until the mid-1970s show how Iraq's development path has been hugely influenced by outside events, notably in the period from 1900 to 1950.[35]

Chapter 6 discusses the status of women. In Iraq, as in practically everywhere in the developing world (and often beyond), there are perceptible and often enduring gender inequalities. However, much like for males, the capabilities of women have both intrinsic and instrumental value, and the performance of these capabilities is worth examining.

The particular ways in which gender inequities are expressed are explored in the context of cultural and religious realities. I argue that such expressions are similar to those found elsewhere in the developing world. Of interest, however, is how the developmental and political priorities of the state have interacted with the cultural and social landscape to delineate the outcomes in human development for women, and this is analyzed in detail.

To some extent these development priorities are themselves constrained by the availability of funds, which in Iraq's case largely has depended on the sale of oil. However, resource abundance is often associated with poor economic and political performance, in what is known as the "natural resource curse."[36] The economic component of this is often referred to as the Dutch Disease, whereby an influx of oil revenues increases the price of non-tradable goods (such as real estate or services) relative to the price of manufactures, shifting capital and labor inputs away from domestic agriculture and manufacturing towards construction and services, thereby reducing non-oil exports.[37] The political component of the resource curse is called the "rentier state paradigm." This hypothesis posits that the ability of government to derive rents from the sale of oil allows it to circumvent the populace at large as a source of revenues, ignoring pressures for political reform and change.[38] In the rentier state, a small minority of the population generates wealth, the majority is engaged in its distribution, and economic rents accrue mostly to the state.[39] As these rents substitute for taxation in government finance, governments are released from accountability, so much so that the state may become independent of society.[40] Or, alternatively, the lack of taxation hinders the development of solidarities along economic lines,[41] while oil rents augment the state's capacity to co opt and/or repress political opponents.[42] Whichever version of rentierism one finds convincing, the conclusion is that natural resource revenues have a negative influence on democratization and political rights.

Chapter 7 thus assesses the political dimension. Entitlements to political rights and freedoms have intrinsic significance: to be politically active or receive information about politics and such rights as freedom from torture or arbitrary arrest are undeniably valuable in themselves. Questions over the instrumental significance of these rights and freedoms are more controversial. Issues concerning the impact of democracy or political liberty on economic development or about the appropriateness of democratic political systems in regions with little cultural or historical affinity to the ideals of political liberalism remain in dispute. In the specific case of Iraq, the point has often been made that to maintain order in that volatile society, stern governance is required.[43]

The reluctance to embrace political rights, implied in the fierce conception of development, arises in the context of the impasse that governments of the newly independent (and mostly poor) nations have faced when implementing public policy and the difficulties associated with promoting investment and economic growth. It is thought that established social groups work to exploit democratic structures in order to defeat or subvert needed reforms and protect their particular interests.[44] Moreover, because competitive political systems require regular elections held at fairly short intervals, it is argued that politicians have an incentive to cater to relatively short-term concerns over long-run development, favoring current consumption over growth-promoting investment.[45] A strong state that could confront special-interest groups, implement vigorous forward-looking public policies, and promote capital accumulation is viewed as desirable. In fact, Samuel Huntington goes so far as to suggest that a single-party state that is able to muscularly enforce social stability, restrain consumption, and implement development policies could act as a vehicle for progress in some developing countries.[46] As proof, South Korea and Taiwan are offered to illustrate the essential compatibility of rapid economic growth and industrialization with authoritarian political arrangements. And, since most people (plausibly) would prefer disenfranchisement to hunger, poverty, or anarchy, the trade-off is one that most are willing to accept.[47]

This ostensibly attractive political bargain is possible in principle as long as the autocratic state deploys policies that are efficient (or at least effective) in achieving development, in other words policies that result in an expansion in incomes and capabilities in society at large, not just for a favored clique. Unfortunately, there is no *a priori* guarantee that autocratic regimes would either formulate the appropriate polices or harbor laudable intensions. Authoritarian regimes may have an enhanced capacity to promote beneficial policies (for example, to invest generously in education and health) or greater ability to repress social groups whose interests are inimical to those of society (such as large landholders that are hostile to land reform or business interests with monopoly power). Whether these regimes act in this way is another matter, for just as these regimes are better placed to promote the public good, they are also well positioned to do the reverse: sponsor policies and narrow interest groups that are harmful to society.

There is, for this reason, little empirical evidence to suggest a robust relationship (either positive or negative) between authoritarianism and economic growth: autocratic regimes do not do better on average at securing growth, as the success stories in South Korea and Taiwan have to be viewed alongside the dismal failures such as Zaire under Mobutu.[48] This is not very surprising as few of the policies that are thought to promote economic growth – namely, the openness to competition, investments in primary health and schooling, successful land reforms, and policies that promote investment – are inconsistent with political liberalism.[49] There is, moreover, some statistical evidence that democracies promote more stable patterns of economic growth, because they, among other things, may nourish better conflict management institutions and are, given extant checks and balances, less likely to experience abrupt policy changes that could discourage investment.[50]

The heightened economic insecurity associated with authoritarianism is brought out in a study by Jean Dreze and Amartya Sen, which compares the performance of China and India in relation to famines.[51] In the study, the authors argue that the democratic institutions and free press have been instrumental in the mobilization of a quick state response to potential famines in India, whereas the absence of similar institutions in China meant that government, untroubled by opposition parties or a critical media, could dogmatically proceed with its chosen policies even when the consequences were dire, as in the Great Leap Forward that resulted in up to 30 million deaths from famine in 1958–61.[52] At the same time, India's democratic institutions have had less success in mobilizing a public riposte to chronic hunger (as distinct from famine) and illiteracy – both comparatively rare in autocratic China.

This discussion brings out key insights at the intersection of political regimes and economic outcomes. Political rights and freedoms can act as powerful catalysts in the development process, helping to identify problems and priorities and marshalling a coalition for their solution. And although authoritarian regimes face fewer constraints in implementing their policies, errors in policy are subject to weaker corrective influences. Indeed, it is not obvious that political autocracy is desirable, even if the potential instrumental benefits of political liberalism are disregarded and were it the case that repressive political arrangements promote economic growth, because of the intrinsic value attached to rights and freedoms. Yet, as noted, this focus on the intrinsic import of rights has been criticized as inauthentic and illegitimate: non-Western cultures place greater emphasis on loyalty and discipline.[53]

Authoritarian leaders (including Saddam Hussein of Iraq) often have been prominent in dismissing concerns over rights and freedoms as a fake (Western) import. This is rather odd though, given the at times less than tolerant history of Western culture and its traditionally ambiguous attitude towards political freedoms and rights. In considering the large compass of history, one finds that long before Western philosophers such as Locke and Voltaire formulated their ideas of "natural rights," the rights of religious minorities in the Abbasid and Ottoman Empires were respected, while minorities in medieval Europe were routinely persecuted. True, ideas about the limited powers of the state and individual rights originated in the age of enlightenment in Europe. However, when such ideas were supposedly implemented – as in post-independence United States where slavery was prevalent and the unpropertied were disenfranchised – they were applied incompletely and selectively. The resulting state of affairs for the majority of the population was little different from the *de facto* despotism in the autocratic states of Europe and Asia. Furthermore, if Western culture is to be credited with giving birth to and nurturing the concepts of natural rights, it also ought to be held accountable for ideas than run counter to these concepts. Bentham described the idea of natural rights as "nonsense," and Marx insisted that such rights follow from, rather than precede, the institution of the state, so these rights were not natural entitlements.[54] And Nietzsche was altogether hostile to such rights because they weakened the will of the morally superior elite.[55] To dismiss the concern for rights and freedoms as a solely imported preoccupation overlooks the tolerant traditions of other societies and obscures the uncertain reverence shown to these rights in the West – even today, as evinced in the moral duplicity of "extraordinary rendition," sadism in Abu-Ghraib and indefinite detention and torture at Guantánamo Bay.[56]

Moreover, the assertion that concerns over human rights and freedoms are secondary considerations outside the non-Western milieu is fantasy. When asked if they thought democracy to be the best form of government, more than three-fifths of respondents in Arab countries, two-fifths of Latin Americans, more than one-third of South Asians, and one-fifth of East Asians answered yes, as compared to one-half in Western Europe and less than two-fifths in the US, Canada, Australia, and New Zealand.[57] Democratic governance and the associated rights and freedoms are thus equally, if not more, valued in some parts on the developing world as in the West.

That the demand for democracy in the Middle East is comparable to that in Europe is not necessarily surprising. In his comparative analysis of social change and modernization, *Tormented Births: Passages to Modernity in Europe and the Middle East*, Isam al-Khafaji shows that there are important commonalities in the processes of economic, political, and social transformation in Europe and the Middle East.[58] Using Iraq (among several subject countries) to illustrate his thesis, al-Khafaji contests the stress that is placed on the cultural distinctiveness of Europe *vis-à-vis* the Middle East, arguing instead that there are broad similarities in the processes related to the formation of social groups, classes, and power relations.

I therefore study the changes in range of political views expressed in society and the government's attempts to shape this expression through political repression using a variety of indicators. Concurrently, issues of sectarian representation in government are addressed. Next, I modify an index of political rights and freedoms, namely the Humana Index, to test hypotheses concerning levels of state repression and centralization as well as questions about the origins of the Iran–Iraq war. Although it utilizes a different methodology, this chapter seeks to understand the trajectory of state centralization that animates the work of Tripp[59] and to appreciate how Iraq's relations with the outside world have influenced its polity, in the spirit of Penrose and Penrose.[60]

The conclusion summarizes and integrates the main findings of the study. Not only does the study elucidate critical aspects of Iraq's development, it also, despite Iraq's distinctiveness, allows us to draw crucial and generalizable lessons that are relevant to the field of development, the specific challenges that oil economies face, and the political economy of the Middle East.

Finally, as every student of Iraq appreciates, the study of Iraq is complicated by the dearth of data, which are often missing, incomplete, and sometimes unreliable. Care is taken to cross-check the data whenever possible. However, the working assumption of this is book is that guarded conclusions based on imperfect data are preferable to saying nothing about this important topic.

2 Social, political, and economic evolution of Iraq, 1920–1990

This chapter tracks key political, social, and economic developments in Iraq from roughly the formation of the state in 1920 to the end of the period of study in 1990. It is necessarily selective and incomplete when read as an historical summary. However, the chapter underscores the extent to which income measures alone are inadequate as indicators of development, and illustrates why the alternative approach using the human development paradigm is preferred.

The first section of the chapter reveals the existence of substantial social cleavages and historically repressive polity. This delineates the initial conditions concerning political and human rights in Iraq and facilitates their comparison through time. In the second section, the study uncovers an economy that, even in 1950, was highly unbalanced, with a large agricultural sector characterized by low productivity, a very small but well developed oil sector, and a weak, underdeveloped industrial sector. As a consequence of these imbalances, the living standards of the majority of the population in 1950 were comparatively low. These original economic conditions help to contextualize both the impressive progress in human development that was subsequently achieved in the period 1950–90 as well as the problems of human capacity-building. The points would be largely obscured in a study of development that relied exclusively on income.

Political and social developments

The modern state of Iraq was formed mostly as a result of British efforts to combine three, somewhat disparate, former Ottoman *wilayets* or provinces – namely, those of Baghdad, Mosul, and Basra. The efforts were motivated primarily by the desire to link the oil fields in the northern province of Mosul with oil reserves assumed (correctly as it turned out) to exist elsewhere in the country.[1] Britain also wanted to be in a position to protect its oil interests in Iran, which were located mainly on the eastern bank of the Shatt-al-Arab waterway, close to Basra in the south. And, the British appear to have attached a "strategic value" to the stationing of the

Royal Air Force (RAF) in Iraq, and considered this an important part of the "British Empire Air route scheme."[2]

In realizing their objectives, the British sought to employ as little direct control and as much of the local administration apparatus and personnel as possible. This was less expensive than direct control and also had the advantage of drawing on indigenous leaders and bureaucrats from within the country. Real control, however, would remain in British hands, as one British official notes:

> What we want to have in existence...is some administration with Arab institutions which we can safely leave while pulling the strings ourselves: something that won't cost very much...but under which our economic and political interests will be secure.[3]

Iraq under the monarchy

With this in mind, the British, in 1921, engineered the election of an Arab, Emir Faisal, who had fought alongside the Allies against the Ottoman Empire in the World War I, as king in Baghdad. Faisal, in turn, brought in Arab (or Arabized) ex-Ottoman officers, who had fought with his Sharifian Army against the Turks to run the government. These ex-Sharifians were quite influential in government, especially in the early decades of the monarchy: the premiers of 16 out of 26 cabinets formed between September 1921 and February 1940 were ex-Sharifians.[4]

The prominence in government of these officers, who with few exceptions came from middle or lower-middle class backgrounds, was looked upon with some envy and displeasure by sections of the religious, propertied, and mercantile groups, as well as by the ex-Ottoman bureaucratic elite in Baghdad. In 1922, a group of 40 tribal leaders went so far as to write to Faisal asking him to appoint persons of noble heritage to high positions in government.[5] The position of Faisal, who claimed descent from the prophet Mohammed, went some way toward blunting such criticism. Opposition from established groups probably gave the ex-Sharifian group its strong cohesion in the early years of the monarchy. This group of officers shared with Faisal ambitions for independence or national union,[6] although their views here were still somewhat vague and ill-articulated. Faisal's own ideas on the subject of Arab union, at this time, were apparently far more developed than those of his officials, and included a proposal for union with Syria.[7] These ambitions often brought Faisal and his ex-Sharifian officers into conflict with the British.

The ex-Sharifians belonged to the same religious sect as Faisal; they were, with few exceptions, Sunni Muslims. However, the religious composition of the ex-Sharifians was not the result of the king's sectarian favoritism, as Faisal appears to have been quite tolerant towards the issue of religion, which helped his candidature as king.[8] Rather, the religious makeup of ex-Sharifians, indeed all officers in the Ottoman military, was a result of a deliberate Turkish policy of discrimination. Although the Ottoman authorities did not interfere with the religious traditions and practices of Shia Islam, they discriminated against the Shia in government and in the army, fearing that the loyalties of this sect resided with the Persian state, rather than their own. The presence in Baghdad of one of the few military preparation schools in the Arab areas of the Ottoman Empire, offering state subsidies to students who attended, gave the children of modest Sunni Muslim families an avenue for upward mobility.[9] In contrast, the children of Shia families were excluded from consideration for positions in the Ottoman military and (to a lesser extent) the bureaucracy.

One result of this Turkish policy of discrimination in Iraq was a military and, to a lesser extent, a bureaucracy, whose sectarian constitution was significantly at odds with that of the country as a whole – a situation which remains to this day. An approximation[10] of the ethnic and religious/sectarian composition of the country in 1947 is presented in Table 2.1.

As is apparent from the table, the Shia Muslim population, which is predominantly Arab, constitutes the majority of the population. They are concentrated mostly in the south of the country, in the old Ottoman province of Basra and in some parts of the province of Baghdad in the center of the country. By contrast, Sunni Muslims inhabit the northern areas of the country, the old Ottoman province of Mosul, as well as the center.

This is noteworthy in light of the perceived tensions between these two Muslim sects. A discussion of the theological differences between Shia and Sunni Islam – while they are significant but sometimes exaggerated – is beyond the scope of this work.[11] It is however important to note that the schism, originating from a seventh-century conflict over the rights of

Table 2.1 Ethnic and religious composition of Iraq

Ethnic/religious group	Percentage of population
Arab Shia Muslims	51.4
Arab Sunni Muslims	19.7
Kurdish Sunni Muslims	18.4
Iranian Shia Muslims	1.2
Turkoman Sunni Muslims	1.1
Turkoman Shia Muslims	0.9
Kurdish Shia Muslims	0.6
Christians	3.1
Jews	2.6
Yezidis	0.8
Sabeans	0.2

Source: Adapted from Abdul Karim al-Uzri, *The Problematic of Government in Iraq*

succession to the prophet Mohammed, has created over the centuries a Shia mentality that has been described as that of the "underdog."[12] The motif of suffering and deprivation that runs through Shia ideology and religious practice has been reinforced by a modest degree of correlation between sectarian and socioeconomic position: the Shia were generally more economically disadvantaged than their Sunni counterparts, and they represented a disproportionate number of the poor. It was not always Sunni domination or exploitation that was responsible for this imbalance, however. As we shall see, Shia deprivation, particularly in the countryside, often resulted directly from the position of their co-religionists.

In addition to the Muslim majority, there were non-Muslim minorities. The Christian population was traditionally concentrated in the north of the country, but also in the cities of Baghdad and Basra, while the Jewish population, very prominent in commerce and the most urban of the groups, was concentrated in the cities of Baghdad and Basra. The Sabeans, a small religious sect, were found mostly in the south and in various cities of the country, while the Yezidis are found in the north. These minorities shied away from the government professions in general but, like the Shia, were tolerated under successive governments.

The religious element discussed above is further complicated by ethnic divisions. A large portion of the Sunni Muslims in the north is composed of ethnic Kurds, as opposed to the rest of the country, which is predominantly Arab. The number of Kurds in the country as a whole, almost one-fifth of the population, is, in fact, roughly equal to the number of Sunni Arabs. Kurds also inhabit the main cities outside the northern region, such as Baghdad, and to a lesser extent, Basra. The Turkomans, a non-Arab population, generally inhabited the north, but were also present in the main cities of Baghdad and Basra. The above discussion illustrates how the joining together of these Ottoman provinces created a country that is highly ethnically and religiously diverse. It also shows that the ethnic and sectarian composition of the country as a whole was at odds with that of the ex-Sharifians, newly prominent in government.

Not only did the creation of the state of Iraq join together ethnically and religiously diverse populations, it also brought together regions with very different, sometimes disparate, economic ties and interests. In the last three decades of the nineteenth century, Iraq became increasingly integrated to international, especially British, markets. The value of seaborne trade tripled between 1880–84 and 1910–13,[13] the British Empire being the destination of half the exports and the source of two-thirds the imports in 1912–13.[14] The main factor in this expansion of trade was the technical improvements in the cargo-carrying capacity of vessels navigating the Tigris River between Basra and Baghdad. These vessels could not navigate north of Baghdad on the Tigris and not at all on most of the Euphrates River, smaller boats being employed in those locations where the use of large vessels was not possible. No data on the provincial origin of exports are available. A breakdown by commodity is available, but not too illuminating. In 1905–9, for example, dates were the biggest export, accounting for about a fifth of the value of all exports. Among the other commodities exported were barley, wheat, and wool. This unfortunately tells us little since, with the exception of dates, which are not grown in large quantities in the north, these commodities are produced throughout the country. Nevertheless, it is likely that the southern and central regions of Iraq became more closely linked to international markets than did the north, whose trade was conducted largely with Syria and Palestine. In fact, it is argued that the receptiveness of the Arab population in northern Iraq to pan-Arabism resides in this region's desire to regain its severed economic links with the Levant.[15] In contrast, the trade relationship between the north and the south of the country was relatively weak,[16] although in the absence of internal trade data no definite conclusions can be drawn.

None of the foregoing implies that the economic interests of individuals within the same region were one, or that single provinces were homogenous. As one would expect, there was a considerable divergence in interests of propertied as opposed to unpropertied persons or merchants as opposed to bureaucrats or artisans. Especially noteworthy, however, were the urban–rural differences. During Ottoman rule, central government authority was limited to the main towns and some agricultural land on their outskirts. The rest of the country came under the control of various competing tribes (or tribal confederations) – a condition that would continue to exist, but to a diminishing extent, after the formation of the Iraqi state. One factor that contributed to the poor development of internal trade was that tribes would levy taxes on goods and persons passing through the territory they controlled.[17] These territories were, in general, in a constant state of flux as tribes, whether they were nomadic or settled, and were constantly in friction (if not conflict) with the central government as well as with other tribes for the control of territory. This fact made tax collection in rural areas difficult and unreliable; indeed, the Ottoman authorities appear to have often relied on rural agents or tribal leaders for tax collection.

The position of the tribal leaders, known as *sheikhs* in the Arabic-speaking regions and *aghas* in the Kurdish regions, in the period from the end of the nineteenth century until the World War I was also in flux. The land that the tribes controlled was held in common by the tribe, as the notion of private property appears to have been, up until the middle 1800s, an alien concept to the tribal population. In the latter part of the nineteenth century, however, the Ottoman authorities, anxious to curtail tribal power and in order to increase revenue, introduced land reforms that required the registration of agricultural land under formal Ottoman control. In the Ottoman conception of land rights, three types of land ownership existed.[18] *Mulk* land was privately owned, and much of the agricultural land surrounding the main cities was of this type. *Waqf* land was land held in trust to be used for pious purposes. The remainder was *mirri* land that belonged to the state. The Ottoman authorities considered tribal land as belonging to this last category of ownership. In addition to these, a fourth type of land right, namely *tapu,* was legislated in 1858. In this type of landholding the state retained ultimate ownership, but individuals were entitled, upon registration of the land, to use or lease the land for purposes of cultivation; furthermore, such rights were heritable. The law's requirements, including proof of actual possession of the land, were quite strict, however, and in many instances the tribal leaders, as custodians of tribal land, were able to come forward and register the land in their name.[19] In other instances, the position of the tribal leader was reduced to that of a common (middle-sized) landholder. At any rate, the Turks discontinued implementation of this law in 1881, fearing that the state had given up "too much of its rights."[20] There is, however, general agreement that one effect of the 1858 law was to diminish the military, social, and political influence of tribal leaders with respect to the Turkish authorities.[21] The sheikhs' prior roles of responsibility for keeping order, defense against external threat, and general organization of agricultural works such as canal building were replaced, to some extent, by a more activist state. At the same time the granting of *tapu* rights to tribal leaders increased their economic power at the expense of their tribesmen, and established the foundations of agrarian power relations in Iraq in the next century. In time, "a society of generally free tribesmen became transformed into one of groups of near-serfs" as "new landlords gained unprecedented legal and economic powers over their peasantry".[22] Tribalism was weakened as the traditional blood or communal bonds that bound tribesmen were replaced by the economic landlord–peasant relationships. But this was achieved by handing over control of the common land of the tribe to the tribal chief.

The decline in the political and military position of the tribal leaders was reversed, artificially, by the British occupation of Iraq from 1915 to 1921 and the subsequent mandate from 1921 to 1932. In the period of direct occupation the British, anxious to reduce the cost of rural peacekeeping and assuming a community of interest between tribe and tribal leader, re-established the political power of the tribal leaders. Such leaders who were friendly to British interests were recognized as "paramount sheikhs," and when this recognition did not meet with the approval of the tribesmen, British forces were used to establish the tribal leader's authority.[23] Furthermore, the Tribal Disputes Regulation, governing disputes in which "either or any of the parties was a tribesman," was issued in 1916.[24] This system of law was later, at British insistence, enshrined in the Iraqi constitution. While in the rest of the country a structure based on the Indian civil and penal system was set up, the Tribal Disputes Regulation gave the tribal leader absolute jural authority over his tribe. Under the regulation no appeals were allowed and there was no *habeas corpus*. Not surprisingly, this legal structure resulted in abuse,[25] with sheikhs often using force with impunity to impose authority on tribesmen. Politically too, the position of tribal leaders was enhanced, and this group received between 15 percent and 20 percent of the seats in the assembly between 1925 and 1933.[26] Under the mandate, the British High Commissioner, who had virtual veto powers over Iraq government policy, would often voice his disapproval when the interests of this class were threatened. Finally, tribal leaders were not, until 1927, subject to property tax, and the rents (for use of government lands) that the sheikhs were obligated to pay the exchequer were reduced even though the British mandatory authorities were apparently aware, as their correspondence indicates, that this was not trickling down to the ordinary tribesmen.[27]

The continuation of British support for this group after the end of direct occupation, when the costs of administration were no longer borne by the British, is explained by the mandatory power's desire to check the nationalist aspirations of the monarch and his officials. In other words, the British sought to maintain an internal balance of power. The legal, and to some extent military and political, independence of the tribes was certainly at odds with the ideal of the unified community that the king represented. And, on a few occasions when the power of certain tribal leaders was thought to be excessive, the British acted militarily against these leaders,[28] the Iraq government not possessing even at the time of independence in 1932 sufficient military strength to stand against the tribes. In general, though, when the monarchy and civil administration attempted to weaken powerful tribal chiefs by either encouraging competitors or breaking up large estates, the British objected.

The tribal elders or officials and politicians were, however, not always unified in their objectives. In the 1920s and 1930s, there was little unity or consensus, even within this group. Tribal leaders habitually encroached on one another's territory, which sometimes required the intervention of the central government (although its powers of enforcement in disputes were often limited). At other times the central government simply "bought" rural peace by giving a powerful tribal leader the right to a certain parcel of land, typically at the expense of another tribe. Politicians too were divided. In 1935, the government of Ali Jawdet, for example, was brought down because its opponents instigated a tribal rebellion in the middle Euphrates region.[29] This discord and fragmentation lead King Faisal to complain:

> There is still – and I say this with my heart full of sorrow – no Iraqi people but unimaginable masses of human beings, devoid of any patriotic idea, imbued with religious traditions and absurdities, connected by no common tie, giving ear to evil, prone to anarchy,

and perpetually ready to rise against any government whatever. Out of these masses we want to fashion a people which we would train, educate and refine...The circumstances being what they are, the immenseness of the efforts needed for this can be imagined.[30]

Faisal died in 1933 and as a result of the ascent of the unqualified Ghazi to the throne the Palace became less influential in politics. At the same time, military leaders became more influential in Iraqi politics. In line with the wishes of the monarchy and ex-Sharifians, but with British resistance all along the way, the size of the Iraqi military grew from 12,000 in 1933, to 20,000 in 1936,[31] and reached 46,000 in 1941.[32] But while the monarchy wanted to use an enlarged army to establish its position as the premier source of authority in the country, the aims of prominent army commanders were not always in concord with those of the monarchy. The military chiefs gave their backing to governments that did not always have royal acceptance, and no government in the period from 1936 to 1941 could stand without the support of key members of the military. These military men had in common the view that the country was most efficiently run by order and decree, rather than endless negotiation and mediation of interests of a plethora of clans and sects – a process that the country's constitution required. Like the ex-Sharifians before them, they were also, by and large, modernizers and looked to Turkey's Kemal Attaturk as an ideal. Many in their ranks saw the Iraqi government as an artificial and imported structure, and thus incapable of delivering progress and modernity. They were also, generally, like the ex-Sharifians, of middle and lower-middle income origin. This group was, however, not a politically or ideologically coherent one, for it is at this point in time, in the middle 1930s, that the distinctions between "Iraqists" and pan-Arabs first becomes apparent. Iraqists were motivated by the desire to rid the country completely of all foreign influence, for although Iraq formally became independent in 1932, the British remained very influential. Under the terms of the 1930 Anglo-Iraqi Treaty, for example, "precedence [was] to be given to the British representative, British officials and the stationing of a British Military Mission," the Iraq government being obligated to provide air bases for the RAF rent free.[33] In contrast, pan-Arabs were motivated by a desire for confederation or union with other Arab nations; complete independence from Britain, as envisaged by the Iraqists was, however, seen as a necessary prelude to Arab union. This distinction between Iraqists and pan-Arabs would later resurface, as we shall see.

The new military officers' political ideologies, while possibly more developed, were not very different from those of the ex-Sharifians. What distinguished the new crop of military leaders from their elders is that the new officers had considerably greater military resources at their disposal than their predecessors, and were not checked in their efforts by a vibrant king. The new officers were eager to establish the army as an authority in the country. While King Faisal was convalescing in Europe in 1933, Bakr Sidqi, then commander of Iraq's northern forces, conducted a bloody suppression, with some consent from the cabinet, of the Assyrians, a small Christian community concentrated in northern Iraq, under the exaggerated pretext that the Assyrians were in rebellion.[34] The military conducted similarly brutal suppressions of rebellious tribes in the middle Euphrates region. Later, in 1936, the same Bakr Sidqi pulled off the Arab world's first military coup. However, like the other military strongmen who were influential in the years 1936–41, he was reluctant to enter government, preferring to pull the political strings from behind the scenes.

In the years 1936–41 cabinets changed as officers of varying shades of pan-Arab or Iraqist leanings came to prominence. In 1940, however, a militant group of pan-Arab officers attained power and a crisis with Britain developed. In 1941, the cabinet, headed by premier Rashid Ali, encouraged by this martial clique declined (or at least did not co-operate fully with) British requests for military assistance as required under the terms of the Anglo-Iraqi Treaty of 1930. In fairness, the language of the treaty was so vague that it supported both the Iraqi and British interpretation.[35] Iraqi military chiefs were undoubtedly emboldened in their intransigence by the allied military failures in Europe and probably overestimated their own strength. The pro-British regent, who acted as the monarch after the death of Ghazi in 1939, fled Iraq, as did many prominent pro-British politicians, mostly ex-Sharifians. The disagreement over the application of the treaty led eventually to British military intervention and the speedy defeat of the Iraqi Army. The defeated military and government leaders fled Iraq; most were recaptured and the *status quo ante* restored.

The quick collapse of the Iraqi Army and the subsequent reoccupation of the country by British forces had important repercussions. First, the fact that the monarchy was re-installed by a foreign force forever tarnished the institution's image in the eyes of the public, and created the impression that the Iraqi ruling classes had become puppets of British imperialism. The underdeveloped nature of politics, and the small size of the governing class, estimated in 1931 to be no more than 300,[36] explains why the majority of the public was indifferent to the ultra-nationalist leanings of the Iraqi government. Even so, this largely apolitical public was also, in general, suspicious of British intentions in Iraq. After 1941, the interests of the monarchy and British imperialist designs came to be seen by the public as one.

With hindsight, the notion that the Iraqi ruling class was an executive of British interests appears unfair. In reality, successive governments had too few tools at their disposal in negotiating the sometimes contradictory demands placed upon them by various interest groups such as the army, tribal leaders, and the British. The historical record does not support the thesis that British interests, and no other, guided Iraqi politicians. The divergence between Faisal's political objectives and those of the British has already been mentioned. Also, commenting on the 1931 oil agreement between the British-controlled Iraq Petroleum Company (IPC) and the Iraqi government, Roger Owen and Sevket Pamuk note that "given the great inequality in power between the two parties, it seems that the Iraqi negotiators drove quite a hard bargain."[37] In fact, Iraqi politicians very shrewdly exploited to their advantage British fears that their influence in Iraq was in decline, in comparison to that of Germany in the 1930s and later with respect to the United States after World War II. But of course, it is the perception of the people that matters in politics, and the perception was that of the Iraqi government as British puppets.

Second, the position of the tribal leaders was strengthened after the Iraqi Army's confrontation with Britain. The position of the former had in fact been checked starting in the middle 1930s, for by that time the Iraqi army was sufficiently powerful as to be able to suppress a rebellion by any configuration of tribes. Indeed, during the 1930s, the army brutally crushed several tribal revolts, although the economic power of the sheikhs remained very strong. With the British reoccupation of the country in 1941, preference was again shown to the tribal chiefs in the countryside with a view to diminishing the political influence of the more nationalist urban centers. Furthermore, after 1941 the monarchy reasoned that it could no longer depend on army support, and came to depend more on the support of tribal leaders. The army was effectively starved of resources between 1941 and 1945,[38] its size being reduced in 1943 to 30,000, of which 20,000 had deserted.[39] The relationship of rivalry between the monarchy and the tribal chiefs that existed in the 1920s and 1930s was thus replaced with one of co-dependence – a situation that would continue until the overthrow of the monarchy in 1958. The enhanced position of the tribal chiefs is reflected in their increased representation in parliament: between 1943 and 1958, tribal leaders constituted between 32 percent and 38 percent of membership in parliament compared with an average of below 20 percent during the 1930s.[40] Efforts to enlarge this group's representation in administration were, however, hampered by the sheikhs' generally low levels of education. Nevertheless, economically the sheikhs were ascendant between 1941 and 1958. This group was consistently shown favor when it came time to re-lease *tapu* land, as Law No. 36 of 1952 redefined "productive use" of land, required under *tapu* grants, to the advantage of the landlord.[41]

This elevation of the landlord class occurred in a period that witnessed an expansion in the size of the urban middle and working classes. In this period, rural to urban migration (explored in greater detail in the next section) swelled the population of the main urban centers. Between 1947 and 1957, the population of Iraq's three largest cities Baghdad, Basra, and Mosul increased by 54 percent, 62 percent, and 33 percent respectively.[42]

In the country as a whole, the urban population as a proportion of the total rose from to 25 percent in 1930 to 38 percent in 1947.[43] The new migrants typically had few resources at their disposal and joined the ranks of the working classes. Concurrently, the growth in public education in this period allowed for the expansion of the clerical and bureaucratic professions and increased the public's susceptibility to political currents and trends.

Neither the working nor middle classes' interests were represented in the extant political structure. These groups were very lightly represented, if at all, in parliament. This was partly due to the electoral system in which elections were not direct but occurred in stages and were generally stacked and manipulated. There was little public confidence in this system, which may explain why, after the army overthrew the monarchy in 1958, there was little or no opposition when the new regime decided to scrap the parliamentary structure altogether. The imbalance in representation is reflected in tax policy of the period 1941–58. The rural chiefs were comparatively lightly taxed, while the urban middle and working classes were more heavily taxed through generally indirect instruments such as excise taxes on sugar and tea, and various consumption taxes.[44]

Even so, attempts at reform were made from time to time. These were generally unsuccessful however. The government of the first *coup d'etat* in 1937 contained liberal and social democratic elements that wanted to reform, among other things, the land tenure system. These elements were, however, forced out when the army, which had backed the government, withdrew its support for the reform program, fearing communist influence. Similarly, the regent after the end of World War II licensed political parties and trade unions, as he had promised to do during the war. When the newly legalized unions struck for better wages and working conditions, though, the government responded by withdrawing recognition and forcefully breaking up strikes.[45] Also, in 1954 when partly as a result of changes to electoral laws a group of 14 reformers were elected to the senate, pro-British politicians and landed interests succeeded in getting the election results nullified and dissolved political parties.[46] The distribution of political power did not evidently support reform, even of the mild variety.

It is not surprising that under these conditions – the absence of constitutional avenues for social change – underground movements and organizations flourished. By far the most important of these organizations was the Iraqi Communist Party (ICP), founded in the middle 1930s. The party attracted elements of the disaffected classes mentioned above; and its members and supporters came from a variety of ethnic and sectarian backgrounds although the party's base was predominantly urban. By the middle 1940s the ICP was an organized and disciplined organization with members in mass organizations of society. The ICP was dominant in the trade unions, and in the brief period in which these were legalized, higher wages and other union demands were attained, although this often occurred at the expense of the withdrawal of government recognition for the union. The ICP's political platform was, however, generally moderate and emphasized, among other things, liberal (democratic) rights, land reform, and freedom from foreign domination.

The party's political program, while it was arguably mild, did not fail to gain the attention of those groups whose interests were tied to the monarchy. The Iraqi police began searching for the leaders of the Party (which had been declared illegal in 1937); their efforts met with some success when in 1947 the leaders of the ICP were captured. This did not dampen Communist activity, however. The Party, led now from jail, agitated and organized mass demonstrations in Baghdad ostensibly against the proposed Portsmouth Treaty – an extension of the Anglo-Iraqi treaty of 1930.[47] The popular opposition to the Portsmouth Agreement was initiated by the right-wing, and officially sanctioned, Independence Party and not the ICP. Once the agitation and demonstrations started though, it became clear that the Independence Party was powerless to end or control them. The ICP was the guiding hand responsible for the continuation of protests and demonstrations. Underlying the mass urban discontent, of course, were the social, economic, and political grievances outlined above. The mass agitation and demonstrations of 1948, known as *al-Wathba* ("the leap"), eventually led to the abandonment of the Portsmouth Treaty and the fall of the government.[48] At its peak in 1959 the ICP could count on 500,000 organized supporters, and throughout the 1950s the ICP was unrivaled in its command of the streets.[49] Indeed, the party was the moving force behind the uprisings of 1952 and 1956 – the latter in protest at the Anglo-French-Israeli attack upon Egypt.

Far less influential than the ICP, at this time, the *Ba'th* (renaissance) party was another clandestine organization that had its origins in Iraq in the early 1950s. Ba'th ideology combined a romantic view of Arab nationalism – for nationalism is about "love before anything else ... [and] He who loves does not ask for reasons,"[50] according to the founder of the party – with vague and somewhat inconsistent conceptions of "socialism" and "freedom". Ba'thist ideology has a generally harmonious view of the nation, and economic differences between individuals are dismissed as false and incidental.[51] Class differences are irrelevant as long as the nation is unified. Nevertheless, the Ba'th advocated, among other things, free access to medical and educational services, a social security system, worker profit-sharing schemes, and economic planning – all arguably aimed to reduce the differences between classes. The need for such programs, in the context of the insignificance of class differences, is difficult to understand. Similarly, there is some difficulty with the Ba'thist conception of freedom. Freedom means first and foremost the nation's ability to choose its own course, but also "sacred" individual freedoms such as the freedom of assembly, belief, and expression as well as property and inheritance rights. Which freedom is paramount, the national or individual freedom, should they come into conflict, is not readily discerned. Ba'thist ideology in general is less the result of a realistic analysis of the Arab situation than a poetic and sometimes disjointed appeal to the imagination. Even so, the emphasis on nationalism and freedom of national action meant that the Ba'th, like the ICP, was stridently anti-imperialist. It was, however, much smaller than the ICP at this time.

Republican Iraq

Neither the ICP nor the Ba'th was involved in the 14th of July revolution in 1958 which overthrew the monarchy, the change of regime being effected by a group of military officers of diverse political inclinations. The new regime scrapped the parliamentary system and ruled through a council composed mostly of military officers.

The tribal chiefs and politicians of the old regime lost political power; the former also lost economic power as the new government soon enacted a land reform program that dispossessed the tribal leaders of control of vast areas of land. The law expropriated privately held landholdings in excess of 625 acres of irrigated land and 1250 acres of rain-fed land, although the landowners were compensated for their loss of land assets. The expropriated land was to be distributed to households in holdings of between 18 and 36 acres in irrigated regions and 36 to 72 acres in rain-fed regions.[52] (Inequalities in the distribution of landholdings before 1958 and the implications of these inequalities are discussed in greater detail in the next section.)

The new regime also attempted to raise the very low living standards of the poor. Bread was subsidized by 20 percent to 25 percent, day labor limited to eight hours per day, and industrial establishments employing 100 persons or more were required to provide housing facilities for their employees.[53] No detailed study has examined the effects of these policies on the living standards of the poor, but it is likely that these policies did much to raise living standards. At the same time, the regime was careful not to penalize domestic capital, and the latter received support in the form of protection from foreign competition and subsidized credit.[54] Finally, the Qassem government pursued a more neutral course in foreign relations, withdrawing from the pro-Western Baghdad pact in 1959.

The military men who came to power were nevertheless divided regarding Iraq's position in relation to other Arab countries. The army, dominated by Sunni Arab officers from northern and central Iraq, had traditionally been arguably more pan-Arab than the rest of the country. The reaction to the loss of trade links with ex-Ottoman Arab regions as well as the Sunni Arab desire to re-enforce their rule, through union with other (predominantly Sunni Muslim) Arab regions, have been suggested as explanations for the region's pan-Arab orientation. Not every officer from this region was pan-Arab, of course, and many military men from the area were indeed Iraqists or independents. Generally, the pan-Arabs in the new government called for immediate union with other Arab countries, while the Iraqists, anxious to preserve Iraqi independence, were reluctant to rush into any union scheme. The Ba'th naturally supported the pan-Arab position. In contrast the ICP supported the Iraqist position. The Iraqi Communists were well aware of the repression the Syrian Communists had faced when Arab nationalists gained power as a result of the formation, in 1958, of the United Arab Republic – from the union of Syria and Egypt.[55]

In the new government the Iraqists, most prominent of which was the new premier and leader of the movement that overthrew the monarchy, General Abdul-Karim Qassem, soon attained the upper hand in this ideological struggle. The new government faced violent opposition from the pan-Arabs and conservatives, however. A coalition of pan-Arab and anti-Communist officers, Ba'thist, and powerful landlords who feared loss of land (as a result of the land reform program put forward by the government) attempted a coup in the northern (nationalist) city of Mosul in March 1959.[56] When this failed, the Ba'th made an attempt to assassinate Qassem in November 1959. The regime was initially successful in defeating its nationalist opponents, for it was very popular and received considerable support from the left, especially the communists; the crushing defeat the nationalists suffered in Mosul, for example, was largely the result of the work of the ICP. Ultimately however, the Qassem regime survived in power by delicately balancing the Ba'thists against the ICP. Thus, when the ICP was thought to have become too powerful, the regime deliberately took measures to reduce its influence: Communist newspapers were suppressed, Communist influence in mass organizations was deliberately checked, and the party was never legalized. The suppression of Communist activity, however, weakened the regime with respect to its Arab-nationalist opponents. The popularity of the regime with the general public could not in the end shield it from attack, and the Qassem regime was overthrown by an alliance of army officers of various political inclinations and the Ba'th in February 1963.

The February 1963 coup ushered in a brief period of state-sponsored violence that the country had not yet experienced. It was the civilian wing of the Ba'th party, the "Nationalist Guard," and not the military that was largely responsible for the excesses and atrocities. By March 1963 10,000 persons had been arrested,[57] too many for existing detention facilities to hold, and consequently sports grounds were utilized.[58] This created fear and disgust for the Ba'th on the part of the public. Even prominent Ba'thists, including the founder of the party, Michel Aflaq, were compelled to criticize the "policy of bloodshed and torture."[59]

The military faction that carried out the coup, while not entirely averse to repressing Communists, manipulated the public indignation at Ba'thist brutalities to their own advantage. The Ba'th was thinly represented in the army at this time, and the majority of the military faction that carried out the coup, while it was mostly composed of nationalists and anti-Communists, was not overwhelmingly Ba'thist. Also the Ba'thists themselves were divided over ideological and policy issues, and the military faction was able to play one Ba'thist faction off against another. In November 1963, the military firmly removed the Ba'th from government.

The nationalist character of the military government that gained power, led by Abdul Salam Aref and later by his brother Abdul Rahman Aref, implied that union with other Arab countries was to be sought. By this time, however, the impracticality of such an undertaking had become evident to the government, the United Arab Republic experiment having failed in 1961. The measures towards union that were taken were thus half-hearted, such as the changing in 1965 of the Iraqi emblem to resemble that of Egypt.[60] Far more important perhaps was the nationalization, along Egyptian lines, of the entire banking and insurance industry as well as 30 large industrial and commercial firms.[61] The regime could reasonably argue that these measures were necessary building blocks for union, although they were in reality attempts by this avowedly nationalist government to deflect the charge that it had abandoned its pan-Arab principles.

The government also presided over the relaxation of the severe political repression that had characterized the period of February to November 1963. Political parties could still not operate legally, but both the Ba'th and the ICP functioned clandestinely with comparatively little government repression, allowing the Ba'th to completely re-form itself and the ICP to temporarily recover. Also in 1965, a civilian was appointed premier who promised greater political liberalization in the form of greater respect for personal (liberal) rights and even free elections. Disagreements between the military and civilian members of the cabinet and within the military itself meant that no consensus was reached on this issue, however.

On 17 July 1968, the Ba'th forced another change of government. This was met with indifference from most of the public and with some trepidation from those segments that had suffered at the hands of the Ba'th in 1963. The new government, headed by president al-Bakr, was aware that its base of support was narrow in the country at large. The army, on which the regime's power ultimately rested, was purged of officers whose allegiance to the Ba'th was suspect. In an effort to widen its appeal in the country at large, the Ba'th government sought to entice, on its own terms and conditions, the Communists into government. With this in mind the Ba'th pursued a dual strategy: the regime terrorized its Communist opponents while at the same time enacting measures that were favorable to the Communists' constituency.

The ICP had in 1967 split into two rival camps: the pro-Soviet Central Committee and the Maoist Central Command. The Central Command formed small, armed groups and openly called for the overthrow of the new regime. Small-scale skirmishes with the authorities and "revolutionary holdups" were however the most that the Central Command could manage. These were certainly not a threat to the stability of the regime; indeed the capture of the Central Command's leadership, by the Ba'th, effectively put an end to this group's activities.

In contrast the Central Committee took no armed action against the regime, believing that such action against a far better armed Ba'thist regime was not wise at that time. The new government actively repressed this group, even though the Central Committee was in agreement with much of the Ba'th's social and economic policies. An amendment, introduced in 1970, to the land reform law enacted under the Qassem government cancelled compensation payments to landlords and expanded co-operative and extension services.[62] This was in line with, and perhaps "went further than the policies envisaged in the Communist [agrarian reform] program of 1960."[63] Labor laws setting minimum wage and working conditions were promulgated. The IPC and its subsidiaries (an international consortium that effectively controlled Iraq's oil production and distribution) were nationalized in 1972. Soviet technical and financial aid had already been sought to develop the Iraqi oil industry outside the IPC concession areas, and this aid continued after the nationalization of the IPC. The improved relations with the Soviet Union and other Eastern Bloc counties culminated in an Iraqi-Soviet "Treaty of Friendship" in 1972. The Ba'th thus continued to repress and harass the ICP while at the same time giving the Communists, in social, economic, and foreign policy, what they had for years been calling for.

This strategy was eventually successful in wooing the ICP into government. Two Communist ministers were appointed to the cabinet in May 1972 and the ICP and the Ba'th formally entered into the "National Patriotic Front" a year later. The regime allowed the ICP to publish its magazines and pamphlets (so long as they were not too critical of the Ba'th). In exchange, the Communists acknowledged, among other things, the "progressive" nature of the Ba'th regime, and accepted Ba'th domination of the mass organizations of society and the army (from which the Communists were not allowed to recruit). The Communists also accepted the "leading" role of the Ba'th in government. Communist ministers received instructions from an all-Ba'thist Revolutionary Command Council (RCC), the highest legislative and executive body in Iraq.

With hindsight, the ICP's decision to enter into an alliance with the Ba'th appears suicidal – an act of inexplicable stupidity.[64] Although a discussion of the merits of the party's decision to enter this alliance is beyond the scope of this work, the alliance gave the ICP the opportunity to operate, albeit with significant restrictions, as a normal political party.

From the Ba'thist point of view, the alliance widened the regime's social base and measurably strengthened its position in its subsequent confrontation with Kurdish nationalists.

The Kurdish population had been demanding autonomous rights from the central government in Baghdad for many years. Faisal, while he tried to include the Kurds in the ruling structure, was reluctant to grant this group autonomy for fear that this would provoke similar demands from Iraq's many other ethnic groups or sects, a situation that may have worked against the integration of his young country. Indeed, the Iraqi army and the RAF defeated Kurdish rebellions, in the 1920s and 1930s, and the leaders of Kurdish nationalist parties were exiled.[65] The 14th of July revolution raised Kurdish hopes that their aspirations for autonomy would be realized, but while Qassem was sympathetic to these aspirations, many of his supporters in the military opposed autonomy.[66] As a result, armed exchanges broke out intermittently between the Kurds and the Qassem government and later between the Kurds and the military-dominated government of 1963–68. The harshness of the mountainous terrain in northern Iraq meant that it was difficult for the central government to extinguish Kurdish resistance completely. Kurdish efforts were however emboldened in the early 1970s by military aid from Iran, and the Kurdish Democratic Party (KDP), the main group engaged in armed conflict with the Iraq government, received Iranian supplies and military advisors.[67] The Ba'th government thus faced a situation where the KDP controlled significant areas of northern Iraq, areas that were, from the central government's point of view, perilously close to Kirkuk, a key oil-producing region. The presence of the Communists, the traditional allies of the Kurds, in government strengthened the position of the Ba'th government, as the latter was able to present a unified front to the Iraqi population and the world at large. In 1975, the government reached an agreement with Iran in Algiers, whereby Iran pledged to end support for the Kurds in exchange for increased access to the Shatt al-Arab. Supplies to the KDP dried up and the Iraq army was able to break Kurdish resistance.

Not all the opponents of the Ba'th were integrated into government in the same way that the Communists were. When the Ba'th came to power in 1968 there were at least nine rival pan-Arab groups.[68] These groups, which contained former Ba'thists who had co-operated with the Aref regime of 1963–68, were crushed. There were rivalries within the Ba'th too, notably a civilian–military one. The Ba'th takeover of power in 1968 had been accomplished through the work of military Ba'thist or military officers who were sympathetic to the Ba'th. These officers had considerable influence since, in the few years following 1968 at least, they were largely responsible for keeping the party in power. This dependence on the military was thought unwise by most civilian and some key military Ba'thists (including President al-Bakr) especially as the Ba'th had lost power in 1963 through the military's intervention. In an effort to Ba'thize the army, Ba'th party commissars were appointed at various levels in the armed forces and military officers whose loyalty was not guaranteed were retired.[69] Civilian apparatuses of the party were also strengthened or, when they did not exist, created. The intelligence apparatuses, for example, were formed in this way. In addition to the institutional there were, of course, personal rivalries. Thus the Ba'thist head of state security, Nadhum Kazar, attempted a coup against the Revolutionary Command Council (RCC) in 1973; his efforts were defeated by the civilian apparatuses of the Ba'th under the control of Saddam Hussein, who became the vice president in 1971.[70] By 1975, the military had been effectively brought under strict (civilian) Ba'th control.

The period from 1968 to 1975 was, in effect, a period of consolidation of power by the Ba'th. In this period, the Ba'th had to deal with a variety of political and military groups that were hostile to its rule as well as with a public that was largely indifferent to its ideology. Even so, the regime's progressive social policies and other actions, such as the nationalization of the petroleum industry, raised its prestige in the country at large. By 1975, the Ba'th had penetrated to virtually every corner of society, and its political authority was now unchallenged. This security was not, however, reflected in greater political openness or lower levels of institutional violence. On the contrary, as we shall see in Chapter 7, the period after 1975 witnessed a definite narrowing in the political sphere and perceptibly heightened levels of political violence.

The Ba'th, it will be remembered, had entered into the National Patriotic Front with the ICP in 1973. Not content with the prohibition on ICP activity in the armed forces and other restrictions, the Ba'th soon began to utilize the front to extend its control in the mass organizations of the country – organizations that had traditionally fallen under Communist influence. "Front" instead of distinctly Ba'th or Communist candidates were put forward in trade union elections.[71] Further, new trade union regulations made it virtually impossible for non-Ba'thists to rise to union leadership.[72] At any rate, soon after the resolution of the Kurdish issue in late 1975 the widely expected turn against the Communists materialized and a number of Communists were arrested. The ICP responded by publicly criticizing Ba'th policies and methods. Relations between the two parties continued to deteriorate for the next two years until, in 1978, a full-scale campaign, comparable to the one conducted by the Ba'th against the Communists in 1963, was launched. This effectively ended the ICP as a force in Iraqi politics in the period under study.

The Ba'th was equally stern in its dealings with the Shia unrest and opposition, both organized and unorganized. The term "Shia opposition" is perhaps misleading for it implies a community of interest within this sect. This opposition was in fact motivated, and sometimes co-ordinated, by Shia religious clerics and it is not clear whether these clerics enjoyed the support of the majority of the sect. Indeed, the traditionally socially and economically underprivileged position of Iraqi Shia made members of this sect especially susceptible to Communist influences; and it is not without irony that some of the Shia clerics, who formed political organizations in the 1950s and 1960s to counteract the iconoclastic influence of Communism upon Shia youth, were later on at the receiving end of Ba'thist repression. These Shia clerics opposed the secular tide that was sweeping the Middle East region in general, and viewed the avowedly secular Ba'th's desire to control all areas of public life as an attack on their traditional position.[73] It was largely due to the machinations of these Shia clerics that anti-government slogans were voiced in a Shia religious festival in February 1977.[74] The more organized political opposition came from groups such as the Islamic *Dawa* ("Call") Party[75] which, emboldened by the Iranian revolution, engaged the regime in conflict by attacking Ba'th party offices and police stations. These movements were, however, never strong enough to endanger the existence of the Ba'th regime, which reacted by simultaneously showing greater deference to religion while hunting down its Islamist opponents. By the early 1980s the Dawa Party had been more or less silenced.

The period after 1975 witnessed significant changes for the Ba'th as well. The rise to prominence of the civilian wing of the party, led by Saddam Hussein, in the early 1970s, has already been mentioned. After the attempted coup of 1973, the intelligence services were reorganized and brought under the control of the then Vice-President Saddam Hussein. Indeed the continued accumulation of power in the hands of Saddam Hussein was such that, by the middle to late 1970s, a cult of personality around his person began to take shape.[76] This gradually replaced, to a considerable extent, party ideology in Ba'thist discourse, as evinced by party pronouncements and publications.[77] Furthermore, until 1978, the state and party apparatuses were, at least in principle though often not in practice, distinct; these two institutions were, however, fused in that year. This formalized a process that had been taking place for some time: the Ba'th Party was becoming less a vehicle for deliberation than a political body that executed its leadership's instructions. Ba'thists who displayed loyalty were rewarded with, among other things, promotion in employment; those who disagreed or were suspected of being disloyal often found themselves the subject of inquiry of the security services.

These expanded throughout the 1970s and, by 1978, employed 125,000 persons, one-fifth of all public employees.[78] This statistic may, however, overstate the extent of the intelligence services' ubiquity in the country since it probably includes support personnel, such as accountants or janitors, and is not an accurate reflection of the number of persons engaged directly in collecting or analyzing information. On the other hand, the statistic excludes the network of secret informers working for the intelligence services throughout the country, and if, as is widely believed, these informers constitute a sizable portion of the total population then the statistic is probably an underestimate. At any rate, any notion that Ba'thists who were not wholeheartedly supportive of their leadership were immune from repression was invalidated soon after Saddam Hussain became president in July 1979. A massive purge of Ba'thists, some of whom were personally close to Saddam Hussain, was conducted on the grounds that they were plotting to overthrow the party leadership. Some of those purged were apparently mildly critical of Hussain's policies or methods[79] or else they may have been viewed as potential rivals to his leadership. Whatever the motivation, the execution of party members thought to have been in Saddam's favor made the point that no opposition would be tolerated.

Under these circumstances it was not surprising that the Ba'th's attack on Iran in September 1980 generated no internal opposition worth noting. A number of explanations for Iraq's attack have been suggested, ranging from the Ba'th's narrow social base in the country and its desire to extinguish Shia unrest,[80] to deep and ancient racial (Semitic-Aryan) and ethnic (Arab-Persian) antagonism and the personal ambitions of Saddam Hussein.[81] While the intention is not to evaluate these, the study of human rights and freedoms in Chapter 7 will allow us to comment on the first thesis.

As we shall see, the war (which lasted from 1980 to 1988) was costly in terms of both resources and human life, forcing the regime to scrap much of its ambitious development and borrow large amounts of money.[82] Although the Ba'th did attempt to insulate the economy by adopting a "guns and butter" policy in the first two years of the war and likely maintained its commitment to social spending, the economic crisis that resulted from the war with Iran is sometimes suggested as a factor behind the regime's decision to attack Kuwait. From the military standpoint, the regime's conduct of the war was very ineffective. Because of the fear of army action against the government, communication between military commanders was restricted and delayed; as a result, co-ordination between military groups and sections was lacking. The army was periodically purged of officers who were used as scapegoats in military defeats, which led to demoralization in the ranks of the Iraqi army. It is estimated that out of a total military strength of 607,000,[83] in 1984, 100,000[84] were deserters; this occurred despite the fact that special military units were set up with orders to locate and shoot deserters on sight. Moreover, the abrogation of the 1975 Algiers agreement with Iran meant that Iranian arms and materiel supplies to the KDP were resumed. Although politically divided (some Kurdish factions were in the pay of the regime), the central government lost control of some areas in northern Iraq. As we shall see in Chapter 7, the Iraqi government, believing that the Kurdish rebels had received civilian support, responded by conducting a massive campaign against non-combatants in the Kurdish region.

The inequities in wealth and power discussed in this section, along with the historically wide gap between the government and the people that have characterized the modern history of Iraq, will be borne in mind throughout this study. Knowledge of these conditions is also critical in the assessment of growth or contraction of capabilities.

The economy to 1950

In this section, the initial economic conditions and structure are assessed. The lack of data about Iraq that was noted in Chapter 1 is notably acute for the period before 1950. Nevertheless, some data about trade and government revenue statistics are available, and are utilized in this section. The study reveals an economy that, even by 1950, was greatly unbalanced: there was a large agricultural sector characterized by low productivity, a very small but modern and well-developed oil sector, and a weak, underdeveloped industrial sector. As a result of these imbalances, the living standards (and human development) of the majority of the population in 1950 were comparatively low, even as per capita incomes were rising. The study of these first economic conditions puts in context the subsequent progress in human development and the difficulties that this process of development encountered.

Agriculture

This sector formed the backbone of the economy in the period before 1950. In fact, the export of agricultural goods was the vehicle through which Iraq came to be connected to the world economy in the late nineteenth century. Such exports increased in the twentieth century, as the sector came to employ most of the workforce, as shown in Table 2.2. These estimates suffer from a number of shortcomings. First, no reliable data on overland trade are available before 1914, only estimates of Iraqi seaborne trade through the port of Basra. Second, trade statistics suffer from frequent changes in definition. Export figures before 1937 include re-exports, but re-exports are excluded thereafter; since re-exports were a small portion of total exports, however, this is unlikely to distort the statistics by very much. Also, although exports were quoted f.o.b., in many instances they were underestimates.[85] Finally, the export statistics presented in the table do not include petroleum exports, which appear as oil revenue in the government's budget accounts and are examined later.

Despite these shortcomings, it is apparent that agricultural exports dominated trade in the period 1900–50. The value of non-oil exports, as expressed in £ sterling – and equivalent to one Iraqi Dinar (ID)[86] – increased in this period, although there was a slight decline in the 1930s. This decline did not result from diminished quantities but from significant declines in the international price of Iraq's main exports, brought about

Table 2.2 Value and composition of exports, 1900–50

Period	1900–4*	1910–13*	1927–30	1931–9	1940–5	1946–50
Value of non-oil exports in current in million £ or ID	1.53	2.70	3.98	3.58	6.74	13.07
As a proportion of non-oil exports (%)						
Dates	21	18	34	33	27	36
Grain, pulses, and flour	16	29	23	32	36	42
Raw wool	12	10	15	12	13	7
Live animals and meat	na	na	4	6	6	7
Sub-total	na	na	76	82	83	74
Ceramic products	0	0	0	0	1	1
Oil revenues as a proportion of date exports (%)	0	0	1	107	115	74

* Refers to seaborne exports from Basra only

Sources: Roger Owen, *The Middle East in the World Economy 1800-1914*, Tauris and Co. Publishers, New York, 1993, p. 275; Principal Bureau of Statistics, *Statistical Abstract 1939*, Government Press, Baghdad, 1941, p. 127; Joseph Sassoon, *Economic Policy in Iraq*, p. 191; and Hanna Batatu, *The Old Social Classes and Revolutionary Movements of Iraq*, Princeton University Press, Princeton NJ, 1978, pp. 106–7.

by worldwide depression. Such disruptions do not appear to have affected the composition of exports: dates; grain, pulses, and flour; raw wool; and, to a lesser extent, live animals and meat continued to be Iraq's main exports. As an annual average, these four items accounted for over three-quarters of exports in the period between 1927 and 1950, and were also a significant part of exports before 1927. The contribution of the largest non-agricultural export, namely, ceramics was, by contrast, negligible.

The oil industry was under the control of foreign companies in this period, and the payments from the sale of oil these companies made to the Iraqi government appear as oil revenue in the government's budget. At no time in the period under consideration, however, do oil revenues exceed agricultural exports. In comparison to dates, a main agricultural export, oil revenues were insignificant before 1930. However, between 1931 and 1945, oil revenues were marginally higher than date exports, while the comparable statistic for the period 1946–50 is three-quarters. In general, therefore, despite the growing importance of oil, agricultural commodities provided significantly more foreign exchange than did petroleum before 1950.

Agriculture also made a significant contribution to government revenues, although this contribution was perhaps less than one might expect given the size and importance of the sector. The average annual contribution of land revenue, which represented revenue from agricultural produce, and oil revenue to public finance are presented in Table 2.3, as is the amount of total revenue. The relative contribution of land revenues to

Table 2.3 Government revenues, 1922–1955

Period	1922–6	1927–30	1931–9	1940–5	1946–50	1951–5
Average annual total revenue (current ID million)	3.99	4.17	5.30	15.15	23.33	67.10
As a portion of total revenue:						
Land revenues	22.9	19.2	8.9	12.9	11.8	3.9
Oil revenues	0	0.3	16.0	12.7	10.6	53.9

Source: Hanna Batatu, *The Old Social Classes*, pp. 106–7

the treasury exhibits a downward trend between 1922 and 1950: it declines from 22.9 percent in the sub-period 1922–6 to 11.8 percent in 1946–50. The sharp decline in land revenues in the 1930s is likely related to depressed agricultural prices, since these taxes were not a fixed amount but were levied in proportion to the value of output. By contrast, the contribution of oil revenues is insignificant before 1930, but averaged between 16 percent and 10.8 percent of total revenues in the sub-periods between 1931 and 1950. After 1950, however, oil revenues increased sharply to over half of total revenue between 1951 and 1955 – and thereafter remained the most important source of income for the treasury. Reasons for the rise in oil revenues after 1950 are explored later in this section.

Except for the sub-period 1931–9, which is associated with depressed prices for agricultural goods, the absolute value of land revenue (in current ID) increased in the period from 1922 to 1950. However, the absolute value of land revenue was stagnant in the sub-period 1951–5, likely because of diminished land productivity. Thus, the sharp decline in land revenue as a proportion of all revenue in this sub-period is not only the result of the unprecedented expansion in oil revenues and hence total revenues, but also the stagnation of land revenues.

Even so, the relatively low and declining contribution of agriculture to public finance before 1950 did not result from the deterioration in agricultural output (which grew in the period) but was a symptom of the severe political imbalances discussed in the previous section. Because of the influence of the landholding tribal leaders in government, agriculture was very lightly taxed, a condition which continued until the overthrow of the monarchy in 1958.

Agricultural output grew as a result of bringing in new land under cultivation, not improved methods of cultivation or a rise in labor or land productivity. Much of the government's capital expenditure focused on flood control and irrigation, which brought new land under cultivation.[87] While flood control was much needed, new irrigation schemes allowed landowners to increase the land under cultivation, and hence output, at the public's expense. Even though land reclamation was often inexpensive, landlords had little incentive to invest in land maintenance. The problem was recognized by a British technical expert, who in 1948 stated:

> I think it a great pity that more attention is not being paid to the reclamation and de-salting of existing lands. This might give us more wheat in a very much shorter time than the big schemes.[88]

Moreover, irrigation schemes often contributed to the problem of salination, which often results from excessive irrigation. The problem of salination was especially acute. A mission organized by the International Bank for Reconstruction and Development (IBRD) estimated that by 1952:

> as much as 20 to 30 percent of cultivated land had been abandoned in the last few decades because of salt accumulation, while on a large part of the remaining land yields have declined by 20 to 50 percent and even more.[89]

But as long as large landholders could rely on publicly funded irrigation schemes, there was little incentive to maintain land productivity. According to the 1952–3 agricultural census, of six provinces with 14.5 million donums (roughly 38.3 million hectares or 56 percent of the country's agricultural land), 13 individuals owned between 50,000 and 100,000 donums, 21 individuals owned between 100,000 and 200,000 donums, and two landowners owned more than one million donums each.[90] The large landholders could thus easily afford to forgo the lost income from land that was not reclaimed, as they could count on the income from their remaining holdings.

The result was that while agricultural output grew, in the first half of the twentieth century, land productivity, on average, declined. Furthermore, as methods of production and working arrangements remained largely unchanged, it is unlikely that labor productivity in agriculture increased. In such circumstances, the material conditions of sharecropping peasants, who formed the vast majority of the rural population (especially in southern Iraq) and probably most of the total population, remained very low (and perhaps regressed) in this period, while the holders of land were enriched.

There is some dispute regarding employment in the agricultural sector. Joseph Sassoon estimates that the sector absorbed roughly 57 percent to 60 percent of the entire workforce in 1947.[91] As Sassoon notes, however, his estimate is partly based on census data in which female agricultural labor is thought to have been greatly understated. According to an estimate by K.G. Fenelon, agriculture absorbed 79 percent of the workforce in 1956,[92] while the sector contributed only 25 percent of GDP in 1953, the first year for which data containing a sectoral breakdown of output are available.[93] Whichever estimate is correct, clearly most of the population was engaged in agriculture before 1950 and that the sector was characterized by very low productivity.

The depressed conditions in agriculture encouraged migration from rural areas to the urban centers, Baghdad and Basra in particular. Table 2.4 contains data on the size and urban–rural distribution of the population. Whereas the statistics for 1947 onwards are based on census data, the statistics that predate 1947 are estimates and doubts about the accuracy of these estimates have been raised.[94] Also, the estimates from 1957 onwards exclude the nomadic population, although the size of this population was, by then, relatively small. Despite these difficulties, the statistics provide a rough idea of the size and distribution of the population.

The proportion of the population that is urban was constant between 1867 and 1930, but increased steadily thereafter. But the proportion of the population that is nomadic declined from roughly one-third of the population in 1867 to only 7 percent in 1930. That is, there was a shift from nomadic livestock and overland camel transport activities to settled agricultural and other rural activities. Developments in river transport reduced the demand for overland trade, which the nomadic tribes depended upon for their livelihood.[95] In time, these tribes settled in rural areas to practice agriculture.

The statistics suggest that there was considerable rural to urban migration after 1930. More than two-thirds of the population was rural in 1930; this proportion declined to roughly one-half in 1965, and was less than one-third in 1987. In Baghdad province, for example, 22 percent of the population in 1947 was composed of immigrants from other provinces, wheras the comparable statistic for 1957 was 25 percent.[96] In

Table 2.4 The population of Iraq, 1867–1987

Year	Total population (million)	Proportion of population		
		Urban (%)	Rural (%)	Nomadic (%)
1867	1.3	24	41	35
1890	1.8	25	50	25
1905	2.3	24	59	17
1930	3.3	25	68	7
1947	4.8	38	57	5
1957	6.3	39	61	
1965	8.0	51	49	
1977	12.0	64	36	
1987	16.3	70	30	

Sources: M. S. Hasan, 'Growth and Structure of Iraq's Population, 1867–1947', *Bulletin of the Oxford University Institute of Statistics*, XX, 1958, pp. 339–52; Directorate General of Census, *Abstract of the General Census of 1957*, Vol. 2, Baghdad, 1964, p. 24; Central Statistical Organization, *Annual Abstract of Statistics 1971*, Baghdad, Undated, p. 51; and Central Statistical Organization, *Numbers and Indicators: Population and Workforce*, (In Arabic), Baghdad, Undated, pp. 4–5.

general, the rate of migration was highest from regions, such as Amarah province in the south, where the concentration of power in the hands of tribal sheikhs was extreme.[97] Interestingly, this rural to urban flow apparently continued after the revolution of 1958, which indicates that wages and living conditions in the countryside remained poor relative to those in urban areas. Indeed, as we shall see in the coming chapters, although there is evidence of improvements in rural areas after 1958, there is also evidence of stagnation in agriculture and persistent urban–rural disparities.

Oil

The oil industry was under the control of foreign companies in this period, and the payments from the sale of oil these companies made to the Iraqi government appear as oil revenue in the government's budget. As shown in Table 2.2, at no time in the period before 1950 do oil revenues exceed agricultural exports. In comparison to dates, a main agricultural export, oil revenues were insignificant before 1930, only marginally higher than the exports of dates between 1931 and 1945, and lower for the period 1946–50. Therefore, despite the growing importance of oil, agricultural commodities provided significantly more foreign exchange than did petroleum before 1950.

The petroleum sector became the driving force in the economy only after 1950, as the output of this resource and per barrel income that the government received from its sale increased sharply. Oil was discovered in the late nineteenth century, but only began to be produced in significant quantities after the discovery of a large oil field at Baba Gurgur in northern Iraq in 1927. Figure 2.1 shows the daily average output of petroleum. In 1928, the first year for which production statistics are available, 2,700 barrels per day or 0.0027 million barrels per day (MBD) were produced. Output increased rapidly after the middle 1930s, and averaged 0.075 MBD in the period 1935–44 and 0.094 in the period 1945–49. After 1950, oil output rose sharply, averaging 0.53 MBD in the period 1950–59 and 1.23 MBD in the period 1960–69.[98]

The increase in output after 1950 was accompanied by improved per barrel revenue. Favorable international circumstances, such as the 1951 nationalization of the oil industry in Iran and the adoption of the principle of profit sharing between some of the oil companies and the Venezuelan and Saudi governments, strengthened the hand of the Iraqi government with respect to the oil companies.[99] A series of negotiations between the oil companies and the Iraq government were initiated, culminating in a new agreement in 1952 whereby the government would receive, annually, 50 percent of the profits of the oil companies as well as other advantages.[100]

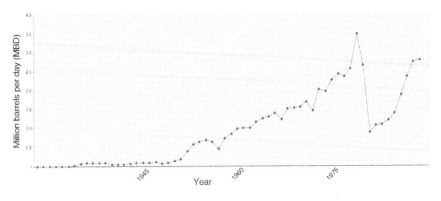

Figure 2.1 Production of crude petroleum, 1928–89

Source: Organization of Petroleum Exporting Countries (OPEC), *Annual Statistical Bulletin 1994*, Vienna, 1995, p. 47

This replaced an earlier concession agreement of March 1931 whereby the Iraq government received a fixed payment of ID 0.2 per ton.[101] The change effectively raised revenue per barrel of oil fourfold between 1950 and the period 1952–9,[102] while a subsequent change in 1971 increased the government's share of profits further.

Oil revenues thus rose substantially after 1950, as oil became the driving force of the economy. As Table 2.3 illustrates, oil revenues were roughly 10 percent of total revenues in the period 1946–50 but more than 50 percent in the period 1951–5, increasing further thereafter. As a proportion of GDP, oil revenues increased from 3 percent to 18 percent from 1950 to 1955.[103] Meanwhile, per capita income, according to calculations made by K. G. Fenelon, increased (in constant 1950 prices) from ID 32 in 1950 to ID 49 in 1956.[104]

The explosion in oil revenues meant essentially that the government was able to finance development spending with a much-alleviated capital constraint. The Development Board was set up in 1950 with a view to directing oil funds towards productive investments. When first erected, the board was empowered to invest the entire portion of oil revenues. This was later reduced to 70 percent in the middle 1950s and further still to 50 percent in the late 1950s, the remainder being diverted to the government's current budget. After the 1958 revolution, the development board was scrapped and replaced with a Ministerial Committee. In time, successive Iraqi governments came to rely increasingly upon oil revenues to finance current expenditures.

Industry

Industrial activities include mining activities such as oil extraction. For the purposes of this work, however, it is useful to distinguish between oil extraction activities, which were highly developed, and other industrial activities, which were in their infancy and comparatively poorly developed. As in other developing countries, the industrial development in Iraq was hindered by lack of infrastructure, capital (especially before 1950), and skilled labor, but also by the small size of the internal market and the low level of purchasing power, not helped by the very low incomes that obtained in the sector that employed the largest number of people, namely agriculture. Nor did government policy before 1958 emphasize the development of the industrial sector, as capital investments in flood control were favored to the exclusion of industrial development. Indeed, between 1931 and 1950, less than 5 percent of the government's capital expenditures were allocated to industrial development,[105] while this percentage was roughly 11 percent in the period 1950–58.[106] After 1958, however, industrial development was emphasized.

Even so, some import-substituting industries had, by 1950, been established, including in textiles, shoes, building materials, and tobacco. The development of these industries was helped in no small measure by the supply disruptions brought about by the advent of World War II, as the lack of access to imported consumer goods provided an incentive, in the form of higher prices, for domestic supply to expand. Despite modest levels of tariff protection, however, the output of these industries did not always fulfill domestic demand at the prevailing price. Not surprisingly, the sector was not a large employer and is estimated to have employed only between 5 percent and 7 percent of the workforce in 1947.

With the possible exception of the oil sector, conditions of work and pay were low. Oil workers were better paid and received superior fringe benefits, including free medical care.[107] But while oil was the driving engine in the economy after 1950, the sector was (and remains) capital intensive and employed relatively few people. The oil companies in Iraq employed an annual average of 3,500 persons in the period 1927–33 and 4,500 in 1938.[108] This increased to 16,000 in 1958, most of whom were local workers.[109] Despite this increase, oil workers were a small proportion of the economically active population, which according to the 1957 census, was roughly 1.8 million people.[110]

Wages and working conditions of urban workers in other sectors were quite low and often fell below the standard set for subsistence. For example, one study in 1953 found that while the subsistence wage for a worker with a wife and two children was ID 0.33 per day, Baghdad rates for unskilled labor were between ID 0.2 and ID 0.25.[111] Given the continued mass migration from rural to urban areas after 1930, living standards in the countryside were surely lower still.

The flow of labor to urban areas tended to depress real wages, especially for unskilled workers, as the growth in labor supply outpaced the growth in demand. Wages failed to keep pace with the inflation that accompanied World War II. General prices rose by more than 500 percent between 1939 and 1948, and the price of foodstuffs (a larger item of expenditure for the poor) increased by more than that, while the wages of unskilled labor increased by far less.[112] Thus, even by the middle 1950s, real wages had not recovered their level of 1939. The decline in real wages affected not only unskilled laborers but also affected other workers who were on fixed incomes, such as government employees. By contrast, merchants and landholders are thought to have profited from war inflation.

The picture that emerges then is of a highly unbalanced developing economy with a large agricultural sector that is characterized by very low productivity; a small and largely underdeveloped industrial sector; and a very small but highly developed oil sector. Under such circumstances, the living standards of the majority of the non-merchant and non-landowning classes were, as the IBRD observed in 1952, "extremely low."[113] Despite the availability of water resources, large amounts of agricultural land and an emerging oil sector, per capita income in 1950 was ID 32 (or US$ 89),[114] low by international standards and slightly lower than (but broadly comparable to) that of Iraq's neighbors Syria (US$ 100) and Lebanon (US$ 115).[115] The corresponding human development outcomes for Iraq lagged behind those of its neighbors, perhaps by more than the respective gaps in per capita incomes. Adult literacy was 18 percent in Iraq in 1957[116] compared with an estimate of 30 percent in Syria for 1960.[117] Infant mortality was 139 per 1000, 132 in Syria, and 68 in Lebanon in 1960.[118] These disparities would later recede and (in many instances) be reversed, as we shall see in Chapters 5 and 6. The numbers, nevertheless, illustrate how per capita income and human development can diverge.

3 Economic growth, consumption, income distribution, and capital formation

Introduction

This chapter assesses economic growth and the distribution of income. An increase in income acts as an instrument to attain desired functionings, whose expansion in the long-term may depend on sustained growth in income or GDP.[1] And, if growth in GDP is relevant to the expansion of some desired functionings, then it must be associated with an enhanced ability to purchase commodities that are relevant to the attainment of those functionings. That is, GDP growth must be associated with a rise in consumption of goods and services. The study of public and private consumption is therefore relevant, especially so in oil-exporting economies such as Iraq, where a rise in price or exported volume of the resource, and consequent expansion in GDP, are not always associated with increased final consumption, as we shall see. The examination of consumption is also important because the rentier state hypothesis predicts governments in oil-exporting countries to deploy oil revenues to bribe or pacify their populations, buttressing the position of the state with respect to society. In that case, one would expect rising oil revenues to be associated with expanded levels of consumption.

Moreover, estimates of GDP and public and private consumption are mean national aggregates that may hide substantial variation. If rising incomes accrue primarily to the rich, then average incomes will exhibit a rise, but the typical person may not be better off and rising aggregate incomes will not be associated with a decline in poverty. In that case expanded aggregate incomes would not imply an enhanced ability to purchase commodities or resources – necessary for the attainment of functionings – for the general population but for only a fairly select few. A study of the distribution of income is thus required.

On the other hand, if all of revenues from the sale of the natural resource are consumed and none invested, then a country would be liquidating its natural capital without any compensating accrual of other forms of (manmade) capital. The resulting net reduction in capital stock would diminish the prospects for consumption in future. A limited study on this very topic, however, concluded that Iraq was in fact not consuming its capital stock in the period 1955 to 1990. Investment in physical capital more than offset the depletion of natural assets, implied in the extraction of oil.[2] Nevertheless, a study of capital formation in Iraq is important because productivity-enhancing investments in physical and human capital are ways that mineral-exporting countries can escape the effects of the Dutch Disease.[3]

As noted in the introduction, the Dutch Disease emanates from the spending of oil revenues in the domestic economy, which is presumed to increase the price of non-tradable goods (such as real estate or services) relative to the price of tradable goods. The (domestic) supply of non-tradable goods is constrained whereas tradable goods can always be imported. Increased demand arising out of the expenditure of oil revenues raises the relative price of non-tradable goods, diverting capital and labor away from (tradable) domestic agriculture and manufacturing towards non-tradable construction and services. Although this reduces non-oil (agricultural and manufactured) domestic output and exports, the migration of productive factors to the sectors that value them most is not necessarily a problem in itself: economic activity is responding to changed incentives in the form of relative prices. However, if the tradable goods-producing sectors are the sources of technical progress and innovation in the economy, the Dutch Disease can stifle economic growth by depriving these sectors of needed resources.

Investing in both tradable and non-tradable goods sectors and subsidization of production of tradable goods that are relevant in terms of innovation helps avert this outcome. To the extent that investments increase productivity, they lower costs, making the domestic production of tradable goods more attractive, inducing resources to flow to these sectors, and reducing prices of non-tradable goods. The level and sectoral distribution of investment are therefore of interest.

The chapter thus consists of the following. First, the trajectories of per capita GDP as well as public and private consumption are analyzed. Second, the distribution of income is examined. This is followed by an assessment of investment in physical capital, including its composition, in the third section. Changes in economic structure are assessed next. Concluding remarks are presented in the final section. Again, because the data are often missing, incomplete, and sometimes contradictory, cross-checking is done when possible.

GDP per capita, private and government consumption

There was a steady and more or less sustained rise in national income per capita from the 1950s until roughly 1980. However, in the context of the Iran–Iraq war and declining oil prices, GDP declined during the 1980s.

Economic growth characterized the decades of the 1950s and the 1960s. K. Haseeb authored the most authoritative early study of national income for the period of the 1950s. He found that in real terms – that is, adjusting for price inflation–national income in Iraq rose by 7.4 percent per annum between 1953 and 1961 (evaluated in constant 1956 prices). Taking into account population increase in this period, this translates to a 5.3 percent annual increase per capita and corresponds to a nominal – inflation-unadjusted – expansion in per capita GDP from Iraqi Dinar (ID) 42 to ID 71 in the same interval.[4] This is a reasonably high rate of growth by most standards. Other (less comprehensive) studies report broadly similar growth rates in income for the period. K. G. Fenelon reports that in real terms (of constant 1956 prices) national income increased from ID 165 million in 1950 to ID 303 million in 1956, which corresponds to an annual rate of growth of more than 10 percent. Likewise, Maniakin calculates that national income increased from ID 292 million in 1956 to ID 422 in 1960 (also in constant 1956 prices), an annual rate of increase of 9.6 percent.[5]

Lower rates of growth in GDP are, however, evident for the 1960s. In constant 1966 prices, GDP increased from ID 578 million in 1960 to ID 975 million in 1968, an annual rate of growth of 6.8 percent.[6] Given that population increased by more than 3 percent per annum over this interval, real per capita GDP grew at 3.5 percent per annum in this period.[7] Moreover, there is evidence that GDP grew at a slower pace in the second half of the decade in comparison with the first: according to IMF statistics, per capita GDP (in constant 1975 prices) increased from ID 259 in 1965 to ID 288 in 1970, a rate of increase of roughly 2.1 percent per annum.[8]

Parallel to the expansion in GDP, the evidence suggests that there was a sustained increase in real government consumption but not in household consumption or investment in the period prior to 1970, although incomplete data do not allow one to make definitive judgments. Table 3.1 contains estimates of government and household expenditure as well as gross fixed capital formation (additions of newly produced fixed assets such as machinery, buildings, and vehicles purchased by businesses,

Table 3.1 Per capita government and household consumption and gross fixed capital formation, in constant 1975 prices (ID), 1955–70[10]

Year	Consumption			Gross fixed capital formation
	Final	Government	Household	
1955	78	17	61	24
1960	97	26	70	30
1965	126	36	91	26
1970	120	37	82	26

Note: Final consumption may not equal the sum of government and household consumption because of rounding

Source: Calculated from IMF, *International Financial Statistics Yearbook 1986*, pp. 398–401

household, and government) used here to indicate investment, all in per capita 1975 prices. There was an uninterrupted rise in government consumption, but household consumption actually declined between 1965 and 1970 and gross fixed capital formation declined between 1960 and 1970. Consequently, final (government plus household) consumption declined between 1965 and 1970. Nevertheless, all these aggregates increased over the longer period 1955 to 1970.

The rise in government consumption is not surprising as the toppling of the monarchy brought about increased social spending and greater state involvement in the economy, emblematized in 1964 by the nationalization of major enterprises in manufacturing, banking, and insurance, as noted in the previous chapter. But the decline in household consumption and gross fixed capital formation may have been related to political instability in the period between 1958 and 1970. Frequent changes in government and consequent disruption to administrative apparatuses as well as conflict in the Kurdish region likely had the effect of depressing consumption and dampened the ability of government to carry through its development plans.[9]

There is likewise a lack of (short-run) correspondence between growth in consumption and GDP for the period 1970 to 1990. This is not, however, the most striking feature of the findings in Table 3.2, calculated from UN data that have updated recently (after the Iraq war in 2003). Calculations based on the new data indicate that final consumption, notably government but also to a lesser extent household consumption, actually increased in the 1980s – that is, in the context of the Iran–Iraq war. This challenges prior conclusions based on previous UN data that indicated that consumption expenditures had risen sharply in the 1970s but declined during the 1980s.[11]

The disparity in findings underlines the data issues concerning Iraq, but the new findings are arguably plausible. The revised data are evidently in

Table 3.2 Per capita GDP, government and household consumption and gross fixed capital formation, in constant 1990 prices ($ US), 1970–90

Year	GDP	Consumption			Gross fixed capital formation
		Final	Government	Household	
1970	670	253	101	151	73
1975	865	235	106	129	174
1979	1384	232	101	131	259
1980	1304	202	98	104	239
1981	1030	517	278	240	415
1982	1001	690	339	351	398
1985	858	310	115	194	141
1989	955	338	214	124	174

Source: Calculated from UN, National Accounts Aggregate Database, available at http://unstats.un.org, accessed 07-12-09

part the result of updated price index estimates, whose revision has changed the final data.[12] The updated statistics are credible because they are reasonably consistent with the economic and political developments at that time, and also with the available household expenditure data, as we shall see.

These data show that, in $US terms, real GDP per capita doubled between 1970 and 1979 but declined during the 1980s to roughly its level in 1975 by the late 1980s.[13] The rise in GDP is associated with the increase in price and exported volume of oil, which accounted for 92.9 percent, 98.6 percent, and 98.6 percent of all exports in 1965, 1975, and 1983, respectively.[14] As exports are – along with private and government consumption, investment, and imports – one of the items of GDP expenditure, changes in the value of petroleum exports are reflected in altered GDP.

The value of exports rose sharply in the 1970s as oil prices and exported volumes of oil expanded. The price of OPEC's "Arab Light" crude, for example, more than tripled from an annual average of US$ 3.05 per barrel in 1973 to US$ 10.73 in 1974, and rose sharply again from US$ 12.70 in 1978 to US$ 28.64 in 1980.[15] At the same time, Iraq's crude oil exports increased, aided by the nationalization of the oil industry in 1972. Prior to nationalization, international oil companies controlled the production and sale of this resource. Aware of the economy's reliance on oil, when negotiating with the Iraq government, the companies often deliberately constricted output to obtain drilling or pricing concessions. For instance, during such negotiations, in 1972, petroleum output declined by 13.5 percent over the previous year.[16] Infighting within the Iraqi government over oil policy, especially during the 1960s, also contributed to the low rate of growth in petroleum exports. In fact, according to Paul Stevens, the failure to greatly raise production levels in the period 1961 to 1976 was due less to the machinations of the oil companies than to the failure of successive Iraqi governments to confront the companies.[17] Nationalization gave the Iraqi state direct control over output. Although membership in OPEC made oil exports subject to a quota, Iraq was able to obtain quota increases in the 1970s. When, in the context of its revolution in 1978, Iran reduced oil output and exports, Iraq, along with other OPEC countries, were able expand their oil output to take advantage of the resulting shortfall in supply. Thus, Iraq's output of oil increased from 1.47 million barrels per day (MBD) in 1972 to 2.42 MBD in 1976, and reached 3.48 MBD in 1979.[18]

By contrast, petroleum prices and output declined in the 1980s, resulting in economic contraction. The international price of oil decreased from an annual average of US$ 32.51 per barrel in 1981 to US$ 13.53 in 1986, but recovered slightly to an average of US$ 16.43 in the years 1987–89.[19] Moreover, the Iran–Iraq war, which began in 1980, caused severe disruptions to petroleum exports.[20] Iraq's export facilities in the Arabian-Persian Gulf were destroyed, and one of its pipelines to the

Mediterranean was closed. As a result, petroleum output fell to 0.9 MBD in 1981, but rose gradually to 1.22 MBD in 1984 and reached 2.74 MBD in 1988.[21] However, because of the decline in the price of oil in the latter part of the 1980s, the increase in output translated into only slightly increased revenues. Exports declined from ID 10 billion in 1980 to ID 3.6 billion in 1981, averaged ID 3.5 billion in the years 1982–85, reached a low of ID 2.4 billion in 1986, and recovered to an average of ID 4.0 billion in the years 1987–88.[22]

Whether they result from a tax on oil companies' output (or profits) or from the direct sale of oil to international buyers, oil revenues usually accrue directly to the state in oil-exporting economies. Depending on the priorities of government, these revenues may be retained as foreign currency, used to purchase foreign financial or physical assets, spent on current domestic consumption, or capital formation (both human and physical). In the case of Iraq, oil revenues financed a significant portion of the state's "ordinary budget" (which includes recurrent expenditures) and almost its entire "development budget" (investment spending). In fiscal year 1972–3, for example, income from oil constituted 40 percent of total revenues for the ordinary budget and increased after the oil price rise to reach 80 percent in fiscal year 1974–5, the last year for which such a breakdown in revenue is available.[23] However, the correspondence between types of budget and classes of spending is imperfect: the purchase of new equipment for state enterprises or the construction of public schools was often paid out of the ordinary budget, even though these are investment activities. In contrast, almost all the activities paid out of the development budget were investments. Indeed, the size of the development budget was often based on the expected receipts from oil, rising in anticipation of higher oil revenues.[24]

Returning to the substance of Table 3.2, we notice that there was stagnation in per capita consumption in the 1970s, but increase in the 1980s. Per capita government consumption, which excludes military expenditures,[25] remained roughly steady from 1970 to 1980, exploded in 1981 and 1982, and subsequently declined but not to its level in the 1970s. Because the government consumption figures exclude military expenditures, they understate any rise in government consumption that resulted from the Ba'th regime's military buildup in the 1970s and subsequent war with Iran in the 1980s. According to Abbas Alnasrawi, military expenditures increased during the 1970s and averaged roughly a quarter to three-fifths of GDP in the 1980s.[26] Yet the exclusion of military expenditures is useful in that it gives an indication of civilian expenditures, at least for the 1970s. Part of the costs of the war with Iran in the 1980s was likely borne by the state's civilian organs, notably the Ministry of Industry and Military Industrialization (founded in the 1980s), that controlled a variety of military and civilian activities.[27] Consequently, the government consumption figures for the 1980s may include some military expenditure, which suggests that state spending on civilian goods is lower than the estimates of government consumption for the 1980s indicates.

The stagnation of government consumption in the 1970s runs against prior conclusions[28] based on earlier data that indicated a large rise of more than 10 percent per annum in government and household consumption between 1970 and 1980.[29] There was undoubtedly an increase in state expenditures during the 1970s. As a result of the oil price explosion in the early 1970s, for example, nominal expenditures in the ordinary budget almost tripled between fiscal years 1972–3 and 1974–5.[30] However, the revised figures indicate that these expenditures buttressed investment (as we shall see), not consumption. If the noted rise in ordinary budget expenditures went to finance investments rather than consumption, the estimates of consumption presented in Table 3.2 are plausible.

Government consumption rose sharply in the first two years of war with Iran (1981 and 1982), only to return to roughly its former level later in the decade. This is because the Ba'th regime pursued a policy of "guns and butter" from the start of the war in 1980 until 1982. The regime used its foreign currency reserves (accumulated mostly during the 1970s and almost depleted by 1983) to shield the public as much as possible from the privations of war (for example, using the state's monopoly on foreign trade to import consumer goods that were by comparison scarce before the start of the war), carrying out its ambitious development program, and vigorously prosecuting with Iran. With the exhaustion of currency reserves, decline in oil revenues and unsure about when the war would end, the regime changed course in 1983. It implemented austerity measures, reduced its social spending, slashed its developmental budget, and borrowed heavily from abroad to finance expenditures that it deemed essential, notably those relating to the war effort and expenses that promoted social stability (which arguably accounts for the rise in food imports, as noted later). Consequently, foreign exchange reserves, conservatively estimated to have been US$ 36 billion in 1980, were essentially wiped out, as the small public debt of US$ 2.5 billion in 1980 ballooned through heavy borrowing.[31]

Turning to household expenditure, Table 3.2 indicates that it declined between 1970 and 1980, increased markedly in 1981 and 1982, and declined thereafter to roughly its level in 1975. Even if the household consumption level is overstated for 1970, the estimates suggest that household consumption likely was stagnant during the 1970s, an interesting finding and contrary to earlier conclusions. The figures are plausible because they are consistent with economic and political realities as well as policies at the time. The ongoing conflict in the northern Kurdish region in the early 1970s likely repressed household consumption.

Interestingly, the stagnation of consumption coincides with the expansive development plans of the state, which, as we shall see, increased after the rise in oil prices in the 1970s and aimed for unprecedented levels of investment. The enlarged investment spending during the 1970s placed severe strains on available resources: bottlenecks were exacerbated further during the Iraq–Iraq war as labor was conscripted into the armed forces and transport systems became even more congested.[32] In the 1970s, spending on consumption was arguably not only secondary to the first priority of capital accumulation, but also competed with investment for scarce resources and unlike investment raised domestic prices but not productive capacity. In fact the regime was so concerned about the inflationary pressures that might arise out of such bottlenecks that (much like other Gulf oil exporters) it imported labor and avoided large pay rises in the public sector, in order to restrain the growth in wages and salaries, which started to increase in real terms in the late 1970s.[33] In contrast, the increase and subsequent decline after 1982 in household consumption may represent the regime's attempt to shield the public from the privations of war. Although foreign reserves were exhausted by 1983 and despite the financial demands of war, reduced oil earnings, and plummeting GDP, the state buttressed per capita household consumption during the 1980s, partly by importing consumer goods (notably food, as we shall see) and selling the goods at subsidized prices. As a result, per capita consumption levels in the middle to late 1980s were not lower than the levels in the late 1970s. Thus, although growth of consumption was constrained during the booming 1970s, it was buttressed during the stagnant 1980s.

There is tentative support for this conclusion from surveys of household expenditure conducted by the CSO and presented in Table 3.3. Deflating the expenditure data by the GDP price deflator provided by the UN yields estimates of real household expenditure. This indicates that whereas real household expenditure increased in the second half of the 1970s, household expenditure expanded during the 1980s. However, these results

Table 3.3 Household expenditure surveys, 1971–2 to 1988

Year	Nominal expenditure (ID)	UN GDP price deflator (1990 = 100)	Real expenditure (1990 ID)
1971/2	6.66	15.1*	44.1
1976	12.93	31.8	40.7
1979	19.32	44.8	43.5
1984/5	43.34	79.9*	54.2
1988	54.65	79.0	69.2

* Obtained by averaging the two relevant years

Sources: For expenditure data: CSO, *Annual Abstract of Statistics 1993*, Baghdad, undated, pp. 388–92. For price deflator: UN, National Accounts Aggregate Database, available at http://unstats.un.org, accessed 07-12-09

are partly sensitive to the choice of price index that is used. Because other indexes are incomplete, the UN series (available for all the data points in the table) is used. Partial consumer price data from the IMF, for example, suggest that there was a rise in household consumption between 1971–2 and 1976.[34] CSO price index data[35] nonetheless confirm that there was no decline in household consumption between 1979 and 1988.

The distribution of income

Although no single study examines consistently the changes in the distribution of income in Iraq through the period, some have examined income distribution at distinct points in time. The studies are summarized in Table 3.4. The estimates for 1956 are for economically active individuals and suggest a high degree of inequality by most standards: while the bottom 40 percent of income earners received 6.8 percent of total income the top 20 percent received 68 percent, and corresponds to a Gini coefficient of 0.61.

The estimates for 1971, which were calculated from the Household Budget Survey of that year, suggest a fundamental change in income distribution. For the country as a whole in 1971, the bottom 40 percent of households received 15.9 percent of total cash income, while the top 20 percent received 47.1 percent. When income is adjusted to include imputed rent and income in kind, this ratio becomes 18.3:44.1 percent respectively. For individuals, the cash earnings of the bottom 40 percent were 20.8 percent, while the top 20 percent received 40.7 percent. When income is

Table 3.4 Indicators of income inequality

Year	Ratio of bottom 40 percent to top 20 percent			Gini coefficient		
	Country	Urban	Rural	Country	Urban	Rural
1956	6.8/68.0			0.61		
1971	*Households:*					
Cash	15.9/47.1					
Adjusted	18.3/44.1	17.7/44.6	19.4/42.2	0.36	0.37	0.34
	Individuals:					
Cash	20.8/40.7					
Adjusted	23.9/37.3			0.26		
1976	*Households:*					
Adjusted				0.37	0.34	0.40

Sources: For 1945: Michael P. Todaro, *Economic Development in the Third World*, Longman, New York, 1985, p. 150. For 1971: Shaker M. Issa, 'The Distribution of Income in Iraq, 1971', in *The Integration of Modern Iraq*, Abbas Kelidar (ed.), Croom Helm, London, 1979, pp. 123–34. For 1976: Ismail Aubaid Hummadi, *Economic Growth and Structural Changes in the Iraqi Economy with Emphasis on Agriculture: 1953-1975*, Ph.D. Dissertation, University of Colorado: Boulder, 1978, p. 169

adjusted this ratio becomes 23.9:37.3 percent, which indicates that the average income of the top 20 percent was roughly double that for the bottom 40 percent. The corresponding Gini coefficients for adjusted household income were 0.37 for urban areas, 0.34 for rural, and 0.36 for the country as a whole, compared with 0.26 for adjusted individual income. The greater equality in the distribution of income for individuals is a result of variation of household size with income: the average size of households for the lower-income groups was smaller than that for the higher-income groups. The inequality estimates for 1976 are derived from the Household Budget Survey of that year and are adjusted to include income in kind. These give Gini coefficients of 0.34, 0.40, and 0.37 for urban, rural, and country.

The apparent rise in rural inequality between 1971 and 1976 may be due to the different sampling methods employed in successive household budget surveys, from which the estimates of inequality are derived: the 1976 survey is thought to have been far more complete.[36] Even so, there is little doubt that the distribution of income improved between 1956 and 1976 and, indeed, compared favorably with that of many developing and some developed countries.[37]

This improved income distribution was not accidental but was the result of the emphasis on social welfare that successive governments after the 1958 revolution put into practice. In rural areas, land reform enacted in 1959, and amended in 1970, redistributed land assets, which equalized incomes within rural areas. Also, after 1958, greater resources were devoted to health and education, as we shall see. To the extent that the provision of these services disproportionally benefited the poor – directly by heavy subsidization of goods that the poor purchase or indirectly as enhanced educational and health outcomes promote higher labor productivities, access to employment and hence income – it promotes a more equal distribution of income. Finally, the expansion of the public sector, where wage and salary differentials were deliberately curtailed, was another factor that likely contributed to lowering income inequality.

Nevertheless, there are reasons to believe that the disparity in incomes increased after the middle 1970s, although data are unavailable to confirm this. Increased oil revenues permitted the state to expand the provision of health and education goods, but windfall revenues also allowed the state to embark on an ambitious development program that often utilized the services of domestic contactors. According to Isam al-Khafaji, the Ba'thi state used such development expenditures to reward particular groups: contractors, importers, and industrialists with close ties to the regime.[38] Moreover, there was a perceptible pro-market policy reorientation beginning in the late 1970s. Market liberalization and privatization of state assets began in 1983 in agriculture and was extended in 1987–9 to manufacturing and services sectors: public enterprises were sold to investors, pro-capitalist labor laws enacted, and some price controls eased.[39] The privatization measures failed in terms of their primary goal – to induce private capital to increase the domestic supply of goods, either by investing in goods producing activities or through use of (by the late 1980s) scarce foreign exchange to finance imports; consequently some of the measures were reversed.[40] But by concentrating profits and wealth, the privatization measures along with the favor shown to well-connected contractors likely worsened the distribution of income.

Formation of physical capital

Table 3.2 indicates that there was a rise in investment in physical capital following the oil price rise of the 1970s. Indeed, per capita real gross fixed capital formation more than doubled between 1970 and 1975 and had more than doubled again by the early 1980s. However, investment declined during the 1980s, falling to its levels in the middle 1970 but still higher than the level in the 1970s, before the rise in oil prices.

Since the 1960s public investment has accounted for most of national investment.[41] By 1980, the public sector was responsible for 78 per cent of gross fixed capital formation.[42] Thus, changes in the levels of public investment account for the rise in the nation's level of physical capital formation during the 1970s and its subsequent decline in the 1980s. Augmented oil revenues allowed the state to greatly expand its investments during the 1970s; the regime pursued its development plans until 1983, when they could no longer be funded. Even after the reduction in public investment, in 1985, the government still accounted for 72 percent of total investment, the lowest proportion in the period 1980–88.[43] It is the reduced levels of public investment are primarily responsible for the depressed levels of capital formation noted above.

The extent of the decline in public investment is indicated in Table 3.5, which contains estimates of development allocations from 1970 to 1983, the last year for which data are available. Although some investment expenditures are recorded in the ordinary rather than development budget, the figures are suggestive and show that the value of development allocations increased more or less steadily until 1983, when there was an abrupt decline in both nominal and real investment expenditures.

In fact these estimates of investment allocations may overstate the actual levels of investment, especially for the 1980s. Abbas Alnasrawi has noted that development spending in Iraq has been hampered by the lack of skilled labor and inadequate infrastructure funding, with the result that development spending has consistently lagged behind development allocations. In the period 1970–74, for example, only 61 percent of the development allocation was spent.[44] Estimates of allocations only (not spending) are available for the period 1976–83, but it is exceeding unlikely that anywhere near the amounts allocated for investment were actually spent. Pressures on infrastructure and shortages of skilled labor

Table 3.5 Development allocations, 1970–83

Year/Period	Nominal allocation (billion ID)	Real (1990 ID) allocation (billion ID)
1970–74	1.93	11.16*
1976	1.49	4.69
1977	2.38	6.80
1978	2.80	7.93
1979	3.28	7.39
1980	5.24	8.19
1981	6.74	12.28
1982	7.70	12.26
1983	5.35	7.68

Note: Because the price index for capital formation is unavailable, the GDP deflator is used to deflate the nominal investment allocations instead

* Calculated by deflating by the average price index for the years 1970–74

Sources: For estimates of investment allocations: Adapted from Abbas Alnasrawi, *The Economy of Iraq*, pp. 71, 82. For the price index used to calculate real investment: UN, National Accounts Aggregate Database, available at http://unstats.un.org, accessed 07-12-09

were greater still in the war conditions of the 1980s. The conscription of men into the armed forces, which numbered 800,000 (or 18.2 percent of the labor force) in 1986, surely exacerbated labor shortages,[45] while the closing of Iraq's seaports during the war necessitated the use of costlier overland transport.

Because productivity-promoting investments (over the long term) in a variety of economic activities could potentially avoid the Dutch Disease that is associated with mineral exports, the sectoral composition of investments is of interest. The (unweighted) average distribution of gross fixed capital formation by economic sector, for the period 1970–85, is presented in Table 3.6. Transport received a relatively large share of investment in each of the three sub-periods, 1970–75, 1975–80, and 1980–85 or 20.9 percent of investment, the highest sectoral share, over the entire period 1970–85. Manufacturing also received a comparatively large proportion of investment, in the sub-periods 1970–75 and 1975–80, but a relatively low share in 1980–85. Over the entire period, 1970–85, this sector's share of investment was second to that of transport. Agriculture received a roughly even share of investment in the three sub-periods, which translated to 11.6 percent of investment over the entire period. Investment in government services shows a consistent increase over time, rising to 20.8 percent of GDP in 1980–85. However, for the entire period, 1970–85, government services received, on average, 15.4 percent of investment. Mining (or oil),[46] electricity, construction, and trade received lower shares of investment.

The manufacturing sector's significantly reduced share of investment in 1980–85 is due to the decline in development spending. Throughout the

Table 3.6 Distribution of gross fixed capital formation by economic sector, 1970–85

Economic activity	Gross fixed capital formation (%)			
	1970–75	1975–80	1980–85	1970–85
Agriculture, hunting, fishing, and forestry	11.3	10.8	12.2	11.6
Mining and quarrying	7.8	8.3	5.3	7.7
Manufacturing	22.5	18.3	8.7	16.3
Electricity, gas, and water	5.3	7.3	10.0	7.6
Construction	2.7	4.5	2.3	3.1
Wholesale and retail trade	4.2	4.2	3.2	3.9
Transport, storage, and communication	18.2	22.8	23.7	20.9
Government services	11.5	14.0	20.8	15.4

Source: Calculated from UN, *National Accounts Statistics: Analysis of Main Aggregates 1985*, New York, 1988, pp. 207–8

1970s and 1980s, investment in manufacturing was largely government financed, accounting for, on average, over 90 percent of gross capital formation in equipment and machinery, a class of producers' durable goods between 1980 and 1988.[47] Reductions in development spending affected manufacturing more than other sectors, reducing manufacturing's share of investment.

The prominence of government services, which received roughly one-seventh of total investment in the period 1970–85, is also noteworthy. The rise in the proportion of investment devoted to government services in the period 1980–85 is not surprising given the government expenditure was rising while GDP was falling in the sub-period. Government consumption as a proportion of GDP rose from 10 percent in 1978 to 27 percent in 1981 and was 15 percent in 1984.[48] However, although some investment in this category was arguably necessary to improve or rationalize public administration, a portion of this expenditure surely served to enable internal repression and therefore cannot be considered as productive investments that expand domestic supply of goods.

Be that as it may, the observed pattern of investment is not one that is concentrated in a particular sector and suggests that the objective of these (mostly public) investments was to diversify economic activity away from reliance on oil. The evidence does not support the view that public investments neglected agriculture and privileged the oil and manufacturing sectors.[49] Agriculture consistently received a sizable portion of investments. And, whereas the shares of investment devoted to the manufacturing and oil sectors declined between 1970–75 and 1980–85, the portion going to agriculture was roughly stable. Indeed, the picture that emerges is that of an economy engaged in rapid capital formation in a variety of economic activities – a "big-push" to establish a variety of industries.

Of course, there is no guarantee that these investments yielded (or even were capable of yielding) the highest social rates of return. Joe Stork has cast doubt on the prospective profitability of the large capital-intensive hydrocarbon-based industrial investments of the state during the 1970s, noting that if the cost of inputs is factored in at international prices (rather than subsidized and hence distorted Iraqi prices), the sector is internationally uncompetitive.[50] While in principle profitability is not the correct gage with which to measure the performance of public-sector firms (concerned as they are with social costs and benefits that may deviate considerably from private measures), attaining profitability under international prices is pertinent because these investments were intended to diversify economic activity and eventually the composition of exports (away from dependence on oil). It is possible (even likely) that the costs in such industries would be initially high (and hence profits low), but costs would be expected to decline as experience in production and development of skills is gained. In fact there exists in general a high degree of complementarity between the accrual of physical capital and human capital (expansion of which is discussed in upcoming chapters): the rate of return on physical capital increases when combined with human capital. This is especially the case in relation to industries (such as petrochemicals) that require specific human capital. One would therefore expect investments in education and health to raise the rate of return to investments in physical capital.

Subsequent scholarship illustrates how selective state interventions (including subsidies) can overcome co-ordination and other failures to promote industrialization.[51] That is, it may be advantageous to deliberately defy comparative advantage in the short to medium term to establish viable industries in the long run. We will never know whether or not Iraq's (presumed) defiance of its comparative advantage was wise: the war with Iran essentially halted Iraq's development and the subsequent invasion of Kuwait and war in 1991 reversed it. Given the supporting investments in human capital and in a wide variety of sectors, the policies may well have succeeded in promoting industrialization and worked to avoid the Dutch Disease. This does not imply that Iraq's implementation of its development strategy was optimal or even that the strategy was the correct one given existing constraints, but that the balance of evidence does suggest that development was vigorously pursued, often at the expense of current consumption (notably during the 1970s), and that had it not been interrupted, the strategy might have resulted in Iraq's successful industrialization and attainment of a diversified economy.

Indeed, the development strategy encountered a number of obstacles and suffered some shortcomings. As regards the general features of the economy, after the early 1960s Iraq was a highly regulated economy, with an overabundance of policy-imposed distortions including detailed price controls on a wide variety of consumer and intermediate goods, restrictions on international trade and defective price signals. Although state intervention in economic activity is often justified in terms of correcting existing (endogenous) distortions, the extent and detail of regulation of Iraq's economy was arguably excessive.[52] It consequently often was difficult to determine which projects had the highest social rates of return. Moreover, the state bureaucracy, which controlled most of (even non-oil) GDP after the early 1970s,[53] was notoriously slow, cumbersome, and inefficient with bureaucrats reluctant to make decisions or take initiative.[54]

As concerns the state's big-push strategy itself, the economy's capacity to absorb investments was limited and it was thus unable to carry through all the planned investment projects. The high tariffs and quantity restrictions on imports promoted import substitution, but along with an overvalued exchange rate also discriminated against exports. Counterfactually, a liberal import policy for consumer goods might have provided more consumption goods and worked to sap inflationary pressures (imports were later liberalized during the 1980s, but the aim then was to attract investment funds from abroad, not to forestall inflation arising out of increased demand). In fact, many of the heavy industries that Iraq sought to develop (such as machinery and petrochemicals) were characterized by increasing returns and, consequently, would be competitive only if the demand generated in the (still narrow but growing) domestic market was sufficiently large or if market-expanding trade agreements were arranged. Finally, given the fast pace of capital accumulation, "turn-key projects," which handed over speedily completed industrial establishments, were often favored because foreign contractors could complete these projects fairly quickly. But turn-keys often involved minimal local technical input and hence constrained the development of local skills and technology. Whatever the difficulties or contradictions of the development strategy, there is no doubt that oil revenues were marshaled to establish a broad array of industries that produced a range of goods.

Economic structure

The contribution of oil revenues to the national economy can be gleaned from examining the contribution to GDP of the various economic sectors including mining, presented in Table 3.7. As noted in the last chapter, the petroleum sector was growing in economic significance before 1950, but still was second in importance to agriculture. After 1950, however, oil became the dominant sector in the economy. By the 1960s, oil generated no less than a third of GDP, as evinced by the percentage contribution of the mining sector. This rose to two-thirds with the rise in output and price of oil during the 1970s, but declined with the reductions in output after 1980. Nevertheless, throughout the period, oil was the largest single sector.

The decline in the relative shares of the main non-oil sectors, agriculture, construction, and manufacturing in the period 1970–80 does not signify an absolute decline in the output of these sectors, but was the

60 *Economic growth, consumption, income, and capital*

Table 3.7 Proportion of GDP generated by type of economic activity, 1960–89

Economic activity	1960	1965	1970	1974	1980	1984	1987	1989
Agriculture (% of GDP)	19	20	16	7	5	13	15	17
Industry	52	47	40	66	65	34	34	37
Mining	41	37	30	60	60	24	20	24
Manufacturing	10	9	9	5	4	9	12	11
Electricity, gas, and water	*	2	1	*	*	1	2	2
Construction	4	4	3	2	8	10	8	7
Trade, restaurants, and hotels	6	9	8	5	5	12	12	12
Transport	8	7	6	4	4	5	7	7
Finance	4	5	6	4	4	10	10	10

* Less than 1%

Sources: For 1960, 1965 and 1970: calculated from UN, *Yearbook of National Accounts Statistics 1975*, New York, 1976, p. 661; for 1974: UN, *Yearbook of National Accounts Statistics 1979*, New York, 1980, p. 585; all other years: UN, *National Accounts Statistics: Main Aggregates and Detailed Tables 1990*, New York, 1992, p. 912

outcome of a higher rate of growth in the oil sector after the early 1970s. In fact, in real terms, construction and manufacturing sectors grew by more than 250 percent each between 1970 and 1980.[55] However, because of the rise in the price and (to a lesser extent) output of oil in the period 1970–80, the (nominal) contribution of the oil sector rose.[56] In contrast, the reduced share of mining during the 1980s was the result of an absolute drop in this sector's output, which declined by 64 percent in nominal terms and by more than 50 percent in real terms between 1980 and 1985.[57] Because other sectors did not decline by as much or grew during the 1980s, their relative contributions rose.

In general, however, the 1980s was a period of economic contraction brought about largely by conditions of war and the associated decline in the output of the oil sector, the relatively robust performance of personal consumption notwithstanding. As shown in Table 3.2, per capita GDP declined by a large margin between 1980 and 1985 and recovered only modestly from 1985 to 1989. Although the rate of growth in the construction sector in the period 1970–75 is most likely an overestimate – a more plausible estimate is an annualized rate of between 10 and 15 percent[58] – Table 3.8 shows the extent of the slowdown in growth of the main economic sectors. Except for agriculture,[59] real rates of growth were negative in all sectors in the period 1980–87: in the case of industry (which includes mining, manufacturing and utilities), wholesale and retail trade, and transport, the rates of decline exceeded 7 percent per annum.

The changed economic fortunes are captured in Table 3.9, which contains estimates of the various types of expenditure on GDP from 1960 to 1988. Summing private consumption, government consumption, investment, and net exports (exports minus imports) yields GDP (although the estimates in the table may not sum to 100 percent because of

Table 3.8 Real rates of growth by activity, 1970–87

Economic activity	Annualized rates of growth (percent)		
	1970–75	1975–80	1980–87
Agriculture, hunting, fishing, and forestry	−0.3	2.3	2.1
Industry	7.1	10.1	−7.9
Manufacturing	10.6	14.3	−1.8
Construction	35.5	18.0	−1.0
Wholesale and retail trade	11.4	24.9	−10.2
Transport, storage, and communication	14.2	20.3	−15.7

Source: UN, *National Accounts Statistics: Analysis of Main Aggregates 1987*, New York, 1990, pp. 172, 179, 186, 192, 199 and 206

rounding). As a proportion of all expenditures, both government and private consumption increased after 1980. As shown earlier, consumption continued to rise (or at least remained constant) as GDP declined during the 1980s. Heavy borrowing and (to a much lesser extent) declining investment levels propped up consumption after foreign reserves were practically depleted in the early 1980s. Consequently, capital formation remained well above 20 percent of GDP during the 1980s, higher than their levels in the 1960s and early 1970s. Also, as a proportion of GDP, both imports and exports declined after 1980. Sharply reduced oil revenues in the 1980s are reflected in subdued levels of exports. However, the figures presented in Table 3.9 understate the level of imports as foreign trade statistics excluded imports of military goods, which were substantial in the 1980s. According to figures compiled by Abbas Alnasrawi based on the US Arms Control and Disarmament Agency estimates, military imports averaged US\$ 5.6 billion in the period 1980 to 1988, were US\$ 2.4 billion (or 17 percent of all imports) in 1980, rose to a high of US\$ 9.2 billion in (or 83 percent of all imports) in 1984, but declined steadily thereafter.[60]

Table 3.9 Expenditure on GDP, 1960–88

Type of expenditure (percent)	1960	1965	1970	1975	1980	1985	1988
Government consumption	18	20	22	na	15	29	31
Private consumption	na	48	46	na	23	52	50
Total consumption	na	68	68	51	38	81	82
Increase in stocks	na	2	1	9	7	−4	*
Gross fixed capital formation	20	15	15	27	24	28	22
Total Investment	na	16	16	35	30	24	21
Exports	42	39	35	58	63	24	19
Imports	28	23	19	45	31	29	22

* Less than 1%

Sources: For 1960 to 1975: calculated from UN, *Yearbook of National Accounts Statistics 1979*, New York, 1980, p. 584; for 1980 to 1988: calculated from UN, *National Accounts Statistics: Main Aggregates and Detailed Tables 1990*, p. 911

In sum, the picture that emerges is that of an economy engaged in frantic capital formation but actively restrained consumption during the 1970s – when oil revenues were plentiful, and high levels of military spending, reduced capital formation but buttressed consumption, in part through the provision of subsidized civilian imports (especially food, as we shall see in Chapter 5) during the 1980s – when oil revenues were constrained and Iraq's war expenses were considerable. This image is not obviously consistent with the rentier hypothesis vision of the rentier state as one that impatiently deploys oil revenues to bribe or co-opt the public at large in order to support its political standing, unless one assumes a developmentally minded general public who values investment spending more than its own current consumption (in the 1970s but not the 1980s). The relationship between oil revenues and outcomes in economic or social policy is not clear or automatic but complex and highly contingent.[61]

Summary and conclusion

Returning to the themes presented in the introduction, the command over resources, implied in per capita consumption, was stagnant but investment was rising rapidly during the 1970s – when GDP was rising, while increased (or at least non-declining) consumption but reduced investments are evident during the 1980s – when GDP was declining or stagnant. The findings concerning consumption, based on revised data, run counter to the prevailing views of broad expansion in the command over commodities and resources during the 1970s and outright contraction during the 1980s. Although these revised estimates need to be treated with care, several points emerge from the discussion in the chapter.

The divergence between national output (and income) highlights a feature of mineral economies, where a large part of national income is derived from rent and substantially unrelated to domestic production. Even if consumption were not stagnant during the 1970s but rising, there is evidence that the state was attempting to repress consumption for fear of fueling inflation arising from its ambitious investment program. At least for the period of the 1970s, these actions run counter to what the rentier state hypothesis would predict, namely that rentier states sponsor consumption to buy political durability.

Abbas Alnasrawi has noted that successive Iraqi governments, including the Ba'th, have failed to diversify Iraq's economic base, with the result that the country had, by the late 1980s, become more rather than less dependent upon oil. He correctly notes the Ba'th regime's heightened politicization of the planning process, with five-year development plans replaced by more politically directed annual objectives.[62] In contrast, we contend that, while there were surely contradictions and inefficiencies (including resources that were arguably wasted on militarization and the noted politicization of development planning) in Iraq's development strategy, the balance of evidence suggests that a serious attempt was made to diversify the economy. Rationalization and reform might have overcome many of the shortcomings associated with Iraq's big-push strategy and avoided the worst aspects of the Dutch Disease.

The course of rapid development pursued in the 1970s may have succeeded had it not been interrupted by Iraq's attack on Iran in 1980. It is this disastrous geopolitical miscalculation to go to war rather than the choice of economic strategy or the skill with which the strategy was implemented that ultimately accounts for Iraq's economic difficulties in the 1980s and 1990s.

4 Education

Education is central to any discussion of human development. Because it is mostly (but not exclusively) the young who acquire education, the impact of the expansion of educational capabilities is substantial in developing countries, like Iraq, where a large portion of the population is under 15 years old.[1] The capacity to read and write is desirable in itself. But, education also raises labor productivity, incomes, and hence the command over goods and services, and allows one to participate more fully in society.

Because of the relative scarcity of education and skills in developing countries, the social rate of return to education typically exceeds those in developed nations. The subsidization of education is therefore highly desirable in developing countries. In fact, the social rate of return to education in these countries quite often surpasses the return on physical capital. Investments in human and physical capital, moreover, tend to be complementary, as the return to investments in physical capital will be higher in the presence of literate and educated workers.[2] Such complementary relationships flourish in relation to distinct outcomes within human development, such as complementarities between education, infant mortality and nutrition, discussed in the next chapter.

Were existing incentives, as reflected in the prevailing set of market prices, relied upon to allocate education resources, too few people would receive instruction and, consequently, society's level of output and income would be lower. Government's extensive subsidization of education, by reducing private costs and thus increasing net private benefits, restores efficiency in this market: more persons are induced to seek instruction and the level of output is, as a result, higher. This, in its simplest version, is the economic justification for state intervention in education.

Yet not all investments in education are equally profitable. Broadly speaking, social rates of return are highest for primary education, lower for secondary, and lower still for higher education – that is, expenditures on primary and secondary education will raise national income by greater increments than equivalent expenditures on university training. In addition, emphasis on primary and secondary education, rather than higher education, necessarily for the few, implies a more equitable spread of educational resources and, to the extent that education is a major determinant of future or expected income, this leads to a more egalitarian distribution of income. It is clear that university education expands one's freedom. But such education is typically many times more expensive than primary or secondary education. The freedom that one individual attains from a university education thus has to be balanced against the freedoms that many would obtain from basic literacy and numeracy associated with primary education. Emphasis on primary education and basic literacy as opposed to higher education is thus desirable.

It is with reference to these themes that the discussion in this chapter will be developed. Trends in literacy rates and enrollment ratios at various levels of education are explored; this is followed by a discussion of the patterns of change in these indicators; the trends are then decoded and explained.

Literacy and enrollment rates

Literacy rates

Literacy rates, calculated from census data, shown below in Table 4.1,[3] illustrate the historically low levels of education in Iraq. The Ottoman provinces that were later joined together to form the country were among the less developed regions of the Empire, and educational institutions were spread very thin. Education received greater emphasis in the period of the British mandate and later after independence in 1932. Still, by the middle of the century, educational achievements were low.

Indeed, only one-ninth of the population was literate in 1947. This proportion increased to 18.3 percent in 1957; in that year, roughly a third of the urban population was literate, whereas the corresponding statistic

Table 4.1 Literacy rates, 1947–87

	5 years and older				10 years and older			
Census	Total population	Urban	Rural	Rural/ urban	Total population	Urban	Rural	Rural/ urban
1947	11.0							
1957	18.3	34.7	7.5	22	18.3			
1965	29.9	43.0	16.0	37	30.3	43.8	15.7	36
1977					47.0	58.7	25.2	43
1987					72.6	77.5	60.6	78

Sources: Calculated from UNESCO, *Basic Facts and Figures 1958*, Paris, 1959, p. 13; Directorate General of Census, *Abstract of the General Census of 1957*; pp. 14, 24; Central Statistical Organization, *Annual Abstract of Statistics 1971*, Baghdad, undated, p. 66; Central Statistical Organization, *Annual Abstract of Statistics 1978*, Baghdad, undated, p. 35; and Central Statistical Organization, *Annual Abstract of Statistics 1989*, Baghdad, 1990, p. 42

for rural areas was one-thirteenth; consequently, the literacy rate in rural districts was 22 percent of the level in urban districts (indicated under the Rural/urban column). Literacy rates continued to improve and, for the 5 years and older population, reached roughly 29.9 percent for the country as a whole, 43.0 percent in urban, and 16.0 percent in rural districts in 1965. The corresponding statistics for the 10 years and older population are almost identical: 30.3 percent, 43.8 percent, and 15.7 percent respectively. In that year, the literacy rate in rural districts was 37 percent of the level in urban districts for the 5 years and older population (36 percent for the 10 years and older population). However, the majority of the population was still illiterate by 1977, as literacy in the country as a whole was 47.0 percent, 58.7 percent in urban, and 25.2 percent in rural areas, and the literacy rate in rural districts was 43 percent of the level in urban districts. By 1987 this disparity had been notably reduced, to 78 percent; in that year, literacy rates for the same groups were 72.6 percent, 77.5 percent, and 60.6 percent.

Literacy was steadily increasing, but the pace of change was uneven. Literacy rates for the entire country increased by 12 percentage points (from 18.3 percent to 30.3 percent) between 1957 and 1965; by 16.7 percentage points (from 30.3 percent to 47 percent) between 1965 and 1977; and by 25.6 percentage points (from 47 percent to 72.6 percent) between 1977 and 1987. In the same period, the rural–urban disparity in literacy declined. The rural literacy rate as a proportion of its urban counterparts was 22 percent in 1957, 36 percent (37 percent for the 5 years and older population) in 1965, 43 percent in 1977, and 78 percent in 1987. The largest decline in the rural–urban disparity in literacy rates occurred between 1977 and 1987.

The improvements in literacy before 1977 are mainly accounted for by a rising proportion of school-age children attending school, rather than an expansion in the number of illiterate adults receiving instruction. In contrast, the gains in literacy and the large decline in the urban–rural disparity between 1977 and 1987 are accounted for by the "illiteracy eradication campaign."

This program was launched in 1978 with Law No. 92, which mandated that illiterate persons between the ages of 15 and 45 (who numbered roughly 2.25 million or 18 percent of the total population)[4] attend literacy classes. The classes taught reading, writing and arithmetic, but also engaged in "political awareness," in particular "the achievements and aspirations of the BASP [Ba'th Arab Socialist Party]."[5] Incentives to participate in these classes included reductions in prison sentences and the availability of nurseries near illiteracy centers, which encouraged women to attend.[6] Punishments in the form of ineligibility for bank loans or termination of government employment were legislated. However, it appears that peer pressure typically sufficed to ensure participation, and there was evidently a strong desire on the part of illiterates to learn to read and write, as testified by the fact that roughly 9 percent of those who attended the program were over 45 years old and so not required to attend.[7] Within the targeted population, 84 percent attended classes and, on the whole, the dropout rate was very low.[8]

The adult literacy campaign succeeded in substantially raising literacy rates, especially in rural areas where a disproportionate part of the targeted population lived and also, as we shall see in Chapter 6, for women. Although average rates of literacy were on the decline before the implementation of the program, Table 4.2 shows that the absolute number of illiterates continued to increase. Between 1977 and 1987, however, the absolute number of illiterates declined for the first time, from roughly 4 million to less than 3 million. The program effectively reversed the hitherto existing trend of rising number of illiterates in the country and, largely as a result of the program, Iraq's gains in terms of literacy were higher than any other Middle Eastern or Arab country in the period 1957 to 1983.[9]

Enrollment rates

Enrollment rates in primary education show clear improvement in the period under consideration. As illustrated in Table 4.3, net enrollment[10] for the 7 to 12 years old population increased quite steadily from 1950 to 1968.[11] For the 6 to 11 years old population, net enrollment increased steadily from 48 percent in 1960 to 99 percent in 1980. It then declined slightly to 93 percent in 1985, but recovered to 96 percent in 1987 and 94 percent in 1988. The gross enrollment rate for the same population exhibits a similar trend over this period.

Two points are of interest. The net enrollment rates for the 6 to 11 years old population in 1960 (48 percent) are significantly lower that that for the 7 to 12 years old population in the same year (67 percent). This suggests that parents were deferring primary schooling for their children: parents were sending their children to school at an age above the minimum age of admission. Also, the increase in enrollment was uneven:

Table 4.2 Illiterate population, 1957–87

Census	Illiterate population (million)	
	5 years and older	10 years and older
1957	4.18	
1965	4.52	3.61
1977		4.00
1987		2.91

Sources: Directorate General of Census, *Abstract of the General Census of 1957*; p. 24; Central Statistical Organization, *Annual Abstract of Statistics 1971*, p. 66; Central Statistical Organization, *Annual Abstract of Statistics 1978*, p. 35; and Central Statistical Organization, *Annual Abstract of Statistics 1989*, p. 42

Table 4.3 Enrollment rates in primary education

Year	Primary (6–11 years of age) Gross	Net	Primary (7–12 years of age) Gross	Net
1950				24
1955				36
1960	65	48		67
1965			72	57
1968				69
1970	69	55		
1975	94	79		
1976	99	81		
1980	113	99		
1985	104	93		
1987	109	96		
1988	107	94		

Sources: UNESCO, *Statistical Yearbook 1970*, Paris, 1971, p. 97; UNESCO, *Statistical Yearbook 1974*, Paris, 1975, p. 148; UNESCO, *Statistical Yearbook 1977*, Paris, 1978, p. 158; UNESCO, *Statistical Yearbook 1984*, Paris, 1985, 3-49; UNESCO, *Statistical Yearbook 1988*, Paris, 1989, 3-47; and UNESCO, *Statistical Yearbook 1994*, Paris, 1995, 3–48

there was a significant rise in enrollment between 1955 and 1960 and large gains between 1970 and 1980, although there was also a slight, but perhaps significant, decline in enrollment between 1980 and 1988. Even so, net enrollment rates were well above 90 percent in the 1980s.

Similarly, secondary school enrollment increased in this period. As shown in Table 4.4,[12] net enrollment for the 13 to 18 years old population increased from 5 percent in 1950 to 8 percent in 1955, to 17 percent in 1960 and reached 26 percent in 1968. Likewise, net enrollment for the 12 to 17 years old population increased from 19 percent in 1970 to 25 percent in 1975 to 47 percent in 1980 and stood at 40 percent in 1988. Again the improvements in enrollment were uneven, with the largest increases occurring between 1955 and 1960, and between 1975 and 1980.

These statistics include enrollments in vocational and teacher training, as well as general secondary enrollment. Vocational and teacher training were a small proportion of total secondary enrollment. In 1975, for example, 23,775 students were enrolled in vocational training, which represented 4.5 percent of total secondary enrollment; the number enrolled in teacher training was lower still.[13] However, as the economy's need for skilled labor became increasingly apparent to the government, enrollment in vocational training increased rapidly, even during the 1980s when enrollment in total secondary education stagnated. The number of students in vocational training grew from 9,700 in 1970 to 54,000 in 1980 and reached 160,300 in 1988 – at a much faster rate than the total number of secondary students, which increased from 314,000 to 1,033,400 to 1,116,900 during the same years.[14] In contrast, teacher

Table 4.4 Enrollment rates in secondary education

| Year | Secondary (12–17 years of age) | | Secondary (13–18 years of age) |
	Gross	Net	Net
1950			5
1955			8
1960			17
1965			23
1968			26
1970	24	19	
1975	35	25	
1976	38	28	
1980	57	47	
1985	55	na	
1987	49	41	
1988	48	40	

Sources: UNESCO, *Statistical Yearbook 1970*, p. 97; UNESCO, *Statistical Yearbook 1974*, p. 148; UNESCO, *Statistical Yearbook 1977*, p. 158; UNESCO, *Statistical Yearbook 1984*, 3-49; UNESCO, *Statistical Yearbook 1988*, 3-47; and UNESCO, *Statistical Yearbook 1994*, 3-48

training grew at a lower rate, roughly parallel to the rate of growth of total secondary enrollment.

Enrollment rates in higher education increased markedly in this period. As Table 4.5 points out, the proportion of the 20 to 24 years old population enrolled at university increased from 2.0 percent in 1960 to 5.2 percent in 1970, to roughly 9.0 percent from 1975 to 1980. This rose sharply to 12.4 percent in 1985 and reached 13.8 percent in 1988. Thus, in contrast to primary and secondary education, the enrollment rate in higher education rose during the 1980s.

Despite the decline in primary and secondary enrollment in the 1980s, the general picture that emerges is one of the enhanced spread of education in the period under study. But, the statistics examined give little indication of the changes in the quality of education. The question of whether or not the quality of education has been maintained is an

Table 4.5 Enrollment rates in higher education (20–24 years of age)

Year	Gross
1960	2.0
1965	4.1
1970	5.2
1975	9.0
1980	9.3
1985	12.4
1988	13.8

Sources: UNESCO, *Statistical Yearbook 1977*, p. 158; UNESCO, *Statistical Yearbook 1984*, 3-49; and UNESCO, *Statistical Yearbook 1988*, 3-47

important one, especially since rapid expansions in enrollment have often been associated with declines in standards.[15]

To the extent that the quality of instruction is a function of, among other things, the degree to which students have access to teacher resources, increases in the pupil–teacher ratio would suggest a reduction in teacher access and hence a decline in the quality of education. Moreover, the question of whether there has been a decline in the standards to which students are held is of interest. In this regard, changes in the failure rate on national examinations as well as the ratio of repeaters to all students in the last year of primary and secondary education are evaluated. All other things remaining constant, a relatively unchanged failure rate and constant ratio of repeaters would suggest that standards were maintained in the period. Of course, it is possible that factors such as the degree of difficulty in passing national examinations and the quality of students might have changed in this period and these issues are also discussed.

Table 4.6 shows that the pupil to teacher ratio in primary education was remarkably stable in this period. It actually declined slightly between 1958 and 1962 when primary enrollment increased rapidly from roughly 527,000[16] to 850,000,[17] as the number of teachers increased at a still higher rate. The ratio increased marginally between 1975 and 1980, when there was a similar rise in enrollment, but returned to its previous level by 1982. Over the entire period, though, no deterioration in the student to teacher ratio in primary education is apparent; if anything, the long-term trend points to improvement.

Table 4.6 Pupil to teacher ratios in primary and secondary education, 1950–88

Year	Primary	Secondary
1950	29	16
1955	32	na
1958	33	23
1960	30	29
1962	30	32
1965	22	32
1968	22	28
1970	22	24
1975	25	24
1980	28	31
1982	24	28
1985	24	28
1988	23	22

Sources: UNESCO, *Basic Facts and Figures 1960*, pp. 32, 41; UNESCO, *Statistical Yearbook 1965*, Paris, 1966, pp. 167, 195; UNESCO, *Statistical Yearbook 1970*, Paris, 1971, pp. 190, 219; UNESCO, *Statistical Yearbook 1985*, Paris, 1985, III–93 and III–175; UNESCO, *Statistical Yearbook 1992*, Paris, 1992, pp. 3–91, 3–75

In contrast, the pupil to teacher ratio in secondary education is considerably less stable. The ratio increased rather sharply following the expansion in enrollment after 1958, from 23 in that year to 32 in 1962. It declined gradually and returned to its 1958 level in 1970, but increased sharply again between 1975 and 1980, as the number of enrolled students nearly doubled from 525,000 to 1,066,000.[18] This ratio soon began to improve again, and in 1988 was roughly equal to the ratio in 1958. Despite these fluctuations, the pupil to teacher ratio did not show marked deterioration over the entire period; short-term deteriorations in the ratio, when they occurred, were gradually reversed. Moreover, there is no evidence that the quality of teachers at any level declined in the period; to the contrary, the training of teachers became more systematized. There is therefore little evidence to suggest that a permanent deterioration in the student–teacher ratio in either primary or secondary education occurred over the long term.

Problems of education in Iraq have typically surfaced in the shape of inadequate curricula and other structural rigidities rather than an insufficiency of teachers. The primary school curricula were formulated in the 1920s and were largely modeled after nineteenth-century French curricula, which stressed uniformity in methods of instruction.[19] Little attempt was made to apply what was taught in schools directly to pupils' lives; students in rural districts, for example, were by and large taught the same skills as their urban counterparts. Few elective courses were available, even in secondary education. Moreover, instruction centered on memorization rather than analysis or enquiry. As a result, Iraqi schooling has suffered from being simultaneously theoretically quite demanding but rather ineffective in imparting practical and analytical skills.[20]

This, along with a rigid graduation structure, has contributed to historically high levels of attrition. Primary and secondary education each consist of six years or grades, and secondary education is divided into two parts, each three years – the first is known as intermediate, the second as secondary. Success at a mid-year and end of year examinations allow entry into the next grade, and failure rates are high, as students who are unable to pass a single subject must repeat the entire grade, including the subjects that they passed in that year. Failure rates are typically higher still in the last year of primary, intermediate, and secondary education when national examinations are administered at the end of the school year. Those who pass these examinations receive a certificate (primary, intermediate, or secondary). Intermediate school certificate holders have the option of entering vocational training in fields such as agriculture, industry, or commerce. But the vast majority of students prefer to enter secondary school where they must choose either a scientific or literary specialization, both of which are highly theoretical and academic.

The nature and extent of these problems is reflected in Table 4.7, which contains data on failure rates in national examinations at various levels of

Table 4.7 Failure rates in national examinations, 1937–1975

Year	Primary (%)	Intermediate (%)	Secondary (%)
1937	21	29	19
1955	40	49	52
1956	38	20	51
1957	32	12	42
1958	0	0	0
1959	25	24	34
1960	29	21	30
1967	na	na	40
1973	na	na	37
1975	na	na	38

Sources: Calculated from Bureau of Statistics, *Statistical Abstract for the Financial Years 1927/ 28 to 1937/38*, Government Press, Baghdad, 1939, p. 56; Central Bureau of Statistics, *Statistical Abstract 1960*, Zahra Press, Baghdad, 1961, p. 82; Central Statistical Organization, *Statistical Abstract 1967*, Government Press, Baghdad, 1968, p. 436; Central Statistical Organization, *Annual Abstract of Statistics 1973*, Baghdad, undated, pp. 325–6; Central Statistical Organization, *Annual Abstract of Statistics 1975*, Baghdad, undated, pp. 397–8.

education.[21] With the exception of the year 1958 (when all students were passed in celebration of the revolution) and despite some fluctuation from one year to another, the failure rates on national examinations have been consistently high.

High attrition rates aside, the data provide little evidence of a significant or permanent decline in academic standards. There is a noticeable decline in failure rates, associated with the expansion of enrollment, after 1958 in secondary education; the rates for the years 1956 and 1957 are notably higher than those for 1959 and 1960. This indicates that academic standards in secondary education may have declined. If so, however, these standards appear to have recovered somewhat thereafter, as the failure rates for 1967, 1973, and 1975 are broadly comparable to those for 1956 and 1957. At the primary level, the failure rates show a slight decline after 1958, but again the rates for 1959 and 1960 are broadly comparable to those for 1956 and 1957. By contrast, in intermediate education, there is no indication that standards declined at all after 1958; indeed, the failure rates for 1959 and 1960 exceed those for 1956 and 1957. Overall, then, there is little evidence from failure rates to suggest that there has been a significant or permanent decline in academic standards in the six years of secondary education.

Ideally, the study of failure rates would include the period of the late 1970s and 1980s; unfortunately, no data on failure rates are available for these periods. Nevertheless, data on primary and secondary repeaters – that is, the proportion of all students who failed the national examination in their previous attempt and are thus repeating the grade – are available and presented in Table 4.8. Repeaters declined from 25 percent of all

Table 4.8 Repeaters as a proportions of all students, 1970–1988

Year	Final grade in primary school (%)	Final grade in secondary school (%)
1970	25	41
1975	18	33
1979	7	42
1982	30	41
1985	29	38
1987	25	34
1988	23	42

Sources: UNESCO, *Statistical Yearbook 1985*, III–139, III–233; UNESCO, *Statistical Yearbook 1992*, 3–133 and 3–227

students in the last grade of primary education in 1970 to 18 percent in 1975, and were 7 percent in 1979. But this sharp decline was quickly reversed, and 30 percent of all students in the last grade of primary education in 1982 were repeaters; 23 percent were repeaters in 1988. This implies that the requirements for entry into secondary education (or "intermediate education" as it is called in Iraq) were more stringent in the 1980s in comparison to those in the late 1970s.

The declines in repeaters that occurred between 1975 and 1979 suggest that educational standards declined in this period. The quick reversal of the trend in the 1980s, however, indicates that standards in primary education recovered very quickly. In contrast, the statistics on secondary repeaters indicate that no reduction in standards occurred between 1970 and 1988. The data on repeaters suggests that there were no permanent declines in standards; when standards temporarily deteriorated, the trend was quickly reversed. More generally, none of the indicators of the quality of education that are examined point to deterioration over the long term.

Over the long term, of course, the assumptions made earlier concerning the difficulty of passing national examinations and the quality of students may not hold, and it is possible that the academic ability of students may have declined. In this period of generally rising enrollment rates, the educational system may have been absorbing increasingly marginal or academically less gifted students. In that case, the consistently high rates of attrition, the relatively unchanged failure and repeater rates may indicate that schools have become more effective at imparting knowledge to increasingly mediocre students.[22] This, however, is arguably more likely in a country like the US where most of the school-age population is already in school (and where truant students may avoid school because they are less capable) than in a country such as Iraq (where most of the population has not had access to education and where untapped academic potential remains).[23] More likely, improvements in nutrition and health (discussed in the next chapter) worked to enhance the capacities of students to absorb and retain knowledge; improved school facilities likely worked in the same direction, to improve the academic productivity of students. Similarly, if passing had become progressively simpler, then it is easy to understand how relatively unchanged failure and repeater rates could exist in the context of increasing enrollments: lower standards for passing permit roughly the same ratio of the student population to pass, even if such a population is made up of ever more marginal students. But while there is evidence of grade inflation, there is, as we have seen, little evidence that passing has become notably easier.

This discussion highlights some of the problems involved in assessing educational quality. In our case, an unchanged (or even declining) proportion of repeaters would not necessarily suggest that standards have been maintained (or have fallen) because the native ability of those students may have changed in the intervening period. Poor access to education of a large segment of the school-age population implies that this effect was weak and, if it existed at all, and probably assuaged by improved health, nutrition, and physical facilities. The evidence on balance thus points to increased individual attainment, with the known positive spillover effects to society.

Patterns in improvements and some correlations

The gains in enrollments were uneven. There was a notable expansion in primary and secondary enrollment between 1955 and 1960, the result of increased allocation of resources to education and other social services after the 1958 revolution: new schools were built and more teachers were trained. Although expenditure on education had been growing under the monarchy, especially since the oil boom of the early 1950s, there was a notable increase in spending after 1958. As Table 4.9 shows, from 1955 to 1960 education expenditures increased threefold in nominal terms and by more than two and a half times in real terms; as a percentage of GNP, these expenditures increased from 3.4 percent to 6.8 percent in the same period.

Similar, but not altogether identical, factors were behind the rapid rise in enrollment rates during the 1970s. Although our data concerning incomes in Chapter 3 indicate that personal consumption expenditure may have been stagnant (and were very likely repressed) during the 1970s, there was probably increased demand for education. First, the costs to parents, both directly and in terms of the opportunity cost of foregone child labor, likely declined. Schools were nationalized in 1975, and education at all levels became free of charge. Also, this was a period of continued decline in the proportion of labor that was engaged in agriculture, where household (including child) labor is most intensively used. In fact in 1975, a program was introduced under which meals were provided for rural pupils at the elementary level as well as for pupils in

Table 4.9 Expenditure on education, 1951–60

Category	1951	1955	1959–60
Expenditure in current ID (million)	4.42	9.69	29.25
Consumer price index (1939=100)	523	495	548
Expenditure in constant 1939 ID (million)	0.85	1.96	5.34
As a proportion of GNP (%)	na	3.4	6.8

Note: Total expenditure for 1955 was given at ID 8,000,000. This did not include the expenditure of local government on primary education however. Such expenditure amounted to ID 1,685,000 in 1956–57 though. The last figure was added to the ID 8,000,000 to arrive at total expenditure for 1955.

Sources: Calculated from UNESCO, *Basic Facts and Figures 1954*, Paris, 1955, p. 43; UNESCO, *Basic Facts and Figures 1958*, Paris, 1959, p. 70; UNESCO, *Statistical Yearbook 1965*, Paris, 1966, p. 354; Principal Bureau of Statistics, *Statistical Abstract 1956*, Baghdad, 1957, p. 158; and International Monetary Fund, *International Financial Statistics Yearbook 1985*, New York, 1986, pp. 358–9.

poorer urban districts. By academic year 1978–9, 54 percent of elementary school pupils received meals under this program.[24] While its coverage may have been exaggerated, the program undoubtedly encouraged school enrollment, especially as schools became more numerous and accessible. The number of primary schools rose from 5,617 in academic year 1970–1 to 11,316 in 1979–80, and the number of secondary schools increased from 921 to 1,774 in the same period.[25] Not surprisingly, Table 4.10 indicates that education expenditure increased from ID 140.6 million in 1972 to ID 418.4 million in 1980 in constant (1980) prices. However, because of the massive expansion in both the ordinary and development budgets that accompanied the rise in oil prices in the early to middle 1970s, education spending as a proportion of all expenditures actually declined from 19.3 percent in 1972 to 4.1 percent in 1982.

After 1980, the real value of education expenditures declined too. In 1980 prices such expenditures declined from ID 418.4 million in 1980 to ID 287.5 million in 1988. This decline may, however, overstate the contraction in resources that education received. The vast majority of expenditures on education were recurrent, and most of these (roughly two-thirds in 1976[26] and three-quarters in 1988)[27] were in the form of compensation to teachers. The decline in the real value of education expenditures was thus probably largely translated into a decline in the real earnings of teachers. This may or may not have caused teacher morale to decline, but in the context of shrinking education budgets, the decline in earnings surely implied that the flow of resources to students was greater than would have been otherwise. On the other hand, the considerable expenditures of the anti-illiteracy campaign of 1978 are not included in recurrent expenditures and, judging by the small size of capital

Table 4.10 Expenditure on education, 1971–1988

Category	1972	1976	1979	1980	1982	1985	1988
Total expenditure in current ID (million)	68.9	204.5	314.7	418.4	533.4	550.9	690.1
As a proportion all state expenditures (%)	19.3	6.9	na	na	4.1	6.5	na
As a proportion of GNP (%)	4.8	4.3	3.2	na	4.2	3.8	na
Recurring expenditures	67.8	155.8	306.0	na	na	na	624.9
Capital expenditures	1.1	48.7	8.7	na	na	na	65.2
Consumer Price Index (1980=100)	49.0	68.4	85.5	100	136.0	171.3	240.0
Total expenditure in constant ID (million)	140.6	299.0	368.1	418.4	392.2	321.6	287.5

Sources: UNESCO, *Statistical Yearbook 1975*, Paris, 1976, p. 383; UNESCO, *Statistical Yearbook 1982*, Paris, 1982, IV–14; UNESCO, *Statistical Yearbook 1988*, Paris, 1988, 4–14; UNESCO, *Statistical Yearbook 1990*, Paris, 1990, 4–14; United Nations Economic Commission for Western Asia (UNECWA), *Statistical Abstract of the ECWA Region 1971–80*, 5th edition, Baghdad, 1982, p. 123; United Nations Economic and Social Commission for Western Asia (UNESCWA), *Statistical Abstract of the ESCWA Region 1978–87*, 12th edition, Baghdad, 1989, p. 145; UNESCWA, *Statistical Abstract of the ESCWA Region 1983–1992*, 14th edition, Amman, 1994

expenditures, were not included in the estimates of capital expenditures on education. This is because the costs of the campaign were paid out of the development budget and not from ordinary expenditures. The program is reported to have received an allocation of ID 236 million,[28] but it is not known how much of this was actually spent. The inclusion of the expenditures of this campaign would surely raise education expenditures for 1979 and 1980 (and perhaps for 1981 and 1982) and, consequently, accentuate the decline in spending after 1980.

Even so, there is little evidence that this decline in spending was translated into diminished physical access to education. True, the number of primary schools declined from 11,316 in academic year 1979–80 to 8,141 in 1985–6,[29] but this may have been related to the diminished requirement for schools that accompanied the end of the anti-illiteracy campaign. Of course, the closing of schools may have reduced access to instruction, especially in distant rural areas; information regarding the location of the closed schools is unfortunately unavailable. It ought to be noted, however, that the general decline in primary enrollment rates was the result of a decline in female enrollment; male enrollment ratios in primary education were relatively stable. Net male enrollment ratios, for the 6 to 11 years old population, were 100 percent in 1980, 99 percent in 1985. and 100 percent in 1988, while the comparable statistics for females were 94 percent, 87 percent, 87 percent, respectively.[30] If diminished physical access was responsible for the decline in primary enrollment, then it is not clear why female enrollment alone would decline. Nor is the decline in the net secondary enrollment apparently explained by a decrease in access since the number of secondary schools increased from 1,774 in academic year 1979–80 to 2,209 in 1985–6.[31] Moreover, net enrollment for females in the 12 to 17 years old population remained unchanged at 31 percent between 1980 and 1988, while male net enrollment declined from 62 percent in 1980 to 48 percent in 1988.[32] It is thus exceedingly unlikely that the decline in enrollment is related, proximately, to reduced physical access to instruction or, ultimately, to the decline in educational expenditures.

Neither was the decline in male secondary enrollment apparently the result of the conscription requirements of the war with Iran, which started in 1980 and continued until 1988. Military conscription was restricted to the adult population and deferred for those who attended school, as evidenced by the increase in the gross male enrollment rate in higher education in this period.

The increasingly rigorous requirements of entry into secondary education in the 1980s, implied by the rising proportion of repeaters in the final grade of primary education, may have contributed to the decline in male secondary enrollment. But the increase in repeaters does not explain why female enrollment remained unchanged. Consistently, female repeater rates have been lower than those of their male counterparts.[33] Likewise, females have routinely outperformed males on national examinations. This is not evidence of the superior academic talents of Iraqi women nor is it the outcome of an educational structure that has discriminated in their favor. Rather, the disparity is likely explained by the traditions and social structure that historically have discriminated against females. Parents are more likely to withdraw females of mediocre academic abilities from schools than they are males with the same (or perhaps inferior) talents. This, along with the high attrition rates at all levels of education, implies that extremely academically gifted females and somewhat less gifted males are selected to remain in schools. As a consequence, females who survive attrition in education score higher on national examinations than do males. Even so, both the male and female repeater rates in the last year of primary education increased sharply in the 1980s. The increase may, therefore, partly explain the decline in male secondary enrollment after 1980 but does not explain why female enrollment was apparently unaffected.

As shown in Chapter 3, the state resorted to heavy borrowing during the 1980s and was to some extent successful in buttressing average household incomes and government consumption. However, these aggregates may hide considerable variation and it is possible that the incomes of poorer households declined as average incomes remained the same or rose, if the distribution of income changed in favor of the relatively well-off (as is suggested in Chapter 3). If so, could this account for the observed pattern in enrollment rates? To put the question differently, did some households react to their decline in incomes by withdrawing more of their children from school and sending them to work?

In general, higher rates of economic activity imply lower rates of enrollment, as work arguably reduces the time that children are able to devote to school, but it is also possible for children to increase both their work effort and school attendance. In either case, the study of economic activity rates of children during the 1980s is desirable. The absolute number of economically active persons in the 7 to 14 years old population declined from roughly 165,000 in 1977 to 94,000 in 1987, according to Table 4.11. But the decline in economic activity in this age group was higher for females than for males. This is consistent with the increase in net primary enrollment rates, for the 6 to 11 years old population, from 81 percent (100 percent for males and 61 percent for females) in 1976[34] to 94 percent (100 percent for males and 87 percent for females) in 1988, but does not explain the decline in female enrollment after 1980. It is nevertheless possible that female economic activity in the 7 to 14 years old population declined sharply between 1977 and 1980, but increased thereafter. Females in this age group may have been withdrawn from school to compensate for the loss of household labor of mothers or other female relatives who entered the workforce in increasing numbers after 1980. In that case, the withdrawn females would not appear as economically active because the latter is not defined to include work at home.

Turning to the 15 to 19 years old population, we see that the absolute number of persons who were economically active increased from roughly 251,000 in 1977 to 447,000 in 1987, an increase of approximately 78 percent. Since the total number of persons in this age group rose by 89 percent in this period,[35] the economic activity rate for this population

Table 4.11 Economically active primary and secondary school age population, 1977–87

Age group		1977			1987		
		Number	Agriculture	%*	Number	Agriculture	%*
	Male	93,161	27	8	79,873	21	10
7–14	Female	72,157	91	1	13,918	51	5
years	Total	165,318	56	5	93,791	26	9
	Male	194,703	12	38	414,590	8	60
15–19	Female	56,706	74	4	32,612	34	21
years	Total	251,409	26	30	447,202	10	57

*Percentage engaged in community services
Sources: Central Statistics Organization, *Annual Abstract of Statistics 1978*, pp. 36–7; and Central Statistics Organization, *Annual Abstract of Statistics 1991*, Baghdad, undated, pp. 56–7

actually declined. But these statistics hide considerable disparities: the number of economically active males in this age group increased by more than 100 percent, whereas the number of females declined by about 40 percent. In other words, the rate of economic activity for males increased, while that for females declined substantially. Thus, female net secondary enrollment for the 12 to 17 years old population increased from 18 percent in 1976[36] to 31 percent in 1988, and there was no decline in enrollment between 1980 and 1988. By contrast, net secondary enrollment rates for males in the same age group increased from 38 percent in 1976[37] to 62 percent in 1980, but declined to 48 percent in 1988.

The rise in female enrollment is not surprising given the decline in the absolute number of economically active females in this age group. More surprising perhaps is the increase in male secondary enrollment between 1976 and 1988, which coincided with the rise in both the number as well as the rate of economically active males in the 15 to 19 years age group. This incongruity may reside in the different age groups considered, the 12 to 17 years old population versus the economically active 15 to 19 years old population. The proportion of economically active 15 to 19 years old males engaged in community, social, and personal services (the sector that includes public administration and defense) increased from 38 percent of all employment in 1977 to 60 percent in 1987. This rise is probably associated, at least in part, with the conscription requirements of the war with Iran, although it is not possible to conclude this definitively because no data on the distribution of employment in the various activities within this sector are available. Since conscription into the armed forces started at age 18, it is possible to have, simultaneously, increased rates of economic activity for 15 to 19 years old males as well as increased enrollment rates for 12 to 17 years old males.

However, it is also plausible that the rise in the rate of male economic activity between 1977 and 1987 was associated with other factors as well. That is, perhaps because of pressures on the incomes of some families during the 1980s, more males were simultaneously working and attending school. This was a period when the war with Iran was ongoing and many families lost their main breadwinners. This very likely increased the pressure on some children to enter the workforce, and may explain the declining rates of male secondary enrollment after 1980.

It remains to explain why female secondary enrollment was apparently unaffected by these forces. Because of social custom and traditions, families are less willing to allow females to work outside the home than they are males. Of course, women have always worked in family labor, especially in agriculture. In the early 1970s, for example, women accounted for roughly two-fifths of agricultural labor,[38] but the number of persons engaged in agricultural activities declined substantially between 1977 and 1987 and with it female activity in agriculture in the 7 to 19 years old population.[39] Moreover, because of the possibly manual and generally unskilled nature of employment that school-age persons are likely to find, the return to female employment in these activities was probably less than the return for males. Thus, pressures to enter and possibilities for employment were not as strong for females of secondary school age, which may explain why female secondary enrollment did not decline after 1980.

If our conjecture about association between household incomes and enrollment rates are at all correct, then one would expect the reverse – increased demand for education – to be happening at the other end of the distribution of income. And there is some evidence for this. The children of better resourced families remained in school, as evinced by the increase in enrollment in higher education in this period. This was also a means for males to obtain military service deferments. By contrast, other males, presumably from the poorer classes, were joining the workforce in increasing numbers.

Even so, educational outcomes broadly improved in the period under consideration: with the exception of primary and secondary enrollment in the 1980s, enrollment rates at all levels increased, albeit at a variable rate. Literacy rates expanded greatly in this period, with the largest gains associated with the anti-illiteracy campaign of 1978. Literacy spread to the rural areas, especially in the wake of the adult literacy program, which represents a narrowing of urban–rural disparities in education as regards basic education. And, these occurred with little or no noticeable deterioration in the quality of education.

Human development and the political economy of education

Few of the gains discussed would have been achieved were it not for the active intervention of the state in education. Educational structures were very poorly developed when the country was formed; basic education was available only in urban areas and was usually reserved for the privileged. Under such conditions, private education made a significant contribution to instruction. In 1927, the first year for which such data are available, roughly one-fifth to one-sixth of all primary and secondary schools were private. Because of the low levels of literacy and education, emphasis was placed on primary instruction: out of the 276 public schools in the country, only 11 were post-primary – 8 intermediate and 3 secondary in 1927.[40] Public education grew rapidly, however, and there were roughly 1,900 primary and secondary schools in academic year 1959–60, compared with only 148 private schools.[41] In 1975, education was nationalized; all private institutions of learning, from primary schools to universities, were taken over by the state and, henceforth, all education became public. It has been public education, then, that has made possible the noted improvements in the education indicators.

That this expansion in education has occurred largely through public efforts is not particularly surprising. As noted in the introduction, the public-good nature of education implies that, despite its relatively high social rate of return, too few people would receive instruction were it not for substantial government intervention and subsidization. Yet, subsidization of education in developing countries often results in the overprovision of university education, at the expense of primary and secondary education. Because it is usually heavily subsidized, the private rate of return to higher education is typically very high and substantially exceeds the social rate of return. As a result, governments in developing countries face strong demands, especially from the politically important urban middle and upper classes, to expand university education, and the state is often forced to accede to these demands, even though the social rate of return to primary education is often higher than for secondary and university instruction.[42]

This discussion raises questions about how wisely Iraq has allocated its education resources. Table 4.12 contains estimates of the composition by level of education of recurrent education expenditures, which it will be recalled formed the great majority of all education expenditures.[43] Roughly two-thirds of all recurrent expenditure on education in Iraq went to primary instruction in 1965. This proportion declined to three-fifths in 1970, and was between 45 percent and 50 percent between 1976 and 1988. By contrast, secondary education received roughly 16 percent to 20 percent of all expenditure between 1965 and 1987, but received 27.8 percent in 1988. Finally, higher education received a rising share of

Table 4.12 The composition of recurrent education expenditures, 1965–88

Country	Year	Pre-primary and primary (%)	Secondary, vocational, and teacher training (%)	University and graduate
Iraq				
	1965	67.9	16.6	12.7
	1970	60.1	20.3	17.0
	1976	45.3	16.2	18.1
	1980	47.5	17.3	24.1
	1985	46.5	19.5	25.0
	1987	46.5	19.5	25.0
	1988	49.4	27.8	20.6
India				
	1965	23.3	42.1	23.1
	1975	21.4	40.3	22.0
Republic of Korea				
	1965	66.4	22.2	11.3
	1975	62.4	25.5	12.2

Sources: UNESCO, *Statistical Yearbook 1978–9*, p. 675; UNESCO, *Statistical Yearbook 1988*, 4–49; and UNESCO, *Statistical Yearbook 1990*, 4–49

recurrent expenditures in this period; such expenditures increased from 12.7 percent in 1965 to 25.0 percent in 1987, but declined to 20.6 percent in 1988. The reasons behind the abrupt reallocation of expenditure from higher to lower levels of education in 1988 are not clear. As noted, the inclusion of the costs of the anti-illiteracy campaign would undoubtedly inflate the share of recurrent expenditures going into pre-primary and primary education for 1980. It is thus difficult to use the statistics presented above to study the changes in the composition of expenditures between 1980 and 1985 or 1988. Nevertheless, the comparison of the composition of expenditures for 1970 or 1976 (before the illiteracy eradication campaign was implemented) with that for 1985 or 1988 (after the campaign ended) suggests that there was a reorientation of expenditures away from pre-primary and primary education and towards university training. The rising relative allocations to higher education and declining allocations to pre-primary and primary education in the 1980s occurred in the context of declining primary and secondary enrollments. It is therefore difficult to argue that this reallocation occurred because there was no room for primary and secondary education to expand.

In comparison to South Korea, educational expenditures in Iraq have been top heavy: they tended to favor higher education and have been biased against primary education. Despite South Korea's relatively high adult literacy rate, estimated to have been 95 percent in 1970,[44] primary education in that country generally received a higher portion of expenditures than in Iraq. Rates of return on primary education in South Korea were presumably large enough to justify these allocations, even though the country's stock of literacy was relatively high. In contrast, Iraq's education expenditures have not been as top heavy as India's. In that country, whose adult literacy rate was 37 percent in 1970,[45] the share of expenditures that primary education received has been roughly equal to that for higher education and smaller than the share for secondary education.

Of course, not all countries have the same manpower requirements, and it is possible that the varying composition of expenditures in these countries reflected different labor requirements; in that case it may be argued, for instance, that the relatively high expenditures on higher education in India, and to a lesser extent in Iraq, were justified by the needs of these economies for university graduates.

In reality, however, the pattern of expenditures – namely the rising in the relative allocations to higher education – ran counter to the country's manpower needs. As mentioned in Chapter 3, the lack of skilled labor has been a main constraint on the implementation of development projects; this constraint became quite severe in the 1970s, as government expenditure on development rose markedly. What the country needed, in other words, were skilled workers and middle managers more so than professionals and scientists.[46] According to an estimate made by the

Ministry of Planning in 1977, a shortage of roughly 68,000 "supervisory and skilled workers" and 94,000 "semi-skilled workers" was expected in 1979.[47] The rapidly rising enrollment in vocational education surely worked to alleviate some of the labor shortages, but the conscription of large numbers of males into the armed forces after the start of the Iran–Iraq war in 1980 further exacerbated the shortages. Indeed, by the early 1980s skilled labor shortages were so acute that the Iraqi government was compelled to stipulate that new projects could not utilize labor-intensive methods of production.[48]

Yet primary and secondary enrollment ratios declined in the 1980s while university enrollment ratios expanded as the pattern of education expenditures increasingly gave priority to higher education to the disadvantage of primary and secondary education. The reorientation towards university training probably yielded a rate of return to education expenditures that was lower than what would otherwise have been and worked towards widening urban–rural as well as other inequities. In fact the policies ran counter to the country's labor requirements. The study of the composition of recurrent education expenditures suggests, therefore, that education funds have been badly allocated.

Given these imbalances, it is tempting to conclude that the Ba'th government's education priorities resulted in substantial inefficiencies and bias towards the middle and upper classes and urban areas. Upon closer examination, however, it is not clear this was the case. Between academic years 1967–8 and 1977–8, the number of students attending universities increased by 110 percent, slightly more than the rate of growth in primary education, which was 107 percent. However, net primary enrollment was approaching 100 percent in the latter year and almost everyone who could attend primary school was enrolled. The percentage increase in primary enrollment could not, in other words, have been much higher. By comparison, enrollment in secondary (excluding vocational) education, where full enrollment was not achieved, grew by 162 percent, while pre-primary enrollment increased by 262 percent and vocational education by 244 percent, in the same period.[49] Moreover, it will be remembered that while enrollment ratios in higher education expanded substantially between 1970 and 1975, they increased only marginally between 1975 and 1980, when primary and secondary enrollment ratios grew very rapidly. This perhaps reflected a realization on the part of the government that while the country's needs for university graduates were being met, the supply of skilled labor still had to be enlarged. Indeed, it was with a view to increasing the supply of skilled and semi-skilled labor that the illiteracy eradication campaign was initiated. The campaign ended illiteracy for roughly 2 million people, a disproportionate number of whom lived in rural areas and came from the poorer classes. The campaign was allocated ID 236 million (or roughly ID 110 for every targeted illiterate), not a small sum by any standard, although most development specialists would probably agree that it was a wise investment. Were the costs of the campaign included in the statistics on the composition of educational expenditures, it would surely increase significantly the relative share of pre-primary and primary education for the late 1970s to the early 1980s. All this suggests that, far from favoring a small urban university elite, the Ba'th regime's education policies favored primary education and basic literacy and numeracy, and these polices likely worked to reduce stubborn urban–rural disparities.

Not only did these policies make good economic sense; they were politically expedient as well. The literacy campaign, for instance, increased the skills level of the population, and also had the notable advantage of allowing the regime's written propaganda to reach an audience that was hitherto (because of its inability to read) not easily accessible. In fact, the timing of the campaign neatly coincided with the regime's attainment of a complete monopoly in the mass media[50] and this raises questions about why the campaign was not implemented earlier, especially as the Ba'th party's program had long called for the elimination of illiteracy. Planners were surely aware that the literacy campaign was not import intensive and thus would not have exacerbated the existing transport and other bottlenecks; to the contrary, the increase in literacy would have worked to alleviate skilled and semi-skilled labor shortages. The regime's desire to control the content of the program probably explains why the Ba'th government delayed implementation of the program until it had attained political dominance. Similar concerns over control of content have dissuaded other governments in the Middle East and beyond from pursuing adult literacy.[51]

Parallel to this development, the nationalization of schools in 1975 effectively gave the state a complete monopoly in education. Gradually, controls on what could or could not be taught were tightened and propaganda came to be more widely disseminated at all levels of education. The Ba'th paid special attention to the young and viewed their political education as essential for the regime's consolidation of power.[52] Indeed, the regime appeared to have placed no less emphasis on "political education" in primary or secondary schools than at the universities.

Alas, the happy coincidence of a relatively enlightened development strategy and the political interests of the regime were shattered by the explosion of the Iran–Iraq war in 1980. Although the regime attempted to shield the public from declining incomes, the incomes of some households declined, which necessitated increased male activity in the labor market and declines in primary and secondary enrollment ratios. Although the manpower requirements of the country and the desire of the government to increase the supply of skilled labor remained largely apparently unchanged, the declines in incomes had significant effects on education outcomes. There were political implications to these developments: the reduction in primary and secondary enrollments implied that political influence of the regime on the youth was less than it might otherwise have been.

Given these economic and political disadvantages, it is natural to ask why the regime apparently did little to redirect its shrinking education resources away from higher education and towards primary and secondary education. Why, for example, did the state not use its position of monopoly in education to afford even greater subsidies, perhaps in the form of expanded school meals or other programs, to primary and secondary education – to increase the supply of skilled labor which was greatly needed – and reduce student enrollment at the universities?

The government did attempt to compensate for some of the reduction in supply of skilled labor by expanding vocational training. But the rise in enrollment in vocational training, a small constituent of secondary education, was not large enough to offset the decline in secondary enrollment overall. But the government was unwilling to sacrifice enrollment at the universities in order to stem the tide of declining enrollments in primary and secondary education, for, in the meantime, a significant interest group with demands for the expansion of higher education had coalesced. Centered around urban middle and upper class young males (and by extension their families), this group viewed university education as a way of avoiding military service on the front lines of an increasingly unpopular war. It may be that the regime feared that attempts to reduce university intake or diminish the subsidization of higher education in general might lead to student disturbances in the urban centers of the country. If so, the Ba'th displayed a keen sense of history: university students were active in the demonstrations against the Portsmouth Agreement in 1948 (which eventually brought down the government at the time) as well as in the protests against the Anglo-French-Israeli attack on Egypt during the Suez crisis in 1956. By contrast, secondary school students are less likely to riot and many primary school pupils might prefer to stay at home rather than attend school, if given an option. Moreover, primary and secondary schools are geographically dispersed throughout, while universities are urban and concentrated in the capital. The regime was arguably eager to avoid urban student unrest, even at the cost of neglecting the country's manpower needs and impeding its own educational priorities.

The declines in enrollment at the primary and secondary level and spending constraints notwithstanding, the state's commitment to education remained robust, a commitment shared by all prior republican regimes, as the Ba'th regime attempted to lower both the economic and political costs associated with the decline in enrollments. Vocational education was expanded in this period, providing needed skilled labor. Physical access to primary and secondary education was maintained despite the reduced expenditures on education in the 1980s. But the government was powerless to shield all households from the distress associated with economic stagnation and war, which arguably caused the deterioration in enrollment. The decline occurred in the absence of any perceptible change in the education priorities of the government.

It may be that the regime calculated that a reallocation of resources away from university training and towards primary and secondary education was politically untenable, even though the Ba'th party had by 1980 become completely dominant in political life (as we shall see in Chapter 7). Whether or not the Ba'th was accurate in its appraisal of the political dangers, the regime's unwillingness to redirect education resources illustrates perhaps how no government, however powerful, is completely independent of social forces and undermines the view of the Ba'thi state as independent of society, "hovering" over social groups and forces.[53] It also shows how it is difficult, even for powerful states with apparently equalizing agendas, to avoid urban bias.

Concluding remarks

At one level, Iraq's experiences, particularly in the period before the early 1980s, could be viewed as the successful channeling of oil revenues into human development, with prudent emphasis on primary education and basic literacy and numeracy. Education outcomes clearly improved in the period under study, with the periods of late 1950s and the 1970s registering the most rapid progress. The marginal decline in primary and secondary enrollment after 1980 is not evidence of indifference or change in education priorities, but resulted from the severe declines in income, as families sent more children to work. True, the real value of education expenditures declined in the 1980s, but the regime's commitment to education continued after the outbreak of war with Iran and the contraction of oil revenues.

We conjecture that the regime was unwilling to alter the pattern of educational spending, towards greater emphasis on primary and secondary education, for fear of igniting political instability among the urban middle class. The same desire for power and stability, we argue, impelled the notoriously control-obsessed Ba'th to delay implementation of its anti-illiteracy campaign until it had attained a monopoly in society and the mass media. Even though its own party platform called for ending illiteracy and despite the presence of severe skilled labor shortages, which higher levels of literacy would greatly alleviate, the regime delayed the execution of the program until it was certain it could control the content. This, at another level, illustrates how development outcomes often reflect the sometimes contradictory desires of change and stability – in this case the Ba'th regime's aspirations for rapid modernization on one hand, and for maintenance of political control and stability on the other.

5 Housing, basic services, nutrition, and health

As with education, there is both instrumental and intrinsic importance to human development outcomes associated with the provision of housing, basic services, nutrition, and health. Not only is the ability to live a long, healthy, well-nourished life desirable in its own terms, but there are positive externalities linked to adequate health and nutrition that extend to other dimensions of development: improvement of one's aptitude for learning and work, and an increase in the productivity of labor and hence income.[1]

In general, the provision of health in developing countries, like that for education, tends to be top heavy, and this promotes both inefficiency and inequality in the supply of services. Expensive curative medicines are often preferred to inexpensive, but effective, preventative therapies and primary care, even though the social rate of return to spending on the latter usually far exceeds the rate for the expensive therapies. As a case in point, immunization against six common communicable diseases[2] costs about $1.20 per child, while the cost of treatment of these diseases is many times this amount. Likewise, use of oral rehydration therapy, which costs about $0.10 per patient, can significantly and inexpensively reduce infant deaths.[3] The prevailing pattern of expenditure on health in many developing countries is difficult to justify in terms of efficiency.

Nor is it easy to explain on grounds of equity. A large portion of health budgets, sometimes as high as 80 percent, is spent on hospitals, most of which are located in urban centers, whereas more than a third of the population has no access to primary health care.[4] This distorted pattern of spending stems from the urban bias prevalent in almost all developing countries: the urban population, especially the middle class, being a powerful political constituency, whose demands are difficult to ignore. As a result, a large part of the rural population and the urban poor have no access to the health system.[5]

A more even distribution of health services and greater emphasis on primary care would improve health outcomes, without requiring an increase in expenditures. The reallocation of spending away from large urban hospitals to evenly dispersed health clinics, staffed by paramedics (who are relatively inexpensive to train) rather than physicians; provision of basic generic drugs; improved nutrition, water supply, and sanitation; and the mass immunization of infants can substantially improve health outcomes with no increased costs. Indeed, the pattern of expenditure is so inefficient in some countries that a reallocation of spending could both improve outcomes and lower costs.

This chapter explores these themes of efficiency and equity in the provision of health and related services, namely housing, basic services (such as access to safe water and sanitation), and nutrition. Improvements in these latter areas naturally complement health outcomes, but the improvements also have intrinsic significance. The availability of safe water, for example, reduces the incidence of disease, especially among children, and therefore lowers infant mortality, and gains in nutrition reduce susceptibility to disease. The study of nutrition will also reveal how, even in the context of tight budgets and war austerity, governments may be impelled to augment costly entitlements over food. The chapter charts and analyses the improvements in life expectancy and infant mortality, two main measures of health outcomes. These threads of analysis allow us to understand the complex tapestry of outcomes in health and basic services in Iraq and thus to tell a richer, political-economic story.

Housing and basic services

There were clear improvements in the standard of housing between 1957 and 1988, as shown in Table 5.1. Almost two-thirds of households were inadequately housed in 1957,[6] and a little over a third lived in single-room dwellings, while half lived in homes with two or fewer rooms. By 1977, the situation had improved: households that were inadequately housed declined to 42 percent; the proportion living in a single room was reduced to 5.3 percent and in two or fewer rooms to 22.4 percent. In 1988, the proportion of households that were inadequately housed had

Table 5.1 The adequacy of housing, 1957–88

| | Inadequately housed (%) | | | Proportion of households residing in | |
| | | | | One room only (%) | Two or fewer rooms (%) |
Year	Rural	Urban	Total	Total	Total
1957	na	na	65.0	34.5	50.2
1977	83.0	17.7	42.0	5.3	22.4
1988	33.3	2.8	10.8	na	na

Sources: For 1957: Calculated from Directorate General of Census, *Abstract of the 1957 Census* (in Arabic), Volume 2, Part 16, Baghdad, 1964, p. 29; For 1977: Central Statistical Organization, *The General Census of 1977* (in Arabic), Baghdad, undated, p. 14; For 1987: Central Statistical Organization, *Annual Abstract of Statistics 1989*, Baghdad, 1990, p. 362

fallen to 10.8 percent. Still, the standard of housing in rural areas was notably inferior to that in urban areas. In 1977, five-sixths of all rural families were inadequately housed, while the corresponding urban statistic was one-sixth. Standards in both rural and urban areas had improved by 1988, but the urban–rural gap in housing remained.

These statistics underscore the historically poor standard of housing, especially in rural areas. The housing census of 1956 found that, on average, 5.6 persons inhabited the typically single-room *sarifas* (mud homes) in the Baghdad area.[7] Even by 1977, the average number of occupants of a single-room dwelling, in the country as a whole, was 4.9 persons.[8]

The improvement in the standard of housing between 1977 and 1988 is notable in that it occurred (mostly) during a period of war. Nevertheless, a sizable portion of gross fixed capital formation went into residential construction in the period. As Table 5.2 illustrates, average (unweighted) annual investment in residential buildings accounted for roughly one-sixth of all gross fixed capital formation in the 1970s. However, because of the higher levels of income and investment in 1975–79, the annual real value of residential building investment more than tripled between 1970–74 and 1975–79. The annual real value of investments increased by roughly 20 percent between 1975–79 and 1980–83, but declined substantially thereafter. As a result, residential investments increased from roughly one-sixth of all gross fixed capital formation in the 1970s, to one-fifth in 1980–83, and were roughly a quarter of all gross fixed capital formation in 1984–86.

The reduced levels of real investments in residential buildings in the period 1984–86 were undoubtedly associated with the shrinkage in the government's development budget after 1983. Consequently, as we saw in Chapter 3, the level of gross fixed capital formation and its ratio to GDP fell. In fact, the government's share of investments in residential buildings declined from 30 percent in the period 1980–83 to 24 percent in 1984–86. Even so, investments in residential buildings as a proportion of all gross fixed capital formation reached a peak in the period 1984–86, which indicates that the rate of decline in residential construction was less than the drop in investment in other durable goods, such as transport equipment or machinery.

Two factors account for this disparity in the rates of decline. First, the government continued to invest in residential buildings (albeit at a reduced rate) after 1983, and, second, subsidies, usually in the form of low interest rates, were offered to encourage private investment in residential buildings. This had been public policy since the middle 1970s when, as a result of the infusion of oil funds into the domestic economy, the rental prices of property began to rise sharply.

These numbers provide only limited evidence of rising oil revenues inducing an increased flow of resources to the production on non-tradable goods that is typically associated with the Dutch Disease. Estimates of land prices are unavailable, but anecdotal evidence suggests that there was a sharp rise in land values in the late 1970s followed by a collapse in the 1980s, much like other oil-exporting countries of the Middle East. According to Table 5.2, despite increased oil revenues in the period 1975–79, investment in residential buildings as a proportion of all investment remained constant, which indicates that investment in residential buildings was not crowding out other investments. The proportion of investment going to residential buildings increased in the 1980s, but that may have been the result of a dearth in investment opportunities in other activities and (especially after 1983) with reduced overall level of investment, associated with war conditions, that impacted investment in buildings more slowly than in other activities. Indeed, the real value of investment in residential buildings actually declined in the period 1984–86. This is consistent with data presented in Table 3.6 in Chapter 3, which shows that the share of fixed capital formation going to the construction sector increased between 1970–75 and 1975–80 along with rising oil revenues, but declined in 1980–85 to the same level as 1975–80. That is, if there were any the shift of resources into residential buildings or the construction sector, it was fairly mild and temporary.

The disparity in housing between rural and urban areas is replicated in the provision of basic services, as can be seen in Table 5.3. In 1975–80, almost the entire urban population had access to safe water while the corresponding figure for the rural population was less than a quarter. The situation improved noticeably during the 1980s, and by 1988–90 the statistics shifted to 100 percent and 72 percent, respectively. Even so, as late as 1988–90, only 11 percent of the rural population had access to adequate sanitation, compared to 100 percent of the urban population.

The extension of safe water services to rural areas coincides with the period when the country as a whole was becoming more urbanized: the proportion of the population that resided in rural areas declined from 48.6 percent in 1965[9] to 36.3 percent in 1977 to 28.9 percent in 1987.[10] But it was only during the 1980s that the rural areas began to see

Table 5.2 Investments in residential buildings, 1970–86

Investment in residential buildings per annum	1970–74	1975–79	1980–83	1984–86
As a proportion of gross fixed capital formation (%)	16	15	20	24
In current prices (ID million)	42	271	937	836
In constant (1980) prices (ID million)	150	503	621	420
The public sector's share in (%)	na	na	30	24

Sources: For price deflators: United Nations (UN), National Accounts Statistics: Analysis of Main Aggregates 1986, New York, 1989, p. 396; for all other categories: UN, National Accounts Statistics: Main Aggregates and Detailed Tables 1990, New York, 1992, p. 913

Table 5.3 The provision of basic services, 1975–90

	Proportion of population					
	With access to safe water (%)			With access to adequate sanitation (%)		
Year	Rural	Urban	Total	Rural	Urban	Total
1975–80	22	97	73	na	na	na
1985–88	54	100	87	na	na	na
1988–90	72	100	92	11	100	75

Sources: For 1975–80: United Nations Children's Fund (UNICEF), *The State of the World's Children 1985*, New York, Oxford University Press, 1985, p. 117; for 1985–88: UNICEF, *The State of the World's Children 1991*, New York, Oxford University Press, 1991, p. 106; for 1988–90, UNICEF, *The State of the World's Children 1993*, New York, Oxford University Press, 1993, p. 72

significant strides in the provision of safe water. In the case of sanitation though, practically nothing had been achieved in rural areas, even by the late 1980s.

Nutrition

Despite the historically low levels of nutrition, shown in Table 5.4, there was a rise in nutrition standards between the 1960s and late 1980s. In the 1960s and throughout much of the 1970s, per capita calorie consumption was below daily requirements, as defined by the United Nations Food and Agriculture Organization. In contrast, throughout the 1980s, per capita calorie consumption exceeded requirements.

In comparison with other countries in the Middle East and North Africa (MENA) region and oil exporters, Iraq, in 1965, had lower per capita calorie consumption than the average in the MENA region (where levels of nutrition were traditionally low) but equal to that of oil-exporting countries. But by the middle to late 1980s, calorie consumption in Iraq exceeded that in MENA as well as in other oil exporters (Table 5.4).

There is evidence to suggest that the quality of the diet improved as well. According to the United Nations, daily per capita protein consumption increased from 61 grams in 1970, to 73 grams in 1980, and reached 75 grams in 1988.[11] Similarly, the Central Statistical Organization estimates that per capita protein intake increased from 91.2g in 1980 to 101.6g in 1988.[12] The disparity in the estimates of protein consumption likely stems from differing data sources and means of calculation, but to the extent that these estimates are computed in a consistent manner, the statistics indicate that protein consumption improved over the noted period.

According to these estimates, there was a change in the composition of calories consumed, as the proportion of these calories originating from animal sources declined during the 1980s. In 1980, 9 percent of calories

Table 5.4 Daily calorie supply, 1965–89

Year	Daily calories consumed Iraq	Percentage of requirement	Daily calories consumed MENA	Oil exporters
1961–63	2012	83		
1965	2138	90	2445	2113
1970	2256	94		
1974	2433	101		
1977	2134	90		
1980	2677	111		
1981	3086	127		
1985	2926	122	2671	
1989	2887	120		2721

Sources: World Bank (WB), *World Development Report 1982*, Oxford University Press, New York, 1982, p. 153. WB, *World Development Report 1992*, Oxford University Press, New York, 1992, pp. 272–3. WB, *World Development Report 1979*, Oxford University Press, New York, 1979, p. 169; WB, *World Development Report 1987*, Oxford University Press, New York, 1987, p. 261; WB, *World Development Report 1984*, Oxford University Press, New York, 1984, p. 265; and UN, *Compendium of Social Statistics*, New York, 1977, pp. 254–5

consumed originated from animal sources. This increased to 10.2 percent in 1982, but declined to 7.3 percent in 1988.[13] There was a rise in food prices in the 1980s, but an index of food prices by category is unavailable after 1981. If the increase in the price of staples was lower than the increase in prices of meat and dairy, then this pattern of consumption may reflect the substitution of less expensive vegetable for more costly animal products.

Be that as it may, the rise in per capita calorie consumption in the 1980s did not result from an increase in per capita output of the principal grains: wheat, barley, and rice. These crops traditionally make up the staple diet of the population, and, in the case of wheat and barley, tend to account for the largest portions of the planted area. As Table 5.5 shows, there were, with the exception of barley, sizable per capita declines in the

Table 5.5 Output of cereal crops, 1970–89

Commodity	1970–4	1975–79	1980–89
	(metric tons per 1000 persons)		
Wheat	138	75	58
Barley	62	44	59
Rice	20	14	10

Sources: Calculated from (for output figures) United Nations Economic Commission for Western Asia (UNECWA), *Statistical Abstract of the ECWA Region 1970-79*, Beirut, 1981, p. 107; United Nations Economic and Social Commission for Western Asia (UNESCWA), *Statistical Abstract of the ESCWA Region 1978-87*, Baghdad, 1989, p. 126; UNESCWA, *Statistical Abstract of the ESCWA Region 1983-92*, Amman, 1994, p. 109; and (for population estimates) International Monetary Fund (IMF), *International Financial Statistics Yearbook 1999*, New York, 2000, pp. 524–5

production of these crops.[14] Rice and wheat output declined by more than 50 percent between the period 1970–74 and 1980–89, while per capita barley output was slightly reduced over the entire period, although output rose between 1975–79 and 1980–89.

The decline in cereal output is symptomatic of the general long-term stagnation of the sector. As Table 5.6 illustrates, agricultural output grew at −0.3 percent per annum in the period 1970–75 and at 2.3 percent in 1975–80. As the rate of growth of population was 3.3 percent and 3.5 percent respectively, per capita output declined by 3.6 percent and 1.2 percent, respectively, in the two periods. Between 1980 and 1987, output grew at 2.1 percent per annum; factoring in the rate of growth of population, this translated to a decline in per capita output of 0.9 percent per annum. That is, for the entire period 1970–87, per capita agricultural output declined.

The reasons for the stagnation in agriculture are complex, originating in the first half of the twentieth century. As noted earlier, the high concentration of land along with a political structure that favored large landholders discouraged investment before 1958. Increased output in the sector, before 1950, was mostly due to bringing new land under cultivation rather than an increase in land or labor productivity, as production techniques remained relatively unchanged. As Kamil Mahdi concludes, the existing land tenure structure was "unable to offer any prospects other than low productivity agriculture and gradual decline as the process of expansion [of area cultivated] ran its course."[15]

Land reform enacted after the July 1958 revolution mandated the redistribution of land from large landowners to peasants, but failed to end the long-term decline in the sector. The pace of redistribution was slow, and the reform left rural cultivators with diminished access to services, such as the extension of seeds, loans, and equipment, which landowners had previously supplied. This was aggravated by slow progress in the establishment of agricultural co-operatives, which were intended to replace the dispossessed landowners' services.[16]

Even so, by the late 1960s many of these difficulties had been overcome: agricultural value added was 20 percent higher than the pre-land reform

Table 5.6 Real rates of growth in agriculture, 1970–87

Rate of growth	Annualized rates of growth (%)		
	1970–75	1975–80	1980–87
Agriculture, hunting, fishing and forestry	−0.3	2.3	2.1
Population	3.3	3.5	3.0
Per capita growth in agricultural output	−3.6	−1.2	−0.9

Source: For estimates of output: UN, *National Accounts Statistics: Analysis of Main Aggregates 1987*, New York, 1990, p. 172; population growth calculated from: IMF, *International Financial Statistics Yearbook 1999*, pp. 524–5

peak and rural income per capita had swelled by 50 percent, achieved in large part through greater mechanization. At the same time, however, rural to urban migration continued, as salination and the economic pull of higher wages in the cities impelled the movement of labor away from agriculture.[17]

This relatively vibrant peasant economy was damaged in the 1970s. The state under the control of the Ba'th sought to extend its authority over agriculture, offering heavy subsidies to public-sector agrarian enterprises that typically used capital-intensive techniques of production, while simultaneously repressing the purchase price it paid farmers for grains, thus turning the terms of trade against peasant agriculture. In 1970, the land reform law was amended to further reduce the area that landlords were permitted to hold and eliminate compensation payments for confiscated land, which brought more land under state control. At the same time, and in the context of the rising oil revenues, the Iraqi Dinar was revalued *vis-à-vis* the US dollar by roughly 20 percent between 1970 and 1974.[18] Because the state had by this time attained a monopoly on imports, the revaluation did not immediately translate into increased imports of food. However, domestic agriculture, which once had provided most of the country's foreign exchange, became increasingly uncompetitive under international prices. Agricultural output and employment stagnated, even as the sector received substantial state investment.

This discussion illustrates the effects of the Dutch Disease, introduced in Chapter 1 and developed in Chapter 3. As a primary goods exporter receives rising prices for its primary good(s) and increased revenues from exports over a period of years, the incoming foreign exchange drives up the value of the local currency relative to foreign currencies. Imports become cheaper to obtain and may replace domestic production of (non-primary) tradable goods in both agriculture and industry, reducing both domestic output and exports of these goods. Domestic investments in tradable goods become relatively less profitable and this transfers investment to the production of non-tradable goods such as real estate. Gradually, the country becomes more dependent on imports of the tradable goods that it once produced (often necessities, such as food). Then, as prices for the exported primary commodity fall on international markets and foreign exchange earnings are reduced, the country finds itself in a quandary: it can no longer afford to purchase the same quantity of imports, but its domestic capacity to produce such necessities has shrunk. This process fuelled the debt crises of the 1980s in some developing countries, as governments had to borrow on international markets to finance purchases of essential imports.[19]

These phenomena occurred in Iraq, although the proximate cause was less the decline in price of exported primary commodity than the disruption of primary exports (which resulted in reduced government revenues) as well as the need to finance a costly war with Iran. When foreign exchange became scarce, the government changed its agricultural policies in an attempt to restrain costly food imports. In 1983, the state began to lease public land to private capitalists, who (partly because of the conscription requirements of war) used capital-intensive techniques of production. The government retained a plethora of price controls and input subsidies. But the reforms failed to reverse the decline of the sector, and may have contributed to the long-term problem of salination. The modest improvement in the performance of the sector in the late 1970s and 1980s is not evidence of radical revival, but of incremental gains, probably aided by productivity-enhancing improvements in rural health and literacy.

The enhanced rate of growth of per capita agricultural output does not account for the improved standards of nutrition in the 1980s. Iraq had, by the late 1970s, become dependent on imports of food, particularly grain: net food imports (food imports minus food exports) for the years 1977, 1978, and 1979 were ID 164 million, ID 149 million, and ID 138 million, which constituted 33 percent, 27 percent, and 23 percent of the output of the entire agricultural sector.[20] Given that agricultural output grew at a lower rate than population in the 1980s, food availability would have deteriorated had food imports remained constant.

In fact, food imports increased by more than the growth rate of population, raising food availability and hence nutritional standards in the 1980s. As Table 5.7 indicates, food imports doubled from an annual average of ID 74 million (at current prices) in the period 1970–74 to ID 156 million in 1975–79, and doubled again to reach ID 333 million in 1980–89. A similar pattern of growth is obtained when food exports are deducted from food imports to yield net food imports: these doubled

Table 5.7 Food imports, 1970–89

Indicator	1970–74	1975–79	1980–89	1980–82	1983–89
Food imports (ID million)	74	156	333	187	395
Net food imports (ID million)	62	140	316	173	378
Net food imports per capita (current ID)	6.0	11.6	20.2	12.8	23.3
Net food imports as a % of all imports (%)	12.0	6.5	6.9	2.8	9.0

Sources: For estimates of food imports and exports: Central Statistical Organization, *Annual Abstract of Statistics 1970*, Baghdad, undated, p. 264; Central Statistical Organization, *Annual Abstract of Statistics 1971*, Baghdad, undated, p. 228; Central Statistical Organization, *Annual Abstract of Statistics 1972*, Baghdad, undated, p. 168; Central Statistical Organization, *Annual Abstract of Statistics 1973*, Baghdad, undated, p. 205; Central Statistical Organization, *Annual Abstract of Statistics 1974*, Baghdad, undated, p. 435; Central Statistical Organization, *Annual Abstract of Statistics 1975*, Baghdad, undated, p. 219; Central Statistical Organization, *Annual Abstract of Statistics 1976*, Baghdad, undated, p. 410; Central Statistical Organization, *Annual Abstract of Statistics 1978*, p. 177; UNESCWA, *Statistical Abstract of the ESCWA Region 1978–87*, p. 140; UNESCWA, *Statistical Abstract of the ESCWA Region 1983–92*, p. 121; and (for population estimates) IMF, *International Financial Statistics Yearbook 1999*, pp. 524–5

between 1970–74 and 1975–79 and again between 1975–79 and 1980–89. In per capita terms, net food imports increased from ID 6 in 1970–74 to ID 11.6 in 1975–79, and reached ID 20.2 in 1980–89. However, as a result of the sharp rise in non-food imports associated with the oil price increase of the early 1970s, net food imports as a proportion of all imports declined from 12 percent in the period 1970–74 to 6.5 percent in 1975–79, rising slightly to 6.9 percent in 1980–89.

Estimates of net food imports as a proportion of all imports in the period 1980–89 are comparatively low for two reasons. Due to the fairly good harvests for wheat and barley in the years 1980–82, grain imports were relatively modest. Thus, net food imports were ID 173 million per annum in the period 1980–82 in comparison with ID 378 million in 1983–89, and per capita net food imports were only slightly higher in 1980–82 than in 1975–79. Since despite the war with Iran, the state decided to push ahead with its ambitious development plans, total (and non-food) imports peaked in the period 1980–82 and net food imports were only 2.8 percent of total imports in this period. This results in the fairly low estimate of net food imports, as a proportion of total imports, for the sub-period 1980–89.

A closer look at the period after 1983 is of interest, since this was a period of war austerity and severe balance of payment constraints. Despite the constraints, the regime used its monopoly on foreign trade to import food in record quantities: annual net imports of food were ID 378 million per annum in the period 1983–89, which translates to per capita imports of ID 23.3. In spite of the substantial demands of military imports (they accounted for roughly 60 percent of all imports in the period 1983–88) on the balance of payments, net food imports were 9 percent of total imports in the period 1983–89.

The increase in food imports during the 1980s resulted in enhanced availability of food. As Table 5.8 testifies, the average quantity of barley imports declined significantly between 1977–78 and 1986–8, but the quantity of rice doubled and wheat tripled.[21] The domestic output of wheat rose only slightly; the output of rice declined, as domestically produced quantities of barley doubled. As a result of the imports, per capita availability of the foods increased in this period; in the case of wheat, by more than 50 percent.

The enhanced standard of nutrition in the 1980s – when there were severe current account constraints – was therefore not accidental, but the result of a deliberate policy to import large quantities of food (which were subsequently sold to the public at subsidized prices). In contrast, imports of food and hence food availability was less during the late 1970s, when the country was running current account surpluses. Although it is possible that there was a radical reorientation of priorities between the late 1970s and early 1980s, a more plausible explanation is that the state found it necessary in the 1980s to engage in large imports of food, probably to

Table 5.8 Net imports, domestic output, and per capita food availability, 1977–8 and 1986–8

Item	1977–8	1986–8
Net imports (in thousand metric tons):		
Wheat	945	2834
Barley	145	42
Rice	262	558
Domestic output (in thousand metric tons):		
Wheat	803	896
Barley	538	1075
Rice	186	159
Per capita availability (metric tons per thousand persons):		
Wheat	142.9	226.8
Barley	55.8	67.6
Rice	36.7	43.6

Sources: For imports, exports and domestic output: Food and Agriculture Organization (FAO), *FAO Trade Yearbook 1979*, Rome, 1980, pp. 113, 119, 121. FAO, *FAO Trade Yearbook 1988*, Rome, 1990, pp. 123, 129, 131; UNECWA, *Statistical Abstract of the ECWA Region 1971-80*, Baghdad, 1982, pp. 83, 105; UNESCWA, *Statistical Abstract of the ESCWA Region 1978-87*, pp. 111, 126; UNESCWA, *Statistical Abstract of the ESCWA Region 1983-92*, p. 109; for population estimates: International Monetary Fund (IMF), *International Financial Statistics Yearbook 1999*, New York, 2000, pp. 524–5

forestall the likelihood of public disturbances over food availability (which had occurred before in Iraq's history)[22] and to reconcile people to their sacrifices on the battlefields of an increasingly unpopular war with Iran. Regardless of the motives, the policy raised the nutritional standard of the country to unprecedented levels.

Health

Life expectancy at birth

Iraq witnessed a steady increase in life expectancy, roughly 20 years in four decades: from 44 years in 1950–55 to 63.9 in 1985–90, as shown in Table 5.9. The largest gains were achieved in the 1970s, as life expectancy increased from 53 years in 1965–70 to 61.4 in 1975–80. Less rapid growth followed this period: 61.4 years to 63.9 from 1975–80 to 1985–90, with the increase in the latter part of the 1980s exceeding that for the earlier part of the decade. Throughout the period, female longevity exceeded that of males.

In comparison with other developing countries, life expectancy was 1.5 years higher than the weighted average for all developing countries (as defined by the World Bank) in 1965, but the same in 1985, as Table 5.10 illustrates. In respect to other middle-income economies, life expectancy in Iraq was 2.5 years lower than in other middle-income economies in 1965,

Table 5.9 Life expectancy at birth (in years), 1950–90

Period	Male	Female	Entire population
1950–55	43.1	44.9	44.0
1955–60	46.1	47.9	47.0
1960–65	49.1	50.9	50.0
1965–70	52.1	53.9	53.0
1970–75	56.1	57.9	57.0
1975–80	60.5	62.3	61.4
1980–85	61.5	63.3	62.4
1985–90	63.0	64.8	63.9

Source: Adapted from UN, *Demographic Yearbook Special Issue: Population Ageing and the Situation of the Elderly*, New York, 1993, p. 500

but only one year lower in 1985. Thus, in general, Iraq's performance in terms of improvements in life expectancy has been about average.

Infant mortality

According to data from the World Bank, there was a consistent decline in infant mortality, from 139 per thousand in 1960 to 65 in 1990 (see Table 5.11, which includes UNICEF estimates, given in parentheses).[23] The World Bank places the highest rate of improvement between 1975 and 1980, when infant mortality declined by 25 percent. This fell in the 1980s, as infant deaths declined by only 6 percent from 1980 to 1985 and by 11 percent from 1985 to 1990. However, UNICEF estimates of infant mortality vary markedly from these and show no deceleration in gains in the 1980s.

Iraq's comparatively high income during this period is misleading. GDP per capita was roughly US$3,200 in 1985, much higher than the (weighted average) level of gross national product (GNP) per capita in developing countries as a whole, the MENA region, and oil exporters. However, Iraq's official exchange rate, at 1 ID to US$3.21, was hugely overvalued in the middle 1980s, and the free market rate would have surely reduced the country's per capita GDP (as measured in US dollars) by at least one-half to two-thirds. At this level, Iraq's per capita GDP would be comparable to the level in other middle-income economies and oil exporters, but still higher than the average in developing countries

Table 5.10 International comparison of life expectancy (in years), 1965–85

Period	Iraq			Developing countries			Middle-income countries		
	Total	Male	Female	Total	Male	Female	Total	Male	Female
1965	53	51	53	50.5	49	52	54.5	53	56
1985	61	59	63	61	60	62	62	60	64

Source: Adapted from WB, *World Development Report 1987*, pp. 258–9

Table 5.11 Infant mortality (per 1000 live births) 1960–88

Period	Iraq	Developing countries	Middle-income countries	MENA countries	Oil exporters
1960	139 (117)				
1965	119	118	104	151	140
1970	(90)				
1975	104				
1980	78 (63)				
1985	73	71	68		88
1990	65 (40)		79		
GNP per capita 1985 (US $)	3190*	610	1290		1060
GNP per capita 1990 (US $)				1790	

* Refers to GDP per capita

Sources: WB, *World Development Report 1978*, Oxford University Press, New York, 1978, pp. 108–9; WB, *World Development Report 1982*, pp. 150–1; WB, *World Development Report 1987*, pp. 202–3, 258–9; WB, *World Development Report 1992*, pp. 219, 272–3; and Chapter 3, Table 3.1; Peter Pellet, 'Sanctions, Food, Nutrition and Health in Iraq,' in *Iraq Under Siege: The Deadly Impact of sanctions and War*, Anthony Arnove (ed.), South End

(assuming that the exchange rates of other countries were relatively undistorted).

Iraq's infant mortality rate was roughly the same as that in developing countries as a whole in the years 1965 and 1985, and, likewise, the country had done as well as, but not better than, other oil exporters at reducing infant deaths. However, its rate of improvement had surpassed that of middle-income economies: Iraq's infant mortality rate was 14 percent higher in 1965, but only 7 percent higher in 1985. In this respect, Iraq's experience reflects that of the MENA region as a whole: there was rapid progress at improving health outcomes, but these outcomes were lower than what one would have expected given the region's income level.[24] In respect to MENA countries, infant deaths in Iraq were 27 percent fewer in 1965 and 22 percent lower in 1990.

In principle, countries with higher incomes are able to finance larger public health expenditures and, to the extent that health services are a normal good, individuals will tend to demand more health care as incomes rise. The comparatively poor performance of MENA countries in terms of health outcomes, however, is not the result of meager expenditures on health, but rather how the funds are spent – usually inefficiently on expensive curative medicine.[25] Moreover, health outcomes are not a simple function of spending, but result from the interaction of many different factors. Improved housing and nutrition, the extension of basic services, the spread of literacy (especially female), and national emergencies, such as war, also affect outcomes.

Efficiencies and complementarities

After charting the evolution in housing, basic services, and nutrition, the question remains: how have these factors collectively affected health outcomes in Iraq? Health spending increased from ID 16 million in 1971 to ID 41.1 million in 1976, and reached ID 135.8 million in 1980, or 4.7 percent, 2.8 percent, and 3.7 percent of the ordinary (current) budget.[26] Once adjusted according to the government consumption expenditure deflator, this expenditure becomes ID 36.7 million, ID 59.8 million, and 135.8 million, in constant 1980 ID.[27] It is possible that the real value of public expenditure on health declined after the imposition of war austerity in 1983, but in the absence of health spending data after 1980, it is impossible to say.

If so, the presumed decline in public expenditure was not apparently offset by an increase in private expenditure on health. According to data from household expenditure surveys, presented in Table 5.12, the real value of expenditure on medical goods and services was constant at roughly ID 0.34 per month in 1979 and ID 0.36 in 1988.[28] Because of price controls and heavy subsidization of health care, the price index for medical goods and services grew at a rate that was less than the general rate of inflation during the period 1979–88. Private expenditures on health were stagnant in this period.

As noted earlier, the composition of health spending is often a more important determinant of outcomes than the level of expenditure. In the absence of public health expenditure data after 1980, the study of access to health services is helpful. According to Table 5.13, the ratio of the population to hospital beds remained fairly constant, roughly between 500 and 600 persons per bed, from 1970 to 1988. For a brief period, however – between 1980 and 1984, in the case of the population per physician ratio, and between 1980 and 1982, in the case of the population per dentist ratio – the availability of medical personnel declined, but recovered strongly thereafter. The number of hospitals remained roughly the same between

Table 5.12 Household (private) expenditures on health, 1979–88

| | Monthly health expenditures per capita | | | | | Price index for | |
| | As a proportion of all expenditure (%) | | | In current | In constant | Medical | |
Year	Urban	Rural	Total	(ID)	(ID)	services	General
1979	1.7	2.0	1.8	0.34	0.34	100	100
1984–5	1.6	1.9	1.7	0.73	0.34	215	199
1988	1.6	1.6	1.6	0.86	0.36	239	296

Sources: Calculated from Central Statistical Organization, *Annual Abstract of Statistics 1985*, Baghdad, undated, p. 143; and Central Statistical Organization, *Annual Abstract of Statistics 1989*, Baghdad, 1990, p. 196, pp. 356–60

Table 5.13 Various measures of health services, 1970–88

Year	Hospitals	Number of other health facilities	Population per hospital bed	Physician	Dentist
1970	145	1125	528	4250	35220
1975	167	1505	503	3610	24660
1978	200	1686	502	3200	19480
1979	198	1825	518	2900	16310
1980	201	1845	526	2970	15430
1982	198	1363	570	3030	15730
1984	197	1495	565	3410	15330
1985	216	1602	561	2210	12380
1986	228	1698	501	2100	11980
1988	256	1406	603	1990	11080

Sources: Calculated from Central Statistical Organization, *Numbers and Indicators: Educational and Social Services*, (in Arabic), Baghdad, Undated, pp. 19–22; and (for population estimates) IMF, *International Financial Statistics Yearbook 1999*, pp. 524–5

1978 and 1984, although it is worth noting that this trend began in 1978, before the outbreak of hostilities, and ended in the middle of the 1980s, when the war was ongoing. But the number of "other health facilities" – smaller health institutions, such as medical clinics, child and maternal health centers, and dispensaries – declined after 1980.

The reasons behind the decline in the prevalence of physicians and dentists immediately after 1980, and its sharp recovery thereafter, may have been related to the war with Iran: newly graduated physicians and doctors inducted into military service after the outbreak of the war were likely (correctly) not counted as medical personnel. Their subsequent release from military service and re-entry into the civilian economy (in 1985) may account for the sharp rise in the ratio of physicians and dentists to the general population. Despite the fluctuations, the long-term trend points to the increased availability of medical personnel.

Likewise, the decline in "other medical facilities" may have been related to the war with Iran, especially as the data indicate an abrupt drop in their numbers soon after the war began in 1980. To the extent that many of these were rural and some close to the fighting, hostilities may have closed down a number of health centers. At the same time, the number of hospitals, which had stabilized after 1978, rose sharply in the late 1980s.

At first glance, this appears to be another example of the overfunding of inefficient curative medicine in urban areas to the neglect of more efficient preventative and primary care. One ought to be cautious, however, about making such a judgment, for Iraq's urban population increased by 50 percent between 1977 and 1987, from 7.6 million to 11.5.[29] In this light, the rise in hospitals actually failed to keep pace with the rise in urban population.

In fact, access to health services expanded to reach 93 percent for the country as a whole, 78 percent in rural, and 97 percent in urban areas, in the period 1980–86, and remained constant during the remainder of the decade.[30] This allowed for a sharp increase in rates of immunization. As Table 5.14 shows, there was an increase in the proportion of one-year-old children fully immunized against four main diseases: tuberculosis (TB), diphtheria (DPT), polio, and measles, as well as a rise in the proportion of pregnant women immunized against tetanus during the 1980s. With the exception of immunization against TB, immunization rates were low, by any standard, in 1981. However, by 1988–9, over 80 percent of one-year-old children were immunized against these diseases, while more than 50 percent of pregnant women were immunized against tetanus.

If total expenditure on health did indeed decline, spending likely became more efficient and equitable in the 1980s. At the same time, gains in housing, nutrition, the improved provision of safe water, extension of basic services, and literacy (discussed in the last chapter) were working to improve health outcomes. Insufficient nourishment over long periods of time, especially when accompanied by illness, often leads to death, particularly in infants, and the availability of safe water is highly effective in reducing infant deaths (especially from gastric and parasitic diseases).[31] As regards literacy, it is estimated that Iraq's infant mortality rate declines by 6 per 1,000 for each additional year that the mother spends in school, even when controlling for other variables such as income and (rural/urban) environment, as education and literacy play an important role in the acquisition and dissemination of knowledge about health.[32] Thus, although it is difficult to imagine one-year-old children clamoring for immunization, it is easy to understand how improved parental literacy and hence awareness, along with increased resources for preventative care could radically alter the country-wide rates of immunization during the 1980s.

These factors helped improve health outcomes in the 1980s, but others hindered the process. The war with Iran brought substantial dislocation: increased internal migration, as people who were close to the front lines were evacuated and rural residents sought the safety of urban areas. The war may also have led to a drop in public funding for health. One ought to note, however, that despite financial constraints there was sustained state commitment for health: in 1989, at a time of balance of payments difficulties, imports of food and medicine were US$2.36 billion[33] or roughly 5 percent of GDP.

Table 5.14 Immunization rates in the 1980s

	Proportion fully immunized				
	One-year-old children				Pregnant women
Year	TB	DPT	Polio	Measles	Tetanus
1981	76	13	16	33	4
1988–9	94	83	83	82	56

Source: Adapted from UNICEF, *The State of the World's Children 1991*, p. 106

Prolonged periods of economic downturn are often – but not always – associated with declines in health outcomes. As incomes decline, the command over food, medical, and related resources is reduced and government expenditure on health often declines, which occurred in many developing countries that experienced structural adjustment in the 1970s and 1980s. But reduced health outcomes are not inevitable, as the following examples illustrate.

In Ghana, per capita income fell by one-third between 1974 and 1982, largely as a result of a fall in output of its main export, cocoa. Population growth increased at a higher rate than growth in food output, with the result that total food availability declined to 68 percent of the minimum calorie requirement in 1982. Real expenditure per capita on health declined drastically, as did the attendance at hospitals and health clinics. As a result, infant mortality rose from 80 per thousand in the middle 1970s to 100 in 1980, and reached 110–120 in 1983–4.[34]

A similar pattern of deterioration is evident in Brazil in the early 1980s. In 1980, the government responded to the current-account difficulties and debt crisis by raising interest rates and taxes and reducing expenditure on health. Meanwhile, no attempt was made to adjust the country's notoriously inequitable distribution of health resources, where, in 1981, 6 percent of the total expenditure of the National Health Insurance system was allocated to renal dialysis and coronary bypass operations for 12,000 persons – more than the allocation for basic health care and communicable disease control for 40 million people in the north and north-eastern section of the country.[35] As per capita incomes declined (in the period 1981–3), nutritional standards deteriorated, and these effects were in turn compounded by a measles epidemic in 1984. Thus, infant mortality rates rose in 1983–4.[36]

By contrast, the economic contraction in Zimbabwe in the early 1980s did not result in the deterioration of health indicators. As a result of drought and stagnation of exports, the country entered a severe recession in 1982. Per capita incomes declined and did not begin to rise until 1985. Yet health expenditures actually increased in real terms between 1980 and 1985, as a greater proportion of the expenditure was devoted to preventive rather than curative care. Food programs for children were instituted. As a result, infant mortality continued to fall in this period.[37]

The experience of Iraq in the 1980s underlines the absence of a simple one-to-one relationship between the resources that are devoted to health and health outcomes; how those resources are used is crucially important. As noted, World Bank figures suggest a reduced rate of improvement in health outcomes, while the UNICEF estimates show no deceleration in gains. Given the likely reduction in spending on health and dislocations of war in the 1980s, continued gains in health outcomes, even at a reduced rate, are notable. These gains were realized at least in part because of the more efficient and egalitarian composition of spending on preventative and primary health care. The advances were likely aided by enhanced nutrition, female literacy, and improved access to basic services.

Concluding remarks

The patterns of changes in outcomes in health and education bring forward some motivating observations. It is hypothesized that outcomes in education deteriorated in the 1980s because the existing composition of spending, which was efficient in terms of obtaining human development outcomes, was altered towards more expensive higher education. In contrast, the expenditures on health probably became more efficient during 1980s, as more emphasis was placed on preventative and primary care. Unlike what is postulated *vis-à-vis* education, political considerations did not work to inhibit gains in health; on the contrary, we posit that political concerns explain some of the improvement in nutrition.

One could read the emphasis on preventative, primary, and rural health as a reaction by the state to the financial constraints of the 1980s: to maintain outcomes in health, spending had to be reoriented. However, it is also possible that the re-emphasis occurred before 1980 and was not implemented until later; the unchanged number of hospitals in the late 1970s (in Table 5.13) hints at this. Thus, Iraq's reorientation in spending on health need not have been associated with budgetary considerations at all. This, after all, is the period when it was becoming increasingly clear to development practitioners that education and health expenditures tended to be top heavy, inefficient, and inequitable.

Yet, the changed emphasis in health (and related services) also may have been associated with the realization on the part of the state that curative and urban medicine had been advanced as far as possible. The large gains, for instance, in access to safe water in rural areas – from 22 percent of the population in 1975–80 to 72 percent in 1988–90, according to Table 5.3 – were attained only once safe water was essentially available to all in the cities. If so, the reorientation in health represents less the reversal of urban bias than its completion. As elsewhere, the state in Iraq has not been a disinterested dispenser of the "public interest" but has been negotiating multiple and sometimes conflicting private interests. In Iraq, the adequate provisioning of services in urban areas has been viewed by successive governments, regardless of proclaimed ideology, as necessary for political survival, efficiency and considerations of equity notwithstanding.[38]

6 The position of women

Were gender equality the prevailing norm, a discussion of the position of women would be superfluous. Female capabilities would be studied under their broad headings: female literacy and enrollment in school under general literacy and enrollment, and women's incomes and poverty under average incomes and poverty rates. In the presence of marked and often persistent gender inequality, however, the study of these topics, without reference to gender, would be incomplete and almost certainly misleading.

The intellectual rationale for the study of capabilities of women is to some extent much the same as it is for men. There is no reason to believe that the freedom to live long, healthy, and well nourished lives or the capacity to read and write ought to be intrinsically valued less for females than for males. The latter capability in particular enables women to articulate their priorities more effectively, which can help to highlight female concerns, identify local development priorities, and permit greater women's participation in the institutions of civil society, a gain in its own right.

Indeed, female capabilities may carry greater instrumental significance in comparison with those of men. As Amartya Sen notes, there is a well established association between enhanced female literacy and reduced fertility rates. Moreover, whereas the effects of male literacy or general poverty reduction are relatively modest, female literacy has a significant impact in improving child survival and reducing bias against female children. However, the effects of female employment outside the home on child survival are ambiguous. On one hand, it implies greater independence and influence within the family for women and hence a reorienting of family priorities towards children. On the other, working women are often left alone to the twin tasks of employment outside the home and housework, which induces them to offer fewer resources for their children, as men are often unwilling to assist in housework.[1]

The double shift that women sometimes assume is only one symptom of the general bias against females. Reduced access to education, nutrition, and health care as well a disadvantaged social position *vis-à-vis* men are other indicators of the disparity, present throughout most of the world.

The extent of the bias varies, as is apparent from a comparison of the ratio of females to males in different countries (or geographic regions), although this is an admittedly crude, but nonetheless suggestive, indicator. Across the world, more males than females are born, but women have a higher probability of survival than men when given the same resources and care. Females outnumber males in Europe and North America: the ratio exceeds 1.05 in Britain, France, and the United States. In contrast, in regions where women receive comparatively fewer resources, such as South Asia and China, men outnumber women: the ratio of females to males is 0.90 in Pakistan, 0.93 in India, and 0.94 in China. The Middle East and North Africa have fewer females than males in the population, but the ratios are generally not as low as those found in the countries noted above: in Egypt the ratio is 0.95; in Iraq, it is 0.95 for 1987 and 1.01 for 1997. The last statistic is not evidence of improved conditions for women, but reflects the collapse in health infrastructure and widespread malnutrition that resulted from war and sanctions in the 1990s – all of which disproportionately affected men.[2]

Although expressed distinctively in a wide range of social customs and institutions, this discussion suggests that bias against women in Iraq (and the Middle East in general) is not altogether unique. The disparity is found in other developing countries and, indeed, resembles the preference shown to men in many European countries in the nineteenth and (the greater part of) the twentieth centuries.[3] The discussion also suggests that gender inequality in the Middle East may not be as severe as in other places. In fact, women in the Middle East have made substantial progress in reducing gender disparity in terms of education and participation in the labor force,[4] although female labor force participation in the region is still below what one would expect given incomes and education levels.[5]

Despite this advance, Islam, and the values that it gives rise to, are often invoked to explain the relatively low position of women in Middle Eastern and Muslim countries.[6] Culture and religion are important determinants of social outcomes in any society, so it is worthwhile to briefly consider these to put the discussion in this chapter into perspective.

Cultural and religious contexts

An important feature concerning women in Iraq and the Middle East in general is their historical lack of participation in public life. This condition, to be fair, is not exceptional to the Middle East, but is in evidence in other countries, especially in South Asia, and, historically, in Europe, although there are some who argue that the seclusion of women in Europe was never as great as traditionally practiced in the Middle East.[7] Be that as it may, the isolation of women from the public sphere in the Middle East has resided mainly in the emphasis placed on family "honor" and the importance attached to the preservation of that honor, measured by the degree to which the family is able to protect the sexual purity of its female members. The punishment for a woman found guilty of adultery was death, often at the hand of relatives. Historically, this was practiced in other regions beside the Middle East, and the practice is today in retreat. Nevertheless, prestige was attached then to keeping women secluded at home, and work outside the home was viewed as somewhat shameful, particularly by the middle and upper classes that could afford the seclusion. Thus, when in the latter part of the nineteenth and early part of the twentieth centuries more women sought work outside the home, they came usually from the poor classes of society.[8]

Islam is often viewed as largely responsible for this isolation, but the role of this religion as regards position of women is in fact more complex.[9] Neither the emphasis on honor nor the extreme way in which dishonor is remedied is required by Islam. Two separate verses in the Quran, the Muslim holy book, relate to illicit sexual relations in different ways. According to one verse, persons found guilty of fornication are to be punished by incarceration, perhaps until death. In another verse, adulterous men and women are to be punished by 100 lashes each. The accusation of fornication requires four witnesses, however, and is therefore legally difficult to prove in practice.[10] Moreover, Islamic teachings do not require veiling, a prominent symbol of Muslim women's separation from the public sphere. That is, the lack of female participation in social life has been less the result of religion than social convention.

Even so, in two other social arenas, namely marriage (and divorce) and inheritance rights, Islam arguably shows preference towards males. As Christianity has traditionally, Islam compels a woman to obey her husband in marriage, and she is not allowed to give evidence against him in court.[11] Further, Islam allows males to simultaneously have four wives, while women are required to be monandrous. In general, though, Muslim men have typically taken only one wife; multiple wives have been more a feature of rural areas and the practice is in decline. Only 4.4 percent of all marriages were polygamous in the city of Baghdad in 1947; while in the entire province of Baghdad, which contained rural districts, this statistic was 8.5 percent. In the largely rural province of Muntafik, in the south, however, 12.6 percent of men in 1947 had more than one wife.[12] Even so, one ought to note that under Islamic custom men are bound to provide for their wives and children. So parallel to the preference that Islam shows men in marriage there is greater responsibility for males.

Islamic teachings regarding divorce are more obviously biased towards males. Husbands may divorce their wives simply by saying "you are divorced," and are not required to give an explanation. By contrast, a woman is allowed to sue for divorce only if her dowry had not been paid or if the husband was unable to perform sexual intercourse.[13] It ought to be noted, however, that the position of the Shia religious tradition, a minority in Islam but a majority in Iraq, regarding divorce is different. This tradition does not recognize the man's divorce utterance as sufficient, and requires the presence of a *mujtahid* (religious authority) to validate divorce.[14]

The threat of divorce has often placed the woman in a vulnerable position, since she typically has more to lose. Islamic custom generally gives male parents custody of sons above seven years of age and daughters above nine; and in the Shia Muslim tradition men may claim custody of sons as young as two.[15] Further, men are only required to pay alimony for a period of three months after divorce. The traditional use of *dower* – a payment made to the female's family in compensation for her services to the prospective husband – is sometimes viewed to underline the low status of women. It is tempting to view this exchange as a property transaction that emphasizes the low position of women, but the *dower* has also acted as a deterrent to divorce, since any husband seeking this is required to pay a second *dower*, and has given women access to wealth.[16]

In inheritance laws too, Islam gives precedence to men. Daughters are entitled to only half the son's share in inheritance. If there are no sons, the daughter is restricted to half of her parents' estate, the remainder going to paternal male relatives, such as uncles, as well as to the other parent.[17] But the Shia tradition does not recognize the rights of male agnates, although a woman still receives half the man's share.[18] Also, a widow receives an eighth of her husband's estate if they have children, a quarter if there are no children; and if there is more than one wife, these shares are divided equally between them.[19]

These defined property rights for women compare favorably with the absence of rights in Europe before the advent of modern legislation, and are consistent with social customs that view wives and daughters as the responsibility of their male kin. In practice, however, women in Muslim countries have not received what they are entitled to, as these inheritance strictures have in general been either circumvented or ignored. Parents often signed over their property to their sons or else simply ignored the law. These appropriations have not been confined to Muslims, but have also been practiced by Christian minorities in the Middle East – that is, quite independently of religion.[20] Parents have had little interest in directing resources to daughters since it is the sons that have been required by custom to care for parents in old age; resources channeled to daughters often have been viewed as an undesirable leakage. This may explain the traditional reluctance of parents, especially from the poorer classes, to educate their daughters, since it has usually been her husband, not the parents, who typically received the returns to her education.

Islam shows partiality to men, but it is not clear that in general this bias has been the binding constraint on the advancement of women. Islamic teachings place women in a weak position in marriage; but discrimination against women in birthright has not been the result of "Muslim inheritance law but the opposite – a consequence of its neglect."[21] Also, it is not obvious that the lack of women's participation in social life has been the result of Islamic convention. Certainly, some have exploited Islam to argue against improving in position of women, although there is a substantial diversity of views, even among political Islamists, toward, for example, work outside the home.[22] One need only look at the great divergence in the conditions of women in different Muslim countries, however, to realize that Islam alone cannot account for the gender disparity. Dissimilar economic conditions, historical conjuncture, and state policies and priorities are among some of the reasons for the divergence.

According to the analysis of John Caldwell, the low position of women is the outcome of a social structure in which production is based on the extended family, a form that was not unique to Iraq. In this structure, resources flow from women to men and from young to old. Women are not entirely powerless in this arrangement: older women are highly influential in the family and often tasked with disciplining younger errant females, but derive their power largely from older men. Younger women have few options, however, since their non-participation in family labor would terminate the flow of the few resources they do receive.[23]

Corresponding to this form of production is a "cultural superstructure" which elevates the position of men at the expense of most women.[24] But exponents of this viewpoint recognize that causation is not always unidirectional and changes in production mode translate into transformed cultural or ideological patterns sometimes only with considerable lag. Still, the production form is viewed as mainly responsible for the ensuing cultural patterns. In this regard, the apparent indifference of women in Turkey to issues of women's rights in the early twentieth century, in contrast to the mobilization of women in the struggle for equality in the West, is explained by the observation that, unlike in the West, "the ideological lever [was] operating on a substantially unchanged economic base" in Turkey.[25] Within the same logic, Jacqueline Ismael and Suad Joseph argue that the Ba'th regime in Iraq accelerated the undermining of the family mode of production, a process that was already under way before their advent to power, by reducing the power of patriarchical tribes and elevating the nuclear family, considered necessary for modernization.[26] The present bias against women that is supposedly supported in Islamic teachings, in this view, represents the doomed efforts of an archaic superstructure to reinforce its crumbling economic base.

Yet, the Quran remains for devout Muslims the immutable word of God, and its teachings, as they are understood by Muslims, have come to represent a sort of "cultural authenticity" for societies in the hold of economic dominance and cultural infiltration from the West, according to some authorities.[27] The simplistic formulation outlined above has thus come under attack. From within the paradigm, it has been suggested that the erosion of the economic base of patriarchy, although it has resulted in reduced control of fathers and brothers, has precipitated a conservative social backlash against the emancipation of women rather than demonstrable progress.[28] Far from an extensive change in ideology, some see a "patriarchal bargain" between women of the social elite and the state, whereby these women acquired power and rights so long as they did not endanger the patriarchic social structure and the state.[29] Meanwhile, some radicals outside the paradigm view Islam as irredeemably hostile to the conditions and rights of women.[30]

Although this discussion illustrates the disagreements over what accounts for the gender inequality in the Middle East, it also points to general concord about how this disparity might be assessed. To the extent that women in the region have traditionally suffered from comparative isolation and unequal rights and social status, their progress is likely to be reflected in enhanced access to education, employment outside the home, and in the laws that govern their status. These also reflect, albeit imperfectly, the range of choices available to women and their relative independence.

Women's access to education

Female literacy

The intrinsic and instrumental import to literacy and enrollment in school has already been discussed. We examine these here for women. Beginning from a very low educational base, women's literacy clearly improved in the period under study, as shown in Table 6.1. Following the trend of literacy rates in the population as a whole, female literacy rates (for 10 years and older) increased from about one-eighth in 1957 to one-sixth in 1965, to three-tenths in 1977, and was nearly two-thirds in 1987.[31] But, the gap between male and female literacy has declined through time, at an increased rate between 1977 and 1987. The ratio of female to male literacy rates in the country increased from 29.1 percent in 1957 to 44.6 percent in 1977, and reached 82 percent in 1987.

Increases in female enrollment in primary education account for most of the increase in women's literacy, before 1977, but the acceleration in literacy between 1977 and 1987 was due to the government's illiteracy eradication campaign, discussed earlier in Chapter 4. This program, which was launched in 1978, targeted roughly 2.22 million illiterates in the 15 to 45 year old population: 1.54 million females and 680,000 males.[32] By July 1979, 1.2 million women were enrolled in the program[33] and were the disproportionate beneficiaries of the literacy drive.

Table 6.1 Male and female literacy rates

Year	5 years and older				10 years and older			
	Total pop.	Male	Female	Ratio of female to male rates	Total pop.	Male	Female	Ratio of female to male rates
1947	11.0	19.0	4.0	21.0				
1957	18.3	27.8	8.8	31.5	18.3	28.4	8.3	29.1
1965	29.9	41.9	17.5	41.7	30.3	43.3	16.9	38.9
1977					47.0	65.9	29.4	44.6
1987					72.6	79.8	65.5	82.0

Sources: For 1947: calculated from United Nations Educational Scientific and Cultural Organization (UNESCO), *Basic Facts and Figures 1958*, Paris, 1959, p. 13; for 1957: Directorate General of Census, *Abstract of the General Census of 1957*; for 1965: Central Statistical Organization, *General Population Census of 1965*, Baghdad, 1973, p. 340; Central Statistical Organization, *Annual Abstract of Statistics 1971*, Baghdad, Undated, p. 66; for 1977: Central Statistical Organization, *Annual Abstract of Statistics 1978*, Baghdad, Undated, p. 35; and for 1987: Central Statistical Organization, *Annual Abstract of Statistics 1989*, Baghdad, 1990, p. 42

Enrollment rates in primary education

As with literacy, female enrollment in primary education improved in the period. As Table 6.2 shows, gross enrollment rates[34] for the 6 to 11 years old population increased from 36 percent in 1960 to 41 percent in 1970 to 107 percent in 1980, but declined slightly to 101 percent in 1987 and 97 percent in 1988. Similarly, net female enrollment rates increased from 28 percent to 34 percent to 94 percent and slightly declined to 91 percent and 87 percent for the same years. This mirrored the overall trend (for boys and girls) in the primary enrollment in this period. Yet, female enrollment was catching up with its male counterpart. The ratio of female to male gross enrollment (F/M), for the 6 to 11 years old population, increased from 38 percent in 1960 to 42 percent in 1970 to 90 percent in 1980, but declined to 86 percent in 1987 and 84 percent in 1988; for net enrollment the statistic increased from 42 percent to 45 percent to 94 percent but declined to 91 percent and 87 percent for the same years.

The increase in female enrollment rates was not steady, but accelerated between 1975 and 1980, although there were important gains in the preceding period as well. Net enrollment rates, for the 6 to 11 years old population, increased from 28 percent in 1960 to 55 percent in 1975, and for the 7 to 12 years old population, from 12 percent in 1950 to 41 percent in 1968. Between 1975 and 1980, net enrollment for females, for the 6 to 11 years old population, rose from 55 percent to 94 percent. As a result, the ratio of female to male net enrollment rates increased steadily from 42 percent in 1960 to 55 percent in 1975, but jumped to 94 percent in 1980, but declined slightly thereafter.

Table 6.2 Enrollment rates in primary education

| Year | Primary (6–11 years of age) | | | | | | | | Primary (7–12 years of age) | | | | | | | |
| | Gross | | | | Net | | | | Gross | | | | Net | | | |
	M	F	T (%)	F/M	M	F	T (%)	F/M	M	F	T (%)	F/T	M	F	T (%)	F/T
1950														12	24	50
1955														18	36	50
1960	94	36	65	38	66	28	48	42						37	67	55
1965										43	72	61		35	57	62
1968														41	69	61
1970	96	41	69	42	76	34	55	45								
1975	122	64	94	52	100	55	79	55								
1980	119	107	113	90	100	94	99	94								
1985	116	99	104	85	99	87	93	87								
1987	117	101	109	86	100	91	96	91								
1988	116	97	107	84	100	87	94	87								

Sources: UNESCO, *Statistical Yearbook 1970*, Paris, 1971, p. 97; UNESCO, *Statistical Yearbook 1974*, Paris, 1975, p. 148; UNESCO, *Statistical Yearbook 1977*, Paris, 1978, p. 158; UNESCO, *Statistical Yearbook 1984*, Paris, 1985, table 3–49; UNESCO, *Statistical Yearbook 1988*, Paris, 1989, table 3–47; and UNESCO, *Statistical Yearbook 1994*, Paris, 1995, table 3–48

Enrollment rates in secondary education

Gains in female secondary enrollments show a similar pattern. Net enrollment for females in the 13 to 18 years old population increased from 2 percent in 1950 to 7 percent in 1960 and reached 13 percent in 1968, as illustrated in Table 6.3. For the 12 to 17 years old population, net enrollment of females increased from 12 percent in 1970 to 16 percent in 1975 to 31 percent in 1980, where it remained in 1987 and 1988. As with primary education, female enrollment in secondary education increased rapidly between 1975 and 1980. Unlike primary education, however, the ratio of female to male net enrollment continued to rise in the 1980s: from 44 percent in 1970 to 50 percent in 1980, to 65 percent in 1988, although, as explained in Chapter 4, this rise was not result from higher female enrollment, but from a decline in male enrollments.

Enrollment rates in higher education

As regards higher education, Table 6.4 shows that the gross enrollment rate for females (in the 20 to 24 years old population group) increased modestly from 0.9 percent to 2.2 percent to 2.4 percent in 1960, 1965, and 1970 respectively, but rose sharply to 6.0 percent in 1975 and was roughly 10 percent in the 1980s. As a proportion of male enrollment, female enrollment increased from 29 percent in 1960 to 64 percent in 1988. Unlike in secondary education, however, the rise after 1980 occurred alongside higher male enrollments, from 12.5 percent in 1980 to 16.8 percent in 1988.

Table 6.3 Enrollment rates in secondary education

Year	Secondary (12–17 years of age)								Secondary (13–18 years of age)							
	Gross				Net				Gross				Net			
	M	F	T	F/M	M	F	T	F/M	M	F	T	F/T	M	F	T	F/T
		(%)				(%)				(%)				(%)		
1950														2	5	40
1955														3	8	38
1960														7	17	41
1965														11	23	48
1968														13	26	50
1970	34	14	24	41	27	12	19	44								
1975	48	21	35	44	34	16	25	47								
1980	75	38	57	51	62	31	47	50								
1985	62	39	55	57												
1987	61	38	49	62	50	31	41	62								
1988	59	37	48	63	48	31	40	65								

Sources: UNESCO, *Statistical Yearbook 1970*, p. 97; UNESCO, *Statistical Yearbook 1974*, p. 148; UNESCO, *Statistical Yearbook 1977*, p. 158; UNESCO, *Statistical Yearbook 1984*, table 3–49; UNESCO, *Statistical Yearbook 1988*, table 3–47; and UNESCO, *Statistical Yearbook 1994*, table 3–48

Table 6.4 Enrollment rates in higher education

Year	Gross (20–24 years of age)			
	M	F	T	F/M(%)
1960	3.1	0.9	2.0	29
1965	5.8	2.2	4.1	38
1970	7.9	2.4	5.2	30
1975	11.8	6.0	9.0	51
1980	12.5	6.1	9.3	49
1985	15.5	9.3	12.4	60
1988	16.8	10.7	13.8	64

Sources: UNESCO, *Statistical Yearbook 1977*, p. 158; UNESCO, *Statistical Yearbook 1984*, table 3–49; and UNESCO, *Statistical Yearbook 1988*, table 3–47

The undesirability of overfunding higher education, which ultimately permitted the increased enrollment at the universities, and analysis of the enrollment trends in primary and secondary education during the 1980s are presented in Chapter 4. Still, education, especially at the higher level, expands the opportunities for employment outside the home, and this can have a powerful effect on a woman's independence from her spouse, her influence in the family, and, in due course, can work to change social values and perceptions. That is, female education and employment are likely to increase her bargaining power and so reformulate family and ultimately social priorities.[35] The changed female sway within the family is likely to depend in part on the employment possibilities and thus, to some degree, on educational attainment. A study of the academic fields pursued by women at the university level may therefore be revealing, the efficiency and equity concerns about higher education notwithstanding.

As shown in Table 6.5, the proportion of engineering graduates that were female increased from 4 percent in academic year 1970–1 to 16 percent in 1975–6, and was 20 percent in 1979–80,[36] and the ratio for dentistry increased from 22 percent to 35 percent to 36 percent. Women's representation in the study of medicine remained constant, at 19 percent in 1970–1 and 20 percent in 1975–6. It is likely, however, that female representation in medicine increased thereafter, since the proportion of physicians that were female increased during the 1980s: in 1978, females accounted for 24 percent of all Iraqi physicians, 25 percent of general practitioners and 23 percent of specialists,[37] while by 1989 they accounted for 37 percent of all physicians, 40 percent of general practitioners and 27 percent of specialists.[38] These three fields, whose entry requirements are quite stiff, represent the most lucrative and socially prestigious careers in the country. In other fields, such as administration, law, and pharmacy, there was enhanced female representation as well. Gains in access to education for women undoubtedly worked to increase their independence, stay within the family, and influenced social priorities. But female advances in the leading and most remunerative fields probably also provided a potent symbol for gender equality, even with the urban and class bias associated with university education.

Indeed, in respect to outcomes in education, Iraq experienced a more rapid reduction in gender inequality than most other countries in the region. As Table 6.6 shows, roughly a third as many women as men could read and write in 1970, but almost two-thirds as many were literate in 1985. With the exception of Saudi Arabia, the relative gains of women in

Table 6.5 Female graduates as a proportion of all university graduates in selected fields of study

Field	Ratio of female graduates to total (%)		
	1970–1	1975–6	1978–9
Engineering	4	16	20
Medicine	19	20	na
Dentistry	22	35	36
Pharmacy	41	61	na
Administration and economics	19	32	32
Arts and education	31	43	36
Law	7	na	20
Sciences	36	36	39
All fields	24	31	31

Source: Calculated from United Nations Economic Commission for Western Asia (UNECWA), *Statistical Abstract of the ECWA Region 1971–80*, Baghdad, 1982, pp. 95–6

Table 6.6 International comparison of gender inequality in education outcomes females as a proportion of males (%)

Country	Literacy rate 1970	Literacy rate 1985	Enrollment in Primary 1960	Enrollment in Primary 1987–8	Secondary 1987–8	University 1987–8
Iraq	36	64	38	87	64	64
Saudi Arabia	13	61	na	75	67	76
Turkey	49	73	64	93	60	55
Egypt	40	49	65	79	73	52
Syria	33	53	44	94	44	94
Developing countries	54	66	61	91	70	59

Source: Adapted from United Nations Development Programme (UNDP), *Human Development Report 1991*, Oxford University Press, New York, 1991, pp. 138–9

literacy were better than any country shown. In primary education too, Iraq caught up quickly. As a proportion of male enrollment, female enrollment in primary education increased from 38 percent in 1960, among the lowest in the region, to 87 percent in 1987–8, among the highest in the region, and this despite the decline in female enrollment at the primary level during the 1980s. Likewise, *vis-à-vis* developing nations, gender inequalities in literacy and enrollment were more prominent in Iraq in the 1960s and 1970s, but almost vanished in the 1980s.

Moreover, although the data are incomplete, there is reason to believe that this relative improvement was more efficient and equitable than similar gains in other countries in the region, despite the large increase in enrollment at Iraqi universities that was discussed in Chapter 4. It will be remembered that primary education is usually associated with a higher social rate of return and is spread more evenly throughout the population. Yet, as shown in Table 6.7, enrollment rates at primary schools are far too low and at the universities too high in most countries of the Middle East. Egypt, where in 1985 almost a quarter of girls did not receive even primary instruction but nonetheless sent one in seven women to university, is a case in point. Such educational priorities inevitably mean that many women, who are typically poor, receive no basic instruction, while a few, often members of urban elites, receive subsidized university training. The contrast with Iraq and Turkey – where primary school attendance for females is nearly universal but female attendance at the universities is nevertheless lower – is striking and suggests that educational policies were far more efficient and egalitarian in these countries. This is not to say that policies were optimal in Iraq or Turkey – in fact the reverse was suggested in Chapter 4 – but it does indicate that the impressive gains for women in relation to men were achieved in a more efficient and egalitarian manner than in other countries.

Table 6.7 Comparison of female enrollment rates in the middle east

Country		Primary Gross	Net	Secondary Gross	Net	University Gross
Iraq	1975	64	55	21	16	6
	1980	109	95	38	31	6
	1985	100	92	39	na	9
Saudi Arabia	1975	43	29	15	9	2
	1980	50	37	23	16	5
	1985	61	46	33	23	10
Syria	1975	78	72	28	25	6
	1980	89	88	36	31	11
	1985	101	91	49	43	12
Egypt	1975	60		31		8
	1980	65		41		11
	1985	77		54		14
Turkey	1975	97		19		2
	1980	92		24		3
	1985	112		31		6
Arab states	1975	57		20		4
	1980	68		28		5
	1985	72		38		8

Source: UNESCO, *Statistical Yearbook 1988*, table 3–47 to 3–55 and table 2–35

The accelerated gains in female education after 1975, and the largely egalitarian way in which they came about, were not accidental. As was explained in Chapter 4, private schools were nationalized and education became free at all levels in 1975, which reduced the direct costs, but not the opportunity costs of children's labor, to parents of sending children to school. Although no perceptible change in parents' benefit from female education occurred, the reduction in direct costs worked surely to induce parents to send more females to school. This probably had its greatest impact on the education decisions of the poor classes, mostly in relation to primary and secondary education, as, especially in urban areas, the middle and upper-class families were already sending most of their female children to school at these levels.

Women's access to paid employment

The impact of improved education for women would, however, be limited without correspondingly enlarged access to work, especially outside the home. As in other parts of the Middle East, women have always been engaged in family labor that was typically unpaid, the fruits of labor accruing to the (often extended) family as a whole, usually controlled by family elders. But this type of work is less effective in promoting female independence and puts little downward pressure on fertility rates than employment outside the home.[39] It is work outside the home that is thus emphasized in the discussion that follows.

Female economic activity

According to census data, shown in Table 6.8, there was an increase in female employment between the 1950s and 1980s, as the proportion of the female population that is economically active increased from 2.3 percent in 1957 to 9.4 percent in 1977, but declined to 5.8 percent in 1987.[40] On the face of it, these represent fairly low levels of female participation in the labor market – lesser than the extremely low average for the Middle East where women were 16 percent of the labor force in 1992[41] – but there are reasons to be cautious about the accuracy of the estimates for Iraq. The statistic for 1957 is almost certainly an underestimate, as unpaid female labor in the agricultural sector, the largest employer at the time, was greatly understated. The agricultural census of 1971 revealed that 40.6 percent of agricultural workers were female, but those that received money wages were only 2.5 percent of total agricultural labor.[42] It is thus probable that the 1957 census counted only females that received money wages, a small percentage of the total engaged in agriculture. The figures for 1987 are likewise suspect, especially since women's labor was replacing that of conscripted men during the Iran–Iraq war. In fact, between 1981 and 1985, females accounted for 54 percent of the total number of hires in government, whereas they constituted only 26 percent of these between 1976 and 1980, and only 20 percent between 1971 and 1975.[43] It is plausible therefore that the estimate for 1987 excluded unpaid labor or undercounted work in the informal or private sector.

The reported decline in economic activity for women in the 1980s occurred throughout the various age groups of the population, as illustrated in Table 6.9. The reduced rate of economic activity for school-age females, from 3.8 percent to 1.0 percent in the under 20-year-old age group between 1977 and 1987, is consistent with the enhanced school

Table 6.8 The economically active population of Iraq

Census	Proportion of men (%)	Proportion of women (%)	Proportion of total (%)
1957	54.1	2.3	28.3
1977	41.9	9.4	26.1
1987	41.6	5.8	24.2

Sources: International Labour Office (ILO), *Year Book of Labour Statistics: Retrospective Edition on Population Censuses 1945-89*, Geneva, 1990, p. 61; and Central Statistical Organization, *Annual Abstract of Statistics 1989*, pp. 42–5

Table 6.9 Age group breakdown of the proportion of females that are economically active

Age groups	1977 (%)	1987 (%)
0 to 19 years old	3.8	1.0
20 years old and above	16.8	12.4
20 to 39 years old	18.1	15.5
40 years old and above	15.0	7.2

Sources: Calculated from ILO, *Year Book of Labour Statistics: Retrospective Edition on Population Censuses 1945-89*, p. 61; and Central Statistical Organization, *Annual Abstract of Statistics 1989*, pp. 42–5

enrollment levels for females. But female economic activity supposedly declined for the over-20 population as well, from 16.8 percent to 12.4 percent. Within the latter age segment, female activity rates dropped from 18.1 percent to 15.5 percent in the 20 to 39 years old age group and from 15.0 percent to 7.2 percent in the 40 years and older age group. The estimates are consistent with a systematic undercounting of female labor, brought about by a change in definition of economic activity that excluded unpaid labor or work outside the formal labor market.

Changes in female occupations

Be that as it may, the activities of women in the labor force underwent considerable change in the period. Table 6.10 shows that the proportion of professionals and technicians that is female rose from 21 percent of the total in 1957 to 32 percent in 1977, and was 44 percent in 1987. And, while it has been traditionally low, the proportion of managers that is female increased from 2 percent to 3 percent to 13 percent respectively in the same years. Similarly, female representation in retail occupations was 2 percent, 7 percent, and 9 percent; and in services was 10 percent, 10 percent, and 16 percent of total employment. By contrast, female representation in clerical employment and as laborers and artisans remained roughly constant. Finally, the proportion of all persons engaged in agriculture that were female plummeted from 38 percent in 1977 to 14 percent in 1987, although the extent of the decline may be exaggerated if unpaid female labor in agriculture was uncounted.

Still, structural economic changes may explain part of the recorded decline in female economic activity during the 1980s. According to census data, agricultural employment declined drastically, from 927,000 in 1977, of whom 351,000 were female,[44] to 474,000 in 1987, of whom only 67,000 were female.[45] By contrast, the total number of persons engaged in technical or professional occupations rose from 196,000, of whom 64,000 were women,[46] to 381,000, of whom 167,000 were female in the same period.[47] But recorded decline in female activity in agricultural

Table 6.10 Females as a proportion of all engaged in various economic occupations

Type of occupation	1957(%)	1977(%)	1987(%)
Professionals and technicians	21	32	44
Managers	2	3	13
Retail employees	2	7	9
Services employees	10	10	16
Clerical employees	5	7	6
Laborers and artisans	4	5	4
Farmers and foresters	2	38	14

Sources: For 1957: calculated from table 26 Directorate General of Census, *Abstract of the General Census of 1957*, p. 21; for 1977: table 71 Central Statistical Organization, *The General Census of 1977*, Baghdad, undated, p. 126; and for 1987: table I-18 UNESCWA, *Unified Arab Statistical Abstract 1980–1988*, Baghdad, 1990, p. 76

occupations was not entirely offset by their increased activity in other occupations. As a result, the number of economically active females declined from 534,000 in 1977[48] to 460,000 in 1987.[49]

Many of the women engaged in professional, technical, and managerial occupations were absorbed into government employment, a pattern that is consistent with the experience of other countries in the region. In neighboring Jordan, for example, most of the increase in female labor force participation between 1984 and 1996 was due to the expansion of public employment.[50] In Iraq, women workers increased from 8 percent of the total civil employment in 1960 to 18 percent in 1980, and were 27 percent in 1987, according to Table 6.11. In absolute terms, the number of females employed in government was 17,000, 144,000, and 289,900 in the same years. Not all of these were engaged in professional, technical, or managerial occupations, as 71,000 of the 289,900 (or roughly 25 percent) of the female workers in 1987 had only a primary school education or less.[51] Generally though, literacy and numerical skills are required for employment in government, and 19 percent of the females employed in that year had received a bachelors degree or higher.[52]

Table 6.11 Female employees in government

Year	Number	As a proportion of all public employees (%)
1960	17,000	8
1965	28,800	9
1972	48,100	12
1976	77,800	15
1980	144,000	18
1987	289,900	27

Sources: For 1960: calculated from Central Bureau of Statistics, *Statistical Abstract 1962*, Baghdad, 1963, p. 399; for 1965: Central Statistical Organization, *Statistical Abstract 1967*, Baghdad, 1968, p. 106; and for remaining years: Central Statistical Organization, *Numbers and Indicators: Population and Work Force* (in Arabic), Baghdad, Undated, pp. 14–16.

In fact, the educational attainment of females in government was consistently higher than that of males, resulting in higher average wages for females. According to a survey conducted in 1972, the average monthly pay of women in the public sector was ID 34.7, about 20 percent more than the average wages for males, because 31 percent of women had received "higher" (beyond secondary school level) certificates in comparison with only 14 percent for men.[53] Likewise in 1987, 32.6 percent of women in the public sector, but only 17.4 percent of men, had some form of post-secondary education.[54]

The sharp rise in female employment in government was the result a deliberate state encouragement of women to enter paid employment, especially in government – a policy that predates the Iran–Iraq war and the related need to compensate for the conscripted labor of men. Iraqi women and their families, much like those in other Middle Eastern countries, tend to view work in the public sector as safe, "respectable," offering regular, fairly short working hours, and hence as attractive.[55] Indeed, in the Middle East generally, but possibly not Iraq in this period, government employment had been so sought after that substantial "queuing" among educated female job-seekers occurred, with the result that unemployment rates among women were much higher than for men in the region.[56] And state legislation in Iraq made paid labor for women even more appealing. Social Security Law No. 39 of 1971 mandated equal compensation and retirement pay to men and women and fixed the retirement age at 55 for women, lower than the age for men (which stood at 60), as generous maternity leaves, including two and a half months of fully paid leave and six months at half pay, were legislated.[57] In short, the state embarked on program to attract women into paid labor that was "unique in the Arab World."[58]

Still, one could argue that the entry of women into wage labor, as has been suggested with reference to the West, occurred as a result of the family's requirement for two incomes, rather than the desire of females to work; that is, women were working not for reasons of personal volition but because of economic compulsion. There may be some force to this argument: economic necessity is surely an important consideration in decisions about labor market entry. Yet people are not motivated by monetary considerations only: the desire to have an independent source of income and the dignity and self-reliance that comes along with having a job or pursuing a career are important considerations as well. Were the pecuniary incentives the only determining factor in labor market decisions, one would not expect to see, as one often does in Western countries with generous unemployment insurance schemes, people engage in jobs where the net monetary rewards are small or even slightly negative.[59]

In respect to Iraq, female employment in the public sector was expanding consistently throughout the 1970s and 1980s. It may well be that women were responding to rising relative wages in public employment or they may have felt the need to augment household earnings, especially as men were conscripted with high frequency into the armed forces in the 1980s. Much like other economic actions, the labor market decisions of women probably sought a balance of multiple concerns, over the monetary and non-monetary rewards and the costs, including those to the family. This suggests that one ought to be cautious about assuming the exceptionalism, or even primacy, of pecuniary motivations and, hence, it would be a mistake to think that pecuniary pressures were largely responsible for women's entry into paid labor.

In any case, it is exceedingly likely that the enhanced educational attainment for women improved their job prospects, as women moved from lower-skilled to higher-skilled activities and into government employment, allowing women to attain greater intra-family bargaining power and independence. This is not to say that gender inequality was ended, as social attitudes and perceptions are often long-lasting. Women working outside the home confronted, for example, the "double shift": outside employment and housework, which Iraqi men were generally reluctant to assist in.[60] Inequality in housework is, however, not unique to Iraq, but is evident in many Western countries, including the United States and Sweden, and has started to recede only fairly recently.[61] More important than this bias from our viewpoint is the equality achieved by Iraqi women in respect to law, and this is considered next.

Laws governing the position of women

A variety of laws affect the position of women. Some laws do not reference women directly, but can, nevertheless, have a large impact, on account of the prominence of women in the segment of the population affected by such laws. The Illiteracy Eradication Law of 1978 benefited women because they constituted a disproportionate part of the illiterate population, while making education free in 1975 encouraged female enrollment at all stages of education. By contrast, the Social Security Law of 1971 dealt with women's issues in compensation and retirement benefits directly, as did the law regarding maternity leave. Not discussed so far are the laws than govern women in marriage, divorce, and inheritance.

The Personal Status Law of 1959

Prior to the republican government's enactment of the Personal Status Code of 1959, marriage, divorce, and inheritance laws during the monarchy were based largely on the *Hanafi* school of Islamic law, the principles of which deviate little from the legal conventions discussed earlier in this chapter.[62] The new law permitted marriage with more than one wife, but only with the consent of the courts. Permission was given, however, only if the husband could show financial ability to support more than one wife and if equal treatment of wives was supposable.[63] The minimum age of marriage was set at 18 years, although the courts were empowered to ratify marriages for those who were 16 years of age or older.[64]

The new law also reformed divorce. The divorce utterance, discussed earlier, was not considered sufficient if the man was in a condition of intoxication or otherwise "oblivious of what he is doing by reason."[65] Moreover, a man who wished to divorce his wife was required to register this with the courts within three months of his divorce pronouncement, and marriage retained its validity until annulled by the courts. To the grounds for the wife's initiation of divorce under Islamic law were added the right to divorce if the husband had been absent for two years or longer, if he had been sentenced to a term of imprisonment that exceeded five years, or if he was permanently afflicted with a disease that was dangerous to her wellbeing.[66] Finally, the mother was given custody of the children until age seven, although the courts retained the right to extend this if it was deemed to be in the interests of the child.

The most outstanding departure from Islamic convention was reserved for inheritance. The new Code equated male and female shares in inheritance, and the inheritance rights of agnates were not recognized.[67] Circumvention of this via bequests was made difficult, since, according to the Code, "no more than a third of (the net estate) may be bequeathed without the consent of the heirs, and the State is to be regarded as the heir of one who has no other heir."[68] General Qassem, the Iraqi leader at the time, explained that the: "unification of the matter of inheritance, in the interests of half the Iraqi people, required legislation along the lines of this code."[69]

Amendments in 1963 to the Personal Status Code of 1959

The Ba'th-backed military coup in 1963, which overthrew the Qassem government, contained persons of conservative orientation who were opposed to some of the provisions of the 1959 Law and the existing provisions regarding legacy were amended. The gender equality of the 1959 Code was replaced by the Shia Law of inheritance, whereby a woman receives half the man's share, but the inheritance of agnates was (as in the 1959 Code) prohibited.

Amendments in 1978 to the Personal Status Code of 1959

The 1978 Personal Status Code introduced by the Ba'th contained a number of noteworthy amendments. The minimum age of court-ratified marriage was lowered from 16 to 15, in recognition of the reality of early marriage, especially in rural areas, but marriage for those under age 18 was still subject to the approval of the courts. Also, the issue of forced marriages, which was ignored by the 1959 Code, was addressed, as the amended law specified prison terms for parents and other relatives found guilty of compelling a man or woman to marry.[70]

Concerning divorce, this law gave men and women the right to seek divorce in the case of adultery committed by the spouse, an expansion of women's rights of divorce. The mother was given custody of the children until they reached 10 years of age, with the courts retaining the right to extend custody until the children reached 15, at which point the children were permitted to decide with whom they wanted to live.[71]

These changes in the legal position of women between 1959 and 1978 are summarized in Table 6.12. Concerning personal rights, in inheritance there was regression in the rights of women, but modest improvements in the rights against forced marriages, the custody of children, and the initiation of divorce nevertheless occurred. In 1978, women were able to initiate divorce if the husband was unfaithful, had greater rights of custody of children, and had some legal protection against forced marriage, rights that were unavailable in 1959. Regarding other rights, namely the protection against multiple marriages and the requirement that the validity of divorce required its registration in court, there was no change. Concerning social and economic rights, women had achieved full equality in 1978. Men and women received equal pay and retirement benefits. In fact, women were eligible for retirement at a younger age than were men.

Even though there is a clear disparity between gains in personal versus social and economic legislation, Iraqi laws regarding the personal rights of women, although obviously not egalitarian, are considered to be among the more progressive in the Arab world. With the notable exception of Turkey, this discrepancy is characteristic of the Middle East.[72] Yet, the

Table 6.12 Comparison of the legal position of women between 1959 and 1978

Legal right	Direction of change between 1959 and 1978
A. Personal rights:	
Rights of Inheritance	Diminished
Rights from Forced Marriages	Improved
Rights to Custody of Children	Improved
Rights to Initiate Divorce	Improved
Rights of Protection against Polygyny	Unchanged
Rights to have Divorce Recorded in Court	Unchanged
B. Social and economic rights:	
Rights of Equality with Men in Compensation	Improved
Rights of Equality with Men in Retirement	Improved

Sources: Jamal J. Nasir, *The Status of Women Under Islamic Law*; Amal Rassam, 'Revolution Within'; J. N. D. Anderson, 'A Law of Personal Status for Iraq'; Gabriel Baer, *Population and Society*; and Suad Joseph, 'The Mobilization of Iraqi Women into the Wage Labor Force'

gap between intensity of state efforts to school females and channel them into paid labor, on the one hand, and the partial commitment to personal rights, on the other, is outstanding for the region, and thus of interest.

Women and the state

There are at least two explanations for the comparatively mild nature of the gains in personal rights. First, it is claimed that there is a difficulty in openly contravening Islamic teachings, as this may provoke a popular backlash – a great impediment to the improvement in the personal rights of women. As Saddam Hussain, the President of Iraq (1979–2003), stated: "If we are to deal with women's legal rights, the [1968 Ba'thist] Revolution as a whole will lose the support of half the population."[73] Yet, examples abound, in Iraq and elsewhere in the Middle East, of the open and state-sanctioned breach of Islamic teachings, from the workings of the, often publicly owned, banking systems that charge interest to penal codes that deviate markedly from Islamic custom. In Iraq the state has often shown itself willing to violate Islamic customs and sensibilities, sometimes in an open and deliberate way; hence the noted departures from Islamic tradition in divorce and child custody and, in 1980, the Ba'th's execution of the widely venerated Ayatollah Muhammad Baqir al-Sadr – Shia Islam's highest religious authority in Iraq.[74] By itself, the fear of provoking a social backlash over religion is insufficient to explain the lethargy in gains in personal rights.

A related, but more sophisticated, explanation is given by Amal Rassam. According to her, the disparity in rights stems from the "contradictory demands of modernisation and development and those of 'cultural authenticity'," a phenomenon common to many developing countries.[75] In these societies, aspects of the bias against women often symbolized certain fundamental values of the culture at large. The emancipation of women, implied in the process of development, might therefore conflict with some defining values of society, such as those associated with the Islamic heritage in the case of Iraq. The cautious approach of the state regarding women's personal rights may thus reflect its desire to retain some essential social or cultural traditions.

There is undoubtedly some truth to this view. To the extent that Islamic teachings about the role of women represent certain defining values of Iraqi society, one can see how the disproportion in gains concerning personal versus social and economic rights for women might arise. Islamic traditions do not preclude, for instance, equal pay or retirement but do place constraints on, for example, divorce and inheritance. Within personal rights, however, it is difficult to understand why this desire to retain certain core values is expressed, for instance, in improved rights in initiation of divorce, an obvious departure from Islamic tradition, but not in inheritance.

Suad Joseph's analysis offers a point of departure to the resolution of this dichotomy. According to Joseph, the state's mobilization of women into paid labor under the Ba'th was part of the strategy for development, which required the labor of women, and state-building, which implied a weakening of the traditional ties of the individual to their clans or extended families (even though the Ba'th government relied heavily on clans, notably from Tikrit) while, simultaneously, buttressing the nuclear family.[76] In the political vision of the Ba'th, however, the party and state are synonymous. State-building was thus expressed as the desire of government to control all aspects of social life, including women.[77] This was to be accomplished partly through the weakening of the old ties of individuals to their clans and sects, replacing them with new bonds to the state. The position of women therefore was, to a large extent, shaped and tempered by these priorities of development and the monopolization of political power.

In fact, the outcomes concerning women improved most when they were consistent with the development objectives of the Ba'thist state and its drive for political regimentation. The illiteracy eradication campaign, which significantly improved women's literacy, raised labor productivity, and aided in the successful implementation of the government's development programs.[78] The literacy classes had the added benefit of extending the regime's propaganda among the newly literate population. Indeed, according to Iraqi educators, "In addition to the so-called three Rs, the curriculum of the literacy classes emphasizes political awareness, especially of the achievements and aspirations of the BASP [Ba'th Arab Socialist Party]."[79] Equally, the nationalization of schools, in 1975, offered instruction at all levels free of charge, encouraged parents to send female children to school, and also brought all education under the control of the government. Equality in social and economic rights and generous maternity leaves induced women into paid labor, especially in government employment – surely not a hindrance to their political mobilization. That is, the gains of women in education and paid employment and the egalitarianism of the social and economic legislation were consistent with the extension of the state's control in society.

The same is arguably true as regards some of the legislated personal rights. Empowering women to initiate divorce on the grounds of infidelity, legislating stiff prison sentences for parents who force their children to marry, a custom to which females were especially vulnerable, and the extension of child custody rights in the 1978 amendments to the Personal Status Code, were clearly intended to increase women's autonomy with respect to their male kin.[80] Importantly though, many of these measures also increased the power of state-appointed judges to interfere in what had previously been the family's domain, while Ba'th-controlled "popular committees" were formed to present "written recommendations" to judges in disputes over child custody (although judges retained the authority to make the final decision).[81] In many of these instances, the extension of rights for women was compatible with the expansion of power of the state.

By contrast, the expansion of state power was inconsistent with the equality of women in respect to legacy. Equality in inheritance rights would have channeled greater resources to women and weakened further the economic control of males over their female kin but would have done little to perceptibly augment the control of the state over women or any other group. Under a different political calculus the regime might have legislated equality in legacy, even at the risk of inflaming religious sensibilities in society (although it is unlikely that this would have represented a real threat to the regime). But with no apparent gain in terms of development or politicization priorities, the state had little inducement to enact such law.

Yet, the Ba'th were never hostile or insensitive to the conditions of women, as testified by their more progressive laws in comparison with the Arab world, even in respect to personal rights where the gains in terms of development and state control were fewer. In fact, Ba'thist ideology long stressed the importance of women's rights, for according to the party's Eighth Congress in 1974:

> One of the main aims of the Party is the liberation of women from the chains of economic, social, and legal anachronism, to enable them to play a full part in Arab society and in the Arab renaissance for which the party stands.[82]

The education of women, their entry into paid employment, and equality under (at least some) laws were therefore consistent with the regime's ideology and its view of itself as a progressive and secular party. Still, women were also encouraged in their traditional roles as mothers and spouses. Thus, in a speech delivered to the General Federation of Iraqi Women (GFIW) in 1971, Saddam Hussein stated the following: "An enlightened mother who is educated and liberated can give the country a generation of conscious and committed fighters."[83] This remark is consistent with the state's strategy to elevate the nuclear family at the expense of the extended family and also illustrates the Ba'thist conception of emancipation as regards women. Although it seeks liberation from illiteracy, often oppressive ties of family and archaic custom, the vision is not one that places the agency or freedom of action of women at the center. Indeed, in the same speech Hussein cautioned women against relying on "bourgeois concepts of women's emancipation" because "commitment to the revolution . . . [is] the only way to the liberation of women."[84] This is not evidence of a bias against women: the position of the Ba'th party in respect to other social groups, such as labor and the youth, was much the same.

On the practical plane, the Ba'th sought to organize and control women in the same way as these groups. All independent women's organizations or those that historically came under the influence of rival political forces (such as the Iraqi Women's League, which was formed in 1952 under the influence of the Iraqi Communist Party) were banned.[85] Women have instead been marshaled into the Ba'th-controlled GFIW. Created in 1968, this organization had by the early 1980s a presence in every quarter of the country's towns and cities and in every village. The GFIW offered women valuable child care, educational services (the organization played an important role in incorporating women into the literacy campaign), and information on health, nutrition, and hygiene.[86] In political terms, however, the federation functioned as the party's mobilizing arm for women and aimed to extend the state's control over society.

Concluding remarks

The advancement of the position of women in Iraq proceeded most rapidly when it was compatible with the objectives of development and the monopolization of the political space. Women made significant advances in education, at all levels and in an egalitarian fashion in comparison with other countries in the region. The state's effort to attract women into paid employment was unparalleled in its time in the region. And there was progress for women under law: complete equality was achieved in social and economic legislation but relatively modest gains in personal rights. These gains accompanied and reinforced the government's ambitious development plans and efforts of state-building.

Yet, these failed to bring about unambiguously expanded freedom of action for women. The noted improvements in education capabilities freed thousands of women from illiteracy, with undoubtedly positive results in terms of increasing the life and survival chances of children. These gains in education, moreover, facilitated the entry of women into paid employment, thus expanding the freedom of action of females with respect to their kin, family, or clan. These developments did not lead to increased freedom of action *vis-à-vis* the state, and did not aid in the establishment of independent women's organizations that could voice female concerns and articulate their priorities, which were systematically denied. Quite the reverse, women were corralled into the government-controlled GFIW. Of course, one could argue that so long as women's issues are elevated, such independent organizations of civil society are ultimately unnecessary. But one ought not to be sure, for, although they were arguably responsive to the issues of women, the Ba'th nevertheless had little compunction about denying the rights of females when it was expedient to do so. Thus, in 1990, and in the context of social instability accompanying the demobilization of the Iraqi army at the end of the Iran–Iraq war, the regime, in an effort to ease and redirect the disenchantment of returning troops at the then miserable economic conditions that greeted them, exempted from punishment men who kill women relatives for "honor crimes."[87] Their organizations co-opted and controlled by the regime, there was not a whiff of opposition from women.

The story of women provides a microcosm for what was happening in the country at large under the Ba'th – the smashing of the institutions of civil society along with perceptible material advancement. The denial of an independent voice for women is therefore not the result of a bias against women, as the regime sought to control and mobilize labor and the youth in the same way. In this respect, as in others, the Ba'th was remarkably egalitarian.

7   Human rights and political freedoms

Given the intrinsic value that people attach to human rights and political freedoms and because such rights and freedoms may work to shape outcomes in other areas of development or have implications for governance, a study of rights and freedoms is essential. This is especially so for Iraq, an oil economy, that the rentier state hypothesis would predict to show comparatively low performance in terms of democratization and political rights. How Iraq has performed in respect to such rights and freedoms, their interaction with existing social and sectarian divisions, are the subjects of this chapter.

Such a study presents difficulties that are rarely encountered in the discussion of other dimensions of human development. There is, first, often a divergence between the formal (legal) existence of rights, that is "claims on other people or institutions...in ensuring access to some freedom[s]",[1] and the enforcement or realization of these freedoms. It is thus possible to have a legal structure that upholds human rights but a political reality in which such rights are habitually violated and indeed the reverse – a formally repressive legal structure, but a relatively liberal political context in which such laws are not enforced. In Iraq, the formal rights are quite extensive and compare favorably to corresponding rights in Western democracies. For example, the Interim Constitution of 1969, and later amendments, views the accused as "innocent until he is declared guilty" (Article 20 (a)); requires that "all trials should be open to the public unless declared in camera" (Article 20 (c)); prohibits communal punishments (Article 21 (a)); and forbids any "kind of physical or psychological torture" (Article 22 (a)).[2] With regard to the intrinsic and instrumental import of these rights, however, what matters is whether they are upheld. Thus, it is important to consider both the data about the entitlements under law and information about enforcement.

This leads, second, to related problems concerning the data. The availability of data about human rights and political freedoms is limited, as governments rarely systematically publish information about their violations of rights. Nevertheless, some information about human rights and freedoms is available through independent organizations (such as

Amnesty International and Human Rights Watch). Even when the data are available, however, problems arise concerning the interpretation of specific observations. For example, it is not immediately clear whether an increase in government repression implies the expansion or contraction of the political space – the diversity of political opinion that finds expression in society. The accentuated repression may represent the government's attempt to check the rising political fortunes of the opposition which, emboldened by its growing strength, engages the government in conflict. In this case, an increase in political repression may be correlated to an expansion of the political space. But the increased repression may also result in the silencing of opposition voices, a clear contraction in the political space. Improvements in human rights and expansions in political freedoms need not be correlated with greater variety in political views or activities, at least in the short run. Observations will, as far as possible, be placed in their broader social and political contexts, which Chapter 2 helps in digesting.

Partly as a result of these issues, misconceptions about the nature of state violence and political pluralism (or lack thereof) in Iraq have prevailed, among both the public at large and Western policymakers. The proliferation of erroneous assumptions has had arguably disastrous consequences for both Iraq and the West, most recently in the occupation of Iraq. Some of these misconceptions of Iraq are tackled in this chapter. I use two indicators, namely the variety of expression in mass media and political party affiliation, to study the changes in range of political views expressed in society and the government's attempts to shape that expression through political repression, in the period covering the independence of the modern state in 1932 to the middle to late 1980s. This is followed by a study of changes in the intensity of government repression, as expressed in laws that concern the death penalty and political executions and disappearances, insofar as these reflect the state of other less quantifiable elements of human rights. Finally, I modify an index of political rights and freedoms, the Humana Index, to assess the state of political rights and freedoms in Iraq through time. This methodological exercise is a distinctive addition to the literature on Iraq and allows us to test two hypotheses: one concerning the relationship between the level of state repression and formal institutions of governance and another in relation to the origins of the Iran–Iraq war.

Contracting political space

The mass media

One gauge of the breadth of political opinion and information that is expressed in society is the freedom and diversity of opinion that is articulated in the mass media. There were 69 local newspapers, none with a circulation of more than 500 copies per issue in 1917; only three of which were government owned, according to Table 7.1. At the time of the monarchy in 1952, there were 54 daily newspapers with a total circulation of 108,000 per day. This is not to say that freedom of the press was unrestricted at that time: newspapers were often closed down when they were thought to be too critical of the government, but they often reappeared under a different name. A lively underground press also supplemented the legally sanctioned press. The (banned) Communist Party newspaper *Al-Qa'idah* ("The Base"), for example, boasted a circulation of 3,000 copies per issue, and was probably one of the highest circulating journals in the country at the time.[3] While these figures declined after the monarchy's partial crackdown on civil liberties and the (formal) dissolution of political parties in 1954, there were still 16 daily newspapers with a total circulation of 66,000 copies per day in 1957. In the Qassem years too, 1958–1963, there was a modest amount of press freedom.[4] In this period as well, newspapers that were thought to be too critical of the regime would be periodically suspended. Nevertheless, between 1958 and 1963, 33 new daily newspapers appeared;[5] and in 1962, there were 19 dailies with a total circulation of 78,000 copies per day. These represented a variety of political views including the fiercely anti-Communist and Islamist *Al-Heyad* ("Neutrality"),[6] the mouthpiece of the central committee of the ICP, *Ittihad al-Sha'b* ("The People's Union"),[7] and the independent *Al-Bilad* ("The Countries").

With the coming to power of the Ba'th in 1968, press restrictions were gradually tightened. By 1975, the Ba'th party's newspaper, the daily *Al-Thawra* ("The Revolution"), boasted a circulation of about 50,000 copies per day. This was the period of the Progressive National Front, and the Ba'th were formally part of a coalition government with the ICP and the Kurdish Democratic Party. Hence in 1975, the ICP organ *Tariq al-Sha'b* ("The People's Path") could legally function – on the condition that,

Table 7.1 Number of newspapers and their circulation

Year	Number	Total daily circulation
1917	69	less than 500 copies per issue
1952	54	108,000
1957	16	66,000
1962	19	78,000
1975	7	192,000
1982	5	262,000

Sources: Samir al-Khalil, *The Republic of Fear*, p. 85 Abdul Wahab al-Qaysi, *The Impact of Modernization on Iraqi Society During the Ottoman Era*, PhD. Dissertation, University of Michigan, 1958, p. 54; United Nations Educational Scientific and Cultural Organization (UNESCO), *Basic Facts and Figures 1958*, Paris, 1958, p. 101; UNESCO, *Basic Facts and Figures 1961*, Paris, 1961, p. 120; UNESCO, *Statistical Yearbook 1965*, Paris, 1966, pp. 530–1; and UNESCO, *Statistical Yearbook 1986*, Paris, 1986, table 7.9

among other things, it did not directly criticize the Ba'th government – and sold a respectable 18,000 copies daily, until it was closed down when the ICP's relations with the Ba'th soured in 1978.[8] Independent Kurdish newspapers were similarly suppressed. Thus in 1975, there were 7 dailies with a total circulation of 192,000 copies per day.

Law no. 70 of 1980, however, established the General Federation of Academicians and Writers: all journalists, artists, and writers were required to register.[9] The law abolished all existing cultural and literary organizations, and brought all artistic production, including music, under direct state control. By 1982, there were five newspapers, all government controlled, including a daily in English, with a combined circulation of 262,000 copies per day. The Ba'th had acquired a monopoly of the print media.

In addition to print, the regime also exercised complete control over television and radio. Strictly controlled "political and news" programs were the largest single segment to appear on state television in 1988, accounting for a fifth of all broadcast time.[10] In addition two radio stations, *Sawt al-Jamahir* ("The People's Voice") and Baghdad Radio were controlled by the regime. Consequently, by the early 1980s, the regime exercised a monopoly and close control of information inside the country, and there was a notable decline in the variety of political views that received expression in the mass media.

Membership in and affiliation to political parties

Parallel to the constriction of opinion in the mass media, there was a reduction in diversity as expressed in political party membership and affiliation. Although reliable estimates of legally existing parties at the time of the monarchy and Qassem regime are unavailable, there are some estimates of membership in the banned Ba'th and the ICP, historically among the most influential political organizations in Iraq.

Until 1954, when they were banned, political parties had existed under the monarchy. These parties did not, however, command mass appeal, and were suppressed when their challenge to vested interests became too vocal or threatening.[11] Neither the Ba'th nor the ICP were officially sanctioned. Analysis of the membership of these two parties is complicated by the fact that there were gradations in membership: the Ba'th for example differentiated between, among other categories, "active members," "active partisans," and "candidates";[12] and the ICP had similar categories of "active members" and "organized supporters." Moreover, frequent changes to internal rules periodically altered these categories. Nonetheless, ICP documents seized by the police in 1953–4 revealed the names of 507 active members.[13] This statistic does not, however, include imprisoned Communists who in 1953 numbered 312 persons,[14] although it is not known if all of these incarcerated Communists were active party members. The mentioned statistic also excludes members of political organizations that, while formally independent, were under Communist influence such as the Peace Partisans. Similar documents seized by the police in 1955 revealed that active membership in the Ba'th stood at 289 at that time,[15] although the position of the Ba'th in the mass organizations of the country was then much weaker than that of the Communists.

The release, after the 14th of July revolution in 1958, of political prisoners and the resurfacing of the ICP after years of clandestine activity, along with the ICP's successes against nationalist and conservative elements in Mosul in 1959, greatly raised the prestige of the party. As a result, Communist ranks swelled and in 1959 the party had 25,000 active members and half a million organized supporters,[16] in a country whose population in 1957 was 6.3 million.[17] In contrast, the Ba'th, by its own accounting, could in 1959 count on 2,000 organized supporters and 10,000 unorganized supporters. The Ba'th and the ICP were never legalized by the Qassem government, although five other parties functioned legally for a brief period from 1960 to 1961.[18] From 1959 until the overthrow of the Qassem government in February 1963, the membership of Ba'th grew and that of the Communists stagnated or declined. Even so, on the eve of the February 1963 coup, the Ba'th had only 830 active members and at most 15,000 organized supporters,[19] probably a fraction of the ICP's strength.

The successful Ba'thist coup in 1963 swelled this party's ranks, but with the military takeover of power in November of the same year, the Ba'th was again driven underground. In fact, the military government that ruled the country from November 1963 until July 1968 banned all political parties, although a degree of underground political activity was tolerated.

With the second Ba'thist coup in 1968, the Ba'th party again began to increase its numbers. By 1976, the party had 10,000 active members and as many as 500,000 organized supporters.[20] Though able to function legally at this time, no estimate of ICP membership is available, but it is likely to have been significant, judging by the circulation of its daily newspaper. The suppression of the ICP in the late 1970s, however, effectively put an end to the party in Iraq, although remnants of the organization still existed outside the country. By 1984, the Ba'th were the only political party of note left in the country, and had 1.5 million supporters and sympathizers (roughly 10 percent of the entire population) and 25,000 active members.[21]

The rise in the number of members and sympathizers of the Ba'th since 1968 is not incidental but came about through a deliberate policy of the regime. Iraqis in high schools were encouraged at a young age to join the party, and material rewards, in for example preference in job promotion, were granted to Ba'thists. This probably created a context in which many people were encouraged to join the Ba'th for reasons of personal advancement rather than because of the ideological appeal of the Ba'th.

From the regime's point of view, however, this mobilization was an important way of gaining and maintaining control in the country at large: Ba'thists were routinely required to report on the activities of non-Ba'thists and even fellow Ba'thists. Only tried-and-tested Ba'thists, who worked diligently to carry out the instructions of the party, sometimes over many years, became full (active) members of the party, and then only after they attended a course of instruction at the party's *Madrasat al-Idad al-Hizbi* (School of Party Preparation). This explains why there were, in 1984, 60 Ba'th sympathizers and supporters for every active party member.

Death penalty laws

Along with the constriction of the political space – as expressed in the decline in the membership of opposition political parties and the monopolization of the media by the Ba'th – there was an increase in political repression as reflected in the expansion in the number of infractions, especially political, subject to the death penalty. Many of these new laws were intended to limit the activities of rival political organizations and hence to consolidate the domination of the political space. Others were more opportunistic, making a wide variety of actions punishable by death and allowing the state (increasingly under the control of a narrow leadership circle) unprecedented powers to single out perceived opponents.

The intensity of the use of the death penalty, the ultimate sanction that the state can impose, is in its own right a significant indicator of the extent of political repression, but also is likely to be correlated to other central but less quantifiable indicators of rights such as the frequency in the use of torture or arbitrary arrest (which are briefly discussed later). Despite its merits, a study of the use of the death penalty is hampered by the lack of information, as certain governments, including Iraq's, rarely advertise its use. Still, sufficient data from international human rights organizations are available to permit the examination of the intensity of use of the death penalty through time.[22]

There is often a divergence between legislated punishments and their implementation. Stern laws that appear to be rather repressive are in practice quite restrained, as the legislated measures are seldom put into practice. In both Niger and Senegal, for example, the death penalty is provided for, but, as of September 2002, no executions since 1976 have occurred in Niger, and none since 1967 in Senegal.[23] By contrast, in Iraq, the evidence points to both the more frequent use of the death penalty as well as to an expansion in the number of crimes which are subject to the penalty, as we shall see.

Like many countries, Iraq has traditionally applied the death penalty to certain classes of crimes such as murder and espionage. In addition, armed action directed against the state was also punishable by death. Section 80 of the Baghdad Penal Code, a law introduced under British occupation during 1915–20, prescribed the death penalty for a person "who has any part in the command of an armed body ... using force to overthrow and change the government."[24] Furthermore, in 1937 Article 89a of the Penal Code introduced the death penalty for the dissemination of "Bolshevik Socialism" in the armed forces and the police,[25] as was a civilian who advocated Communist ideas among a group of five or more persons.[26] This was the first instance in Iraqi politics when capital punishment was authorized for non-violent political offences.

With the Ba'th takeover in 1968, the death penalty was expanded. In Penal Code 111 of 1969, the death penalty was widened to include 14 offences relating to external, and nine relating to internal security.[27] Furthermore, a Revolutionary Command Council (RCC) decree of 10 November 1971 expanded the death penalty to include any political activity by members of the armed forces other than activities within the Ba'th Party. Law No. 141 of 1974 mandated the death penalty for persons that have any association whatsoever with foreign intelligence organizations. Also in 1974, Ba'th party members who conceal previous political affiliations, or who become affiliated with other political organizations likewise faced the death penalty.

Between 1978 and 1986 seven new death penalty offences were introduced by the RCC. In July 1978, RCC decree 884 imposed the death penalty on any person who having left or retired from the armed forces, for whatever reason, after 17 July 1968 subsequently engaged in non-Ba'thist political activity.[28] Other, non-political offences such as forgery of official documents, official corruption and theft in time of war also became capital offences. Decrees such as Resolution No. 461 made affiliation to the Da'wa Party punishable by death. At the same time, membership in the Communist Party again became a capital offence. Finally, on 18 November 1986, the RCC amended Penal Code 111 of 1969. Under the amendment, the death penalty was expanded yet again to include persons who "insult or attack" the President of the Republic "with the aim of fomenting public opinion against the authorities."[29]

Parallel to the proliferation of death penalty laws, there was increased reliance on extra-ordinary courts, whose proceedings could be held in secret and were not subject to judicial review. The judiciary in Iraq consisted of religious, civil, criminal, and temporary and special courts. A person accused of murder, for example, was tried by the Higher Criminal Court. If convicted, the court's judgment is automatically reviewed by the Court of Cassation, the nation's Supreme Court. In contrast, most persons accused of political crimes were tried in permanent or temporary special courts. The revolutionary court, for example, is a type of permanent special court set up by law 180 of 1968.[30] In special courts, a panel of three judges decides the verdict, and there is no right to appeal. Although the president of Iraq may commute the sentence, the role of defense attorneys in special courts was often limited to pleading for clemency.

The picture that emerges is of one of the heightened use of laws that prescribe the death penalty to deter people from coming under the influence of rival political loci and to enable the regime to repress any individual or group at will. Thus death penalty offences were expanded to include political actions that were previously not capital crimes, as the imprecise language in laws made a wide range of actions capital offenses. As concerns the expansion of the death penalty, in a country with universal male conscription, RCC resolution 884 effectively made all males who had served in the army after 17 July 1968 and subsequently read a Communist newspaper subject to the death penalty. In respect to the indefinite expressions in laws, Article 164 of the Penal Code provides for the death penalty for "any person who, in time of war, attempts to jeopardize the military, political, or economic situation of Iraq."[31] The language in this statute is so broad that it transformed a range of actions from an error by an army conscript to criticism of the regime into executable offences.

Yet while laws aimed to promote the dominance of the regime in politics, the leadership of the Ba'th party centered on Saddam Hussein was eroding the authority of the party rank and file in the country from the late 1970s onwards. Within the party, debate and discussion were increasingly muzzled as the party was reduced to a means for the carrying out RCC decisions – a process that was accelerated with the ascendancy of Saddam Hussein to the party leadership and the presidency of Iraq in 1979. Ba'thists who were reliable enforcers of the leadership were rewarded, while critical voices were repressed. With an RCC that Saddam Hussein stacked with loyal subordinates and a repressive state apparatus that he controlled through tribesmen,[32] Saddam's cult of personality gradually came to replace official party ideology as the locus of politics. By the 1980s, Saddam could rightly claim that "the ideology of the Ba'th Party was to be whatever he said it was."[33]

Supremacy in politics did not moderate the regime's repression, as the expansion of death penalty laws was accompanied by their active enforcement. As shown, the imposition of the death penalty for political offenses was not new in Iraq. What was distinctive was the controlled and sweeping way in which it was done under the Ba'th, in contrast to earlier periods when the use of this penalty often occurred at the initiative of individuals – rather than an organized campaign by the state – or in periods of intense internal conflict.

During the monarchy, the death penalty was imposed for political action (not always violent) and as *ex post facto* punishment for rebellion (as distinct from deaths that occur in the course of insurrection or internal conflict), and shadows the growth in the influence of the army in politics in the 1930s. The still unchecked proclivities of the tribal population to rebel against central authority occurred at precisely the time when the Iraqi army was anxious to exert its newly found authority. Thus, a tribal uprising in the south of the country in 1935 was ruthlessly suppressed and a court martial (legalized under these circumstances) executed nine people, while another court martial executed another nine persons in 1935 when the minority Yazidi sect peacefully resisted conscription.[34] In 1936, in yet another tribal rebellion in the south, more executions were reported. However, these harsh measures did not always meet with the approval of the cabinet or the king, but were often conducted on the initiative of individuals that were anxious to acquire power, in particular army officers such as General Bakr Sidqi.[35]

The anti-Communist laws promulgated in 1937 soon found practical expression when three soldiers were convicted and sentenced to death for engaging in Communist activity inside the armed forces.[36] Meanwhile, four chief actors in the Rashid Ali government's failed military confrontation with the British in 1941 were executed and Ali condemned to death in absentia under Section 80 of the Baghdad Penal Code.[37] In 1949 again, membership in the banned ICP was the justification for political executions. In the context of acute political turmoil over the Portsmouth Agreement with Britain – during which 400 people died as the police clashed with (the largely ICP inspired) demonstrators and the government fell as the Iraqi prime minister fled Baghdad fearing for his life – three captured Communist leaders were executed; at least two other ICP leaders were executed later in the same year.[38] Similarly, in the context of popular protests organized by Communist, Ba'th, and Independence parties during the Suez crisis in 1956 – when an Anglo-French-Israeli force attacked Egypt – at least two agitators were executed.[39]

With the overthrow of the monarchy in 1958, a Special Supreme Military Court, also known as the Mehdawi Court, was set up by the new regime to investigate and try a wide range of offences including conspiracy "against the safety of the homeland," "forcing the policy of the homeland...contrary to the general interest...," and issuing laws against the public interest.[40] The object behind the formation of this court was the trial of prominent members of the old monarchical regime. Yet, out of more than 100 persons accused, only four death sentences were carried out, largely to pacify public opinion that hated the monarchy.[41]

After the re-emergence of the Nationalist–Iraqist schism soon after the proclamation of the Republic, the Mehdawi Court turned its attention to the nationalist opposition. Thus, in 1958–9, 17 persons (almost all military officers) were executed for their part in the failed Mosul coup of 1959. In response to these executions, the Ba'th party's civilian wing attempted to assassinate Qassem. The attempt failed and the Mehdawi Court delivered death sentences for those responsible, but the sentences were commuted and, in time, all those convicted were freed.

The February 1963 coup against Qassem, unlike the 1958 coup that overthrew the monarchy, encountered stiff resistance from segments of the civilian population,[42] especially in the poorer districts of Baghdad and other major cities, as well as some elements of the military that were loyal to Qassem. The former leaders, including Qassem and Mehdawi, were summarily executed by the new regime, but it was only after two days of fighting that the new government established firm control. With control secured, the new regime, in particular its civilian Ba'thist Nationalist Guard, began to seek out its leftist opponents and, consequently, thousands, mostly Communists, were arrested and many executed. The new government announced a total of 149 executions from February to November 1963,[43] a statistic that is a gross underestimate.[44] A conservative estimate puts the number of opponents executed by the Ba'th in this period at more than 800,[45] while another approximates the figure to be 3,000.[46]

Most of these executions occurred after 10 February, when the mass resistance to the new Ba'thist regime had collapsed: only seven out of the 149 executions occurred in the first month after 8 February, according to official figures.[47] Many of the victims, far from resisting the new regime, were in hiding; they were sought out, and often gunned down, at home or in the streets.[48] The animosity between Communists and Nationalists (growing since the overthrow of the monarchy) explains part of the ferocity in Ba'thist actions. But the Ba'th also clearly intended to deliver a critical blow to their political opponents. In an important sense, the events of 1963 represent a watershed moment: in contrast to their earlier enterprising and disorderly nature, political killings were henceforth increasingly characterized by a pre-emptive and purposive quality, perfected later under the second Ba'thi regime.

Partly because of the general resentment that Ba'thist practices engendered, the military was able to outmaneuver the Ba'th and establish itself in government in November 1963. The military remained in power until July 1968, when the Ba'th staged a successful coup. In the first four months after coming to power, dozens of people were brought before revolutionary courts, accused of espionage for Israel, Britain, and the United States. Many of those brought before the court were Jewish, but suspects also included prominent persons and one ex-premier. Even though most observers agree that the 1969 espionage trials were a sham, no less than 68 persons were executed.

The repression of Iraq's Jewish minority by the avowedly secular Ba'th was not the result of the latter's anti-Jewish feelings, but was motivated by political expediency. With the public's reaction to its return to power in 1968 lukewarm at best, the Ba'th astutely channeled the anti-Zionist feelings in the population at large (exaggerated after the humiliating Arab defeat in the Six Day War against Israel in 1967) into political advantage. In striking a blow against presumed American and Israeli spies – in effect confronting both Israel and US imperialism without entering into open conflict – the Ba'th sought to "legitimate" their rule.[49] If suspect prominent politicians of previous regimes (whom the new regime wanted to eliminate) could be included in the net of spies (as they in fact were), all the better. Equally, the regime executed 41 persons – 12 civilians and 29 military men – in January 1970 for their part in an abortive coup, purportedly sponsored by Iran.[50]

But the new regime struck out against real opponents as well. The leadership of the Central Command, an offshoot of the ICP, which engaged the regime in armed conflict, was arrested in 1969, and 20 members of the Command are believed to have died under torture.[51] The mainstream ICP Central Committee, although it took no armed action against the regime, lost at least four of its members, all killed under torture in the winter of 1970–71. And the regime also faced rebellion from its own ranks: the unsuccessful Nadhum Kazzar coup in 1973 ended with the execution of 36 persons.

The consolidation of power of the Ba'th regime in the second part of the 1970s did not result in reduced political executions. Eight people were executed after anti-government slogans that were shouted in a Shia religious festival in February 1977.[52] Between 1975 and late 1977, 400 Kurds were executed by the regime.[53] And, the Communists, formally in government with the Ba'th, faced a renewed campaign or repression and executions.

The strengthening of Ba'thist power, the resolution of a border dispute with Iran, and the ensuing collapse of Kurdish actions against the regime all meant that the presence of Communists in government was no longer needed. Thus in early 1978, 21 Communist soldiers were executed for organizing in the army (a "contravention" of the terms of the National Front).[54] Further arrests and executions followed.

Even Ba'thists were becoming increasingly vulnerable to repression. A few days after Saddam Hussein became President of the Republic in July 1979, it was announced that a plot was uncovered and 22 senior Ba'thists were executed as a result,[55] the total though is almost surely much higher, perhaps as high as 500.[56] This served a double purpose: it underlined that the leadership of the Ba'th – personified in Saddam – would not tolerate independent thought and action from party members and, by eliminating potential rivals, the executions consolidated the rule of Saddam Hussein.

Subsequently, there was heightened repression. Amnesty International documented 520 political executions from 1978 to 1981, 100 of these in March and April 1980.[57] In the years 1982 and 1983 there were over 600 political executions. In fact, in two days in December 1987, more than 150 political prisoners were reportedly executed and even these figures are likely to be underestimates.[58]

In addition to executions, there were disappearances, whose numbers are believed to be even higher. Although disappearances were not new –

Ba'thist internal security forces were believed to be responsible for abduction and subsequent death of the non-Ba'thist foreign minister in 1968,[59] for example – their scale increased enormously during the 1980s. The central government's loss of authority in northern Iraq (after the second Gulf War in 1991) permitted the disclosure of large amounts of information about the *anfal*[60] campaigns of the late 1980s, a series of massive human relocation and extermination drives conducted against entire villages or tribes in the Kurdish region of northern Iraq. In these campaigns, the regime targeted areas whose residents had allegedly provided aid to anti-government Kurdish rebels, sometimes using chemical weapons.[61] Not all Kurds were attacked though, as Kurdish militia groups that aided the government in its campaigns and those who lived outside the targeted region were left unharmed. According to Kurdish sources, 182,000 persons disappeared (and are presumed dead) as a result of these campaigns, but according to the government official in charge the number "couldn't have been more than 100,000."[62] These trends are shown in Table 7.2. The more conservative estimates for political executions and the lower estimate of 100,000 for *anfal* disappearances are used to yield an average of more than 10,000 political killings per year in the 1980s – a staggering figure when one considers that it is likely an underestimate.

The sectarian composition of government and political executions

The intensified political repression, as expressed in the increased use of the death penalty for political offenses, and narrowing political space evident raise the question as to whether there was a sectarian bias in the application of terror. Certainly, the Kurdish and Shia populations were on the receiving end of state terror, more so arguably than the Sunni Arab minority, whose members dominated successive Iraqi regimes. Under the Ba'th, for example, the Kurds suffered the horrors of the *anfal* campaigns, as the Shia underground movements were ruthlessly suppressed and approximately 50,000 persons of Iranian descent (mostly Shia) were

Table 7.2 Political executions and disappearances in Iraq

Year	Total political executions	Total disappearances	Grand total
1941	4	na	4
1949	5	na	5
1959	21	na	21
1963	800	na	800
1980s average	200–300	10,000 annually	over 10,000 per annum

Sources: Amnesty International, *Iraq Disappearances*; Amnesty International, *When the State Kills*; Public Broadcasting Corporation, "The Survival of Saddam"; Hanna Batatu, *The Old Social Classes*; Majid Khadduri, *Independent Iraq*; Human Rights Watch, *Iraq's Crime of Genocide*; Uriel Dann, *Iraq Under Qassem*; and Samir al-Khalil, *The Republic of Fear*

stripped of all possessions and deported, before the onset of the war with Iran.[63] The question remains whether this emanated from an ethnic or sectarian bias on the part of government.

This issue is central as it is often claimed that successive Sunni-dominated Iraqi governments, the Ba'th in particular, catered to the interests of their own community at the expense of other communities. Indeed, some argue that this asymmetry between the sectarian composition of government and the governed lies at the root of the historically violent and unstable nature of Iraqi politics.[64]

The historical asymmetry between the sectarian composition of government and that of the public at large is easy to show. During the monarchy, out of 16 different parliaments between 1925 and 1958, the number of Shia deputies varied between 28 percent and 43 percent of the total,[65] much less than the proportion of Shia in the country as a whole. In the Qassem government of 1958–63, the Shia were even less represented: 55 percent of cabinet posts were occupied by Sunni Arabs, 20 percent by Shia Arabs, and 17 percent by Kurds. In the period from February 1963 to July 1968, five out of six premiers were Sunni Arabs, while only one premier was from the Shia community, as 53 percent of cabinet posts were occupied by Sunni Arabs, only 33 percent by Shia Arabs, and 10 percent by Kurds.[66]

A similar pattern of inequality is evident with the Ba'th after 1968. As Table 7.3 shows, Sunni Arabs dominated the RCC, the most powerful executive and legislative body in the country. Even though Sunni Arabs are about 20 percent of the population, members of this group held between 93 percent and 56 percent of the seats in the RCC; although the Shia Arabs constitute over 50 percent of the population, they occupied between 0 percent and 25 percent of seats. The Kurds, who account for slightly under 20 percent of the total population, received between 7 percent and 12.5 percent of seats; the Christian population, which is less than 3 percent of the total population, received between 0 percent and 11 percent of RCC membership.

This asymmetry between the sectarian composition of government and Iraq's population often is taken as proof that successive Sunni-dominated

Table 7.3 The composition of the revolutionary command council

Year	Total members	Sunni Arabs	Shia Arabs	Kurdish	Christian
July 1969	15	14 (93)	0 (0)	1 (7)	0 (0)
August 1979	16	9 (56)	4 (25)	2 (12.5)	1 (6)
June 1982	9	5 (56)	2 (22)	1 (11)	1 (11)

Note: The percentage of total members that belong to the relevant ethnic/religious group is given in parenthesis.

Sources: Hanna Batatu, *The Old Social Classes*; and Marion Farouk-Sluglett and Peter Sluglett, *Iraq Since 1958*

Iraqi governments have acted in the interests of that community and to the exclusion of others. Thus, some point to a range of government actions, from discrimination in employment during the monarchy to the 1964 nationalization of large corporations (which they argue disproportionately harmed Shia entrepreneurs) and the expulsion of Shia of Iranian descent.[67]

The most obvious defect in this thesis is that it assumes a community of interests within ethnic or religious groups. In the Iraqi context, however, individual and group interests are often divergent. Before the 1958 revolution, the tribal chiefs, many of whom were Shia, were one of the pillars of the Sunni monarchy, especially after the reoccupation of the country by the British in 1941. These tribal sheikhs controlled vast areas of agricultural land and opposed almost every progressive measure that might have raised the very low living standards of their co-religionist peasants.[68] It was to aid these landlords that the (Sunni-dominated) Iraqi army often had to intervene in order to quell (Shia) peasant rebellions. Although these landlords lost economic and political power after the 1958 revolution, the fortunes of the poorer Shia were ascendant. The Qassem government – in whose cabinets the Shia were least represented – through such initiatives as land reform, increased expenditure on health and education, and bread price subsidies, raised the living standards of the poor, a group in which the Shia are disproportionately represented. Measures under the Ba'th – who deported thousands of Shia of Iranian origin – in education, health, and with respect to women as we have seen, likewise worked to raise the living standards among the Shia population. This is not to deny the socially, economically, and politically, underprivileged position of the Shia, nor does it suggest that the Kurdish population (at least in northern Iraq) didn't suffer under the Ba'th. Rather, it is to suggest that far from acting in narrow communal interests, successive Iraqi governments in general have sought to assuage rather than aggravate inequalities.

The Ba'th provide the most extreme illustration of this. The party's ideology is secular and no more incompatible with Shia Islam than with Sunni Islam. In point of fact, between 1952 and 1963, roughly 54 percent of the party's leadership (the "regional command") was Shia.[69] The decline in Shia representation after 1963 had less to do with Ba'thist discrimination than with internal party politics and the superior connections of Sunni members of the party: when arrested, Shia members of the Ba'th often faced longer prison sentences than their Sunni counterparts, who frequently had relatives in the army or police that could intercede on their behalf and appeal for lighter sentences.[70] The decline in Shia representation did not go unnoticed by senior Ba'thists, however, and in the 1970s deliberate attempts to enlist Shia members were made.[71]

Moreover, while the RCC was Sunni dominated, it was hardly representative of the Sunni community at large. A large number of RCC members came from a specific geographic region: six out of the 15 members of the RCC in 1968, and three out of the five Sunni Arab members of the RCC in 1982 were from the town of Tikrit. The population of the governorate (province) in which Tikrit is located was in 1983 less than 3 percent of the total for Iraq.[72] Assuming that roughly one-fifth of Iraq's population is Sunni Arab, the population of this province represents less than 15 percent of the Sunni Arab population. That is, the RCC was only slightly more representative of the Sunni Arab population than it is of the whole country. However, it was not the whole of Tikrit that sat on the RCC but only a few Tikritis, usually tied by bonds of blood or tribe. And, being Tikriti offered no guarantees of safety. Thus, former RCC member Hardan al-Tikriti was gunned down in Kuwait in 1971 on the orders of a fellow Tikriti, Saddam Hussein,[73] who would later in the 1990s order the elimination of his cousins and sons-in-law, who were also Tikriti.

Even if the RCC did not represent the Sunni Arab community as a whole, it could still of course embody the community's interests. Yet the Sunni Arab community is diverse, and the interests of Sunni Arabs are many. While the regime's social and economic policies raised the living standards of poor Sunni Arabs, the regime simultaneously harassed established Sunni Arab families. Poor Sunni Arab males, unable to take advantage of college deferments or other avenues open to richer or better connected Sunnis, provided the canon-fodder for the war with Iran. True, the Iraqi army's officer corps and security services were dominated by Sunni Arabs. As in the RCC, however, Sunni Arabs were selected for these organizations because of ties of family and tribe rather than sect or ethnicity.[74] In fact, Sunni Arab political opponents of the regime were treated no less harshly than opponents from other sects. It is thus difficult to sustain the claim that the Ba'th represented or fulfilled Sunni Arab interests, especially as the average Sunni Arab was as powerless in respect to the regime as his Shia or Kurd compatriot.

Indeed, the brutal repression of the Kurdish population in northern Iraq did not originate from Ba'thist hostility to Kurdish ethnicity or culture. In fact, the Ba'th supported Kurdish language and culture when it was able to control the artistic output.[75] And, as Kurdish leader (and the current Iraqi president) Jalal Talabani testifies, Saddam Hussein employed in his office people from a variety of ethnic backgrounds, including Kurds.[76]

It was the Ba'th's demand for ideological conformity, unparalleled political control and (later) almost complete submission to the person of Saddam Hussein coupled with resistance to this control in the northern Kurdish and (later) Shia areas of the south that better explain the brutality against these populations. As evinced by the fact that well-connected Kurds who lived outside the northern region faced no more repression than other Iraqis, the Ba'th regime was focused on the political rather than on purely ethnic or sectarian concerns. Of course, for the Kurds on the receiving end of state terror, it is little consolation to be told that they were brutalized, gassed, and killed because of where they happened to live rather than because of their particular ethnicity, but the portrait that takes shape is not one of state-sponsored sectarian bias, even (or especially) under the Ba'th.

Some of the preceding discussion in this chapter is at odds with some common assumptions or views about Iraq. First, because of Iraq's turbulent political history, there has been a tendency (especially in the popular press in the West) to view the extreme political repression of Saddam Hussein's Ba'thi regime as little different from the regimes that preceded it. Indeed, it is sometimes supposed, including by Iraqis themselves,[77] that the repression of freedoms and denial of rights is necessary to maintain stability in an ethnically and religiously heterogeneous society such as Iraq. And it is sometimes assumed, notably in the West, that economic and human development (including the respect of human rights) is compatible only with parliamentary democracy and (bourgeois Western-type) political freedoms. Parallel to this, there is a view that Saddam Hussein's Ba'th used the exigent conditions of war with Iran in the 1980s deliberately to consolidate power.[78] These are empirically evaluated in the next section. First, I test the hypothesis that state repression has been roughly uniform through Iraq's modern history. Second, I test the hypothesis that the Ba'th went to war (or used the war) with Iran to consolidate power, eliminating opponents and attaining a monopoly of political power.

The Humana Index

To test these hypotheses, I use an index of political freedoms and rights that was developed by Charles Humana, who applies the index to different countries at a single point in time.[79] The Humana Index (which is explained in detail in the Appendix) gives an indication of the extent to which various political rights and freedoms are respected.[80] I use this index to compare the state of political or human rights and freedoms at three different points in Iraq's political history: under the monarchy in 1947–8, under the Qassem government in 1958–60, and under the Ba'th in the first part of the 1980s. I choose these periods because they represent difficult periods for the respective regime: the period 1947–8 was a time of agitation against the Portsmouth Agreement with Britain; in 1958–60, the Qassem government was under attack from its nationalist and conservative opponents; and in the early to middle 1980s under the Ba'th, Iraq was engaged in a costly and unpopular war with Iran and the government was forced to implement cuts in its development plan and social spending. One advantage of choosing these periods is that information about rights and freedoms is more available than for other periods.

The application of the Humana Index to Iraq

The total number of rights and freedoms are 40 but not all of these are relevant to Iraq and there is no information about some rights and freedoms. Consequently I assess 29 questions below at the three noted points in time. The questions, relevant scores, and brief discussion about each question are presented in the Appendix.

The results of the computations of the Humana Index indicate that the human rights and political freedoms of Iraqis were most respected by the Qassem government in 1958–60, less respected by the monarchy in 1947–8, and least respected under the Ba'th in the early 1980s, as shown in Table 7.4. The overall scores of this index, which excludes the questions concerning the rights of women (because these were explored in an earlier chapter) and those questions about which not enough information is known, were found to be 42 percent, 50 percent and 16 percent for the periods 1947–8, 1958–60 and the early to middle 1980s, respectively.

With two exceptions, namely the category of questions concerning freedom of opposition and personal rights, the order in the overall scores mentioned above is replicated when the rights are examined in their various categories. Thus, for example, for the weighted questions alone, the results are 28 percent, 39 percent, and 22 percent for the noted periods. In respect to the questions about the freedom of opposition, the results are 42 percent, 42 percent, and 0 percent. As concerns juridical rights, the results were 33, 67 and 0. Only the results of the questions concerning personal rights deviate from this pattern: the results are 50 percent for each of the periods considered, although it should be noted that only two rights were examined in this category, as the other rights are excluded for lack of information.

These results are open to the criticism that they are biased, since they exclude the rights or freedoms regarding women and also those about

Table 7.4 Results of the application to Iraq of the Humana Index

Category	Score (in %)		
	1947–8	1958–60	Early to middle 1980s
All included questions	42	50	16
Weighted rights (questions 7 to 13)	28	39	22
Rights of movement and information (questions 1 to 6)	67	73	20
Freedom from coercion (questions 7 to 18)	38	46	20
Freedom of opposition (questions 19 to 28)	42	42	0
Juridical rights (questions 29 to 35)	33	67	0
Personal rights (questions 36 to 40)	50	50	50

which not enough is known. Furthermore, one might argue that the low overall score received for the early 1980s is explained by the backdrop of war with Iran, in contrast to the periods 1947–8 and 1958–60 when the country was at peace: governments are often forced to take actions that restrict liberties or violate rights because of the emergency of war.

The modified Humana Index

I therefore correct for these possible biases. First, the exclusion of rights about which not enough is known is unlikely to have biased downwards the overall score for 1982. The questions omitted for lack of information are shown in Table 7.5 along with the score received for each period. Six out of the eight questions omitted for this reason receive a score of zero for the early 1980s, and no information at all is available regarding the last question. It is therefore unlikely that these omitted questions introduced a downward bias to the score for the last period. However, on one omitted question (namely the freedom to use contraceptive pills or devices) the early 1980s scores the maximum 3, and this may have caused a slight downward bias in the overall score for this period, but is corrected below.

Second, in order to correct for bias, I give the three questions regarding the position of women along with the question concerning the freedom to use contraceptive pills and devices the maximum score of 3 for the last period and the minimum score of zero for the two other periods of 1947–8 and 1958–60. As we saw in Chapter 6, women achieved significant gains in access to education and paid employment, and attained equality with men as regards social and economic laws in the period roughly

Table 7.5 Questions omitted for lack of information

Question	Score 1947–8	1958–60	Early to middle 1980s
5. Monitor human right violations	NA	NA	0
13. Court sentences of corporal punishments	NA	NA	0
26. Independent radio and television networks	NA	NA	0
31. Free legal aid and counsel of own choice	NA	NA	0
34. From police searches of home without warrant	NA	NA	0
35. From arbitrary seizure of personal property	NA	NA	0
39. Freedom to use contraceptive pills or devices	NA	NA	3
40. To practice homosexuality between consenting adults	NA	NA	NA

corresponding to 1947–8 to the middle 1980s. But women have not attained equality in marriage, divorce, or inheritance rights and it will be remembered that the gender equality in inheritance that was legislated by the Qassem government was quickly overturned after his overthrow by the Ba'th in 1963. In other words, if one were scrupulously objective in scoring these freedoms or rights, it is likely that the time periods associated with the monarchy and Qassem would not score so low and the period associated with the Ba'th not score as high. Nevertheless, in order to remove the possibility of a bias against the score for the last period I use these scores, although this modification will likely create a bias in the other direction, against the scores for the earlier periods.

Third, I also make modifications that correct for the war situation in the early to middle 1980s. The modification envisioned here is to examine the 29 rights in August 1980, one month before the outbreak of war with Iran. Only three rights are affected, namely the rights to travel inside and outside the country and freedom from compulsory work or conscription of labor. So few rights are affected because the policies that are typically enforced under war conditions, such press censorship, were already in practice in Iraq by 1980. Regarding the affected rights, travel inside Iraq was in 1980 generally unrestricted. Furthermore, travel outside the country, although it was restricted, was not banned until 1982. Travel abroad was generally restricted to two trips per year, except for some persons in the armed forces and security services for whom travel was prohibited, exit visas being a requirement for those who traveled outside the country. Lastly, while there was no compulsory conscription of labor in 1980 as there was later, although it was difficult for government employees to leave their jobs; quitting government jobs required official approval and was not given easily. The questions regarding these rights, namely the right to travel in one's own country, to travel outside one's country, and freedom from compulsory work or conscription of labor, will therefore receive scores of 3, 2, and 2, respectively, corresponding to 1980 instead of the scores corresponding to the early to middle 1980s.

Finally, there are rights that the Humana Index does not consider. At least two of these are relevant to Iraq. These include the freedom from collective punishment, and the intensity of the use of the death penalty, not merely if it exists or not. Freedom from collective punishment – freedom of relatives, friends, or neighbors of persons convicted or accused of crimes – is implicitly protected under the Universal Declaration of Human Rights.[81] In general, this right was respected at the time of the monarchy and under the Qassem government, but was violated repeatedly under the Ba'th regime.

The frequency of use of the death penalty is of interest, if to the extent that capital punishment is a violation of rights (namely the right to life), then the more frequent is the application of this penalty, the greater the violation of rights. The death penalty has always been in existence in Iraq, but, as was shown, the frequency of its application increased markedly during the period considered. In the five years between 1933 and 1937, for example, 68 death sentences were passed, although it is not known how many of these, if any, were for political offences.[82] More definite statistics are available from the Qassem era, and indicate that in 1961 and 1962 a total of 34 persons were sentenced to death,[83] although is not known how many of these sentences were carried out. Assuming all were, these would constitute a fraction of the figure for the 1980s: the Ba'th executed an estimated 520 political prisoners between 1978 and 1981,[84] and this does not include the number executed for ordinary crimes.

I therefore give the freedom from collective punishment scores of 3, 3, and 0 for the periods 1947–8, 1958–60 and the early to middle 1980s respectively, and the intensity of use of the death penalty scores of 2, 2, and 0. These rights will receive the normal weight, will not be weighted more heavily than other rights or freedoms, and will be evaluated in addition to the existing 29 rights, not replacing any existing questions in the index. There will thus be a weighted question regarding the existence of the death penalty and another non-weighted question regarding the frequency of its application. These modifications are summarized in Table 7.6.

These modifications change the results by very little, as shown in Table 7.7. That is, if the rights and freedoms of women were fully respected (and equal to those of men) in the middle 1980s and not respected at all in the two periods before, the results of the index overall are as follows: 39 percent, 46 percent, and 24 percent for the periods 1947–8, 1958–60, and the early to middle 1980s respectively. The second modification to the index, regarding the conditions of war, yields the following overall results: 42 percent, 50 percent, and 22 percent respectively. When both of

Table 7.6 Proposed modifications to the Humana Index

Question	Score			
	1947–8	1959–60	Early to middle 1980s	1980
Modification 1:				
21. Political and legal equality for women	0	0	3	
22. Social and economic equality for women	0	0	3	
37. Equality of sexes during marriage and for divorce proceeding	0	0	3	
39. To use contraceptive pills or devices	0	0	3	
Modification 2:				
1. Travel in own country	2	3	1	3
2. Travel outside the country	3	3	0	2
10. Compulsory work or conscription of labor	2	3	1	2
Modification 3:				
Freedom from collective punishment	3	3	0	
The intensity of use of the death penalty	2	2	0	

Table 7.7 Results of the modifications made to the Humana Index

Modification	Overall score (in %)			
	1947–8	1958–60	Early to middle 1980s	1980
Modification 1 only	39	46	24	
Modification 2 only	42	50		22
Modification 1 and 2	39	46		29
Modification 3	44	52	16	
Upper limit range	44	52		29
Lower limit range	39	46		16

these modifications are taken together, the results are as follows: 39 percent, 46 percent, and 29 percent respectively. These two modifications together provide an upper estimate for the last period, early to middle 1980s/1980, and a lower estimate for the periods 1947–8 and 1958–60. The third modification, regarding the right from subjection to collective punishment and the intensity of use of the death penalty, yields the following results: 44 percent, 52 percent, and 16 percent for the periods 1947–8, 1958–60, and the early to middle 1980s respectively. The results of this modification provide the upper limit for the periods 1947–8 and 1959–60 and the lower limit for the period early to middle 1980s/1980.

These results are robust to the three introduced modifications. Whichever modifications or combination of modifications are performed, the results indicate that human rights and political freedoms were most respected under the Qassem regime, less respected at the time of the monarchy, and least respected under the Ba'th. The application of these modifications to the index yields an upper limit score of 29 percent and lower limit score of 16 percent for the last period under examination. This is consistent with Humana's overall score of 19 percent for Iraq in 1986.[85] These results are thus plausible.

The findings bring out two main points. First, the formal structures of democracy appear to be neither necessary nor sufficient to achieve improvements in human rights and political freedoms. According to the results there was greater respect for rights and freedoms during the military regime of Qassem than under the formally democratic monarchy. The Qassem government scores higher than the monarchy in the overall index; it also scores higher in most categories including freedom of opposition, and the same in the two remaining categories, namely juridical and personal rights. Moreover, as Table 7.7 shows, the results are robust to any combination of modifications. This is so despite the fact that there was under the monarchy, at least in legal form, a democratic structure with parliament and elections, but no equivalent institutions in the Qassem government. Clearly, democratic forms alone are not sufficient to realize gains in rights and freedom; nor are they necessary as the noted gains occurred under (formally undemocratic) military rule of General Qassem. This helps explain why there was scarcely any public opposition when the constitutional structures of the monarchy were abolished.

Second, there is no evidence that the Ba'th used the war with Iran to consolidate power. The outbreak of the Iran–Iraq war was not associated with a marked decline in rights and freedoms, as these rights and freedoms were already almost non-existent. The overall scores of 42 percent, 50 percent, and 16 percent for the periods 1947–8, 1958–60, and the early to middle 1980s are broadly similar to the 42 percent, 50 percent, and 22 percent that are attained when the last period is changed to August 1980. That is, the poor state of human rights in Iraq during the 1980s can not be blamed on the emergency requirements of war: many of these, such as state control of the press, were already in place in 1980, before the outbreak of war.

These results cast doubt on the thesis advanced by Thom Workman that the Ba'th regime used the war with Iran to consolidate its position in power, to strengthen its standing *vis-à-vis* opposition political groups and to widen its social base. The war, he claimed, provided the regime with a "blanket pretext to do whatever was necessary to contain its opponents," and thus strengthen its own political position.[86] In support of his position, Workman notes that the position of the Ba'th at the end of the war with Iran in 1988 was as solid as, if not stronger than, at the beginning of the conflict in 1980 – a considerable feat when one considers the huge monetary and human costs of the war. Yet the study of the questions in the index for 1980 as compared to the early to middle 1980s changed the response to only three questions, none of which concerned the rights of opposition; on each of the questions about the rights of political opposition, the Ba'th regime scored a zero in both periods. That is, it is difficult to understand why the Ba'th needed the prevailing conditions of war to crush its political opposition, when the regime had already done so before the onset of war.

Quite apart from its pre-war repression of political opponents, this thesis does not explain why, if the Ba'th was eager to exploit the opportunities provided by war, the regime made repeated attempts to end the conflict. The Iraqi government unilaterally declared numerous cease-fires during the war, all ignored by Iran, in an effort to end the war. Indeed, according to Charles Tripp, at the low point of the conflict in 1982, the RCC along with senior Ba'th party members (but without Saddam Hussein) met to propose to Iran a cease-fire offer that abandoned all of Saddam's prior demands.[87] If true, this proposal illustrates how the regime saw the war as a massive blunder rather than a welcome opportunity. The event also represents possibly the last time that the RCC was able to act independently of Saddam, as the latter would subsequently use Iran's rejection of the offer to consolidate power at the expense of the party.

Concluding remarks

The study of the variety of expression in mass media and political party affiliation as well as the intensity of application of capital punishment indicate that, in the period covering the independence of the modern state in 1932 to the middle to late 1980s, respect for rights and freedoms was lacking. Crucially, however, there were important variations across time. The use of the Humana Index (which I modify) suggests that human rights and political freedoms were most respected under the military dictatorship of Qassem in 1958–60, less respected in 1947–8 under the formally democratic monarchy, and least respected in the 1980s under the Ba'th. That is, in the case of Iraq, for the noted periods, the formal structures of democracy were found to be insufficient to achieve improvements in human rights and political freedoms.

Moreover, the results of using this index show that the Ba'th did not need conditions of war to annihilate its opposition and consolidate power as it had already done so prior to the beginning of hostilities. On the contrary, the findings suggest that the Ba'th went to war with Iran in 1980 from a position of relative domestic strength.

8   Conclusion

What emerges from the study of Iraq's human development is a complex, at times surprising, and uneven process of development, one that is intimately connected with state policies, situated in the broader political economy and not obviously or directly related to the rate of economic growth. The story hints at – and, indeed, Iraq's experience after 1990 would painfully illustrate – the fragility of development and the dire consequences that can occur when political institutions and political decision-making structures fail to keep up with advances in other aspects or dimensions of development. Along the way previously obscured aspects of the development process are illuminated, old questions revisited, and new issues raised. Outstanding among these is the question of whether Iraq had anything to show, in terms of accelerated human development, for its atrocious record in human rights and high levels of political violence.

In assessing economic growth in Chapter 3, we argued that, during the 1970s, the state attempted to restrain the growth in per capita consumption, whose growth provides the material basis for (but, of course, does not guarantee) an expansion in capabilities. The state constrained consumption to maintain price stability in order to realize its first priority of rapid capital formation. Even allowing that some investments were economically inefficient and unproductive, the investment record of Iraq was fine throughout, and especially impressive during the 1970s. Conversely, the state sought to actively buttress consumption to placate a war-weary public during the 1980s. In the context of an economic contraction brought about by conflict with Iran and subsequent reduction in oil revenues, the regime borrowed heavily, in part to sustain consumption. It may be that oil revenues, because they improve access to finance capital, allow the state to smooth consumption (saving when oil revenues are high and borrowing when they are deficient). Nevertheless, the active restraint on consumption is in tension with the vision of the rentier state as one whose concern is mainly and reflexively to buy public compliance with oil revenues: the Ba'thi state was evidently a reluctant consumer when its purchasing power was highest, in the 1970s.

Counterfactually, the rapid pace of development that was pursued in the 1970s, had it been allowed to continue, might have succeeded in transforming the country into a modern and diversified industrialized economy, escaping the main problems associated with the Dutch Disease. To be sure, Iraq's highly centralized and interventionist "big push" strategy of economic development was associated with various problems (including the promotion of inefficient activities and industries), and the high rate of capital formation aggravated some existing bottlenecks (especially in transport). Contrarily, many of the investments in human and physical capital that Iraq carried through are complementary. And some interventions can actually enhance economic efficiency in the long run, aiding industrialization. Of course, existing inefficiencies in principle could have been corrected with reform or rationalization. Whatever the positives or shortcomings associated with Iraq's development strategy, it was the Ba'th's attack on Iran and the protracted war that followed that effectively brought the process of development planning (and the associated high levels of growth and investment) to an end. It was not, in other words, the contradictions arising of the chosen economic development strategy that condemned its implementation, but erroneous political decisions that impelled the state to shelve its development plans and curtail investment in the early 1980s. The country subsequently became arguably more rather than less dependent on oil, as the civilian economy (and its non-oil economic activities) was disrupted and loans (essentially, claims against future oil revenues) were secured by government from lenders.

Yet, the immediate effects of the changed geopolitical position *vis-à-vis* the war with Iran, and corresponding declines in oil revenues, investment levels, and GDP, on human development outcomes were not direct or obvious. As the study of education illustrates in Chapter 4, education outcomes continued to improve throughout the period under study, except for a slight decline in secondary enrollment in the 1980s. In fact, enrollments in higher education reached unprecedented levels. This, however, was contrary to the manpower requirements of the country, which demanded more skilled but not professional labor. And it implied that the allocations of educational resources were neither as equitable nor likely as efficient as they might have been. Increased enrollments at the universities along with reduced high school enrollments also ran counter to the state's own educational priorities, which emphasized enrollments in the lower levels of education. However, it is conjectured that the Ba'thi state was unwilling to intervene to reallocate educational resources away from higher education, perhaps for fear of igniting unrest among urban youths. This underlines the notion that even supposedly powerful states confront limitations in their pursuit of equalizing agendas and contests the notion that the Ba'thi state was so powerful that it was largely independent of society.

In contrast to the case in education, Chapter 5 reveals that the allocation of expenditures and outcomes in health became more equitable and efficient over time, as more emphasis was placed on primary and preventative care (such as immunizations) and extension of basic services (including safe water and sanitation). In fact, some human development outcomes (for example, infant mortality) improved at an undiminished or accelerated pace during the 1980s. Interestingly, standards of nutrition actually increased to unprecedented levels during the Iran–Iraq war in the 1980s, as the regime increased imports of grains to ensure adequate food availability to the general public.

The disparity between the progress of human development outcomes and changes to GDP is striking and illustrates how development outcomes are complex and have multiple determinants, GDP being only one. It may well be that in the very long term the expansion of human development is constrained by economic growth, but it is unlikely that this constraint is binding at any one point in time. State priorities, political exigencies, and the larger political economy are likely to be more important determinants, especially in many mineral-exporting countries where the state plays a prominent economic role and is a large employer.

To the extent that these (somewhat unexpected) development outcomes underline the complex and contingent nature of development, the assessment of the status of women in Chapter 6 portends the vulnerability of that development. Largely facilitated, supported, or directly sponsored through the actions of the state, women gained in terms of educational outcomes and paid employment during the period under consideration. Women also gained to a lesser extent in terms of their status under law. However, mirroring what was occurring elsewhere in society, independent women's organizations were repressed or co-opted and replaced with Ba'th party organs. By the end of the period, no autonomous associations for women were left standing. Consequently, when the regime enacted laws that restricted the freedom of action and standing of women, there was no opposition from women's (or any other) groups to note. The findings support the contention that the status of women has advanced most vigorously when it has been consistent with the aims of the state.

That the same contraction in political space was proceeding in society at large is illustrated in Chapter 7. There was a notable decline in the diversity of expression in the mass media and political party affiliations. This was accompanied by heightened state repression, as expressed in the increased use of the death penalty and disappearances. All these are confirmed by the results of the modified Humana Index. The results of this index show that in Iraq's modern history human rights and political freedoms were most respected during the Qassem regime, less so during the monarchy, and least under the Ba'th. That is, the military dictatorship of Qassem protected more rights and advanced more freedoms than the formal constitutional structures of democracy (and the regular elections) of the monarchy. This illustrates how formal democratic structures and regular election cycles may be neither necessary nor sufficient to advance or guarantee freedoms and rights. The results of the index also cast doubt on the argument that the Ba'th used the Iran–Iraq war to consolidate its hold over power in Iraq, as it is shown that the Ba'th regime was already firmly ensconced in power before the conflict began.

Two salient points emerge from this discussion. The Iraqi state – Ba'thi for most of the period under study – implemented a largely successful and mostly egalitarian strategy for human development. With the exception of human rights and political freedoms, where there was a notable contraction, capabilities expanded more or less uninterruptedly, sometimes at an accelerated and at other times reduced pace. Some of the policies and programs that the Ba'th implemented were proposed before they came to power in 1968. Indeed, support within Iraq for the egalitarian development of human capabilities precedes the Ba'thi regime by decades.[1] Nevertheless, there is no doubt that the Ba'thi regime vigorously pursued long-term development, sometimes at the expense of current consumption, even if the development program that it adopted was not its brainchild. Yet the Ba'th was incapable of tolerating any coherent political opposition.

The second point concerns the putative association between dictatorship and development as it relates to Iraq, a topic explored at the beginning of the book. Although the discussion that is presented here is necessarily brief, this is an issue that needs to be addressed when assessing Iraq's development history. To restate the argument, early development and modernization thinking posited that authoritarian political arrangements – because they neutralize, dissuade, and silence political opposition, impose social stability and peace, and allow the state a free hand to implement its policies – tended to accelerate development. In Iraq, civil society was smashed, human rights were routinely violated, and political freedoms were repressed, and at the same time much was achieved in the material components of development, notably in education, nutrition, various health outcomes, and in relation to the status of women. Because these occur at roughly the same time, it is tempting to conclude that dictatorship boosted development.

This question of whether Iraq's authoritarian polity promoted development devolves into two issues. The first issue concerns whether high and rising political repression allowed the state to implement specific policies or initiatives that it otherwise would not have been able to carry through. Here one is hard pressed to name a single program that conforms to this criterion and some where the Ba'thi state's desire to monopolize the political space might have checked the pace of development. In respect to education, it is argued that the state delayed the implementation of its literacy campaign until it was sure that it could control the content, despite the need for skilled labor and the high expected rate of return from the investment. Concerning this campaign, it will be remembered that coercion appears to have played a minor role only (if any at all), as more people attended literacy classes than were required to do. At the same time, the state appeared reluctant to use its political supremacy to reallocate educational resources to achieve more egalitarian and economically efficient results in the 1980s. In respect to health and nutrition, there is likewise little evidence that development outcomes were improved by increased political repression. Basic services were extended to rural areas, but only after the (politically sensitive) urban areas were generously provisioned. Elevated imports of food did achieve high levels of nutrition but there is nothing inconsistent about increased imports of food and a more liberal polity. As regards the status of women, it is shown that although women gained substantially in education and paid employment, their gains *vis-à-vis* personal rights and laws were less prominent precisely because the Ba'thi state had little interest to advance such rights. That is, despite notable advances in human capabilities, dictatorship and rising political repression appear to have had little positive instrumental effect in the development of human capabilities. Development may have expanded by even more under a less authoritarian polity.

The second issue is more general and concerns whether dictatorial rule, in creating a stable and predictable economic climate, facilitates capital formation and development. The political corollary to this (socio-economic) bonus to authoritarianism, which is sometimes expressed in polite conversation, contends that the high degree of ethno-sectarian diversity in a country such as Iraq requires stern governance. Neither position is convincing. Whatever the perceived benefits to the Iraqi leadership, it is exceedingly unlikely that Iraq's endemic political violence promoted either a stable economy or polity. The Ba'th by the middle 1970s had consolidated its hold on power, established economic and political stability, was perfectly able to (and indeed did) defend basic property rights, and was directing the implementation of a largely successful development strategy. It is difficult to see how the subsequent rise in political repression and violence to unprecedented levels, including the extension of capital punishment to include economic crimes (defined so broadly that they could be used to incriminate almost anyone), served to sustain a predictable economic environment. It almost certainly did the opposite. In respect to the political stability in heterogeneous societies, Sami Zubaida argues that it is precisely state dictatorships in Iraq and elsewhere in the Middle East, which extinguished all alternative centers of power, that have inadvertently nourished sectarianism. Unable to seek assistance or resources from a cross-sectarian civil society, individuals at times of distress inevitably turn to familial, tribal, and ethno-sectarian institutions for help. Although they are secular themselves, totalitarian dictatorships wind up supporting sectarianism.[2]

The very real tragedy for the people of Iraq is that totalitarian political institutions not only slowed the pace of development but also may have contributed to its arrest and reversal. The Ba'thi regime, after consolidating its hold on power (facilitated in part by the impressive expansion in human development) and achieving dominance in the domestic political arena, with a narrowing clique at the apex of government and, critically, with sustenance from abroad, including from key Western countries, embarked on devastatingly costly international misadventures. The state shelved its ambitious development plans during the Iran–Iraq war (1980–88) and the Gulf War that followed the invasion of Kuwait in 1991 obliterated development. We will never know what the alternative course of events would have been under a more liberal polity and there is no guarantee that democracies have protective powers over societies (the findings of Chapter 7 underline their limitations). But the notion that the denial of civil rights or plain civility is necessary or even desirable to promote development or provide stability is one that the people of Middle East appear to be actively rejecting.

Appendix:
The Humana Index

The Humana Index is designed for comparing human rights across different countries at a single point in time, but it may be usefully employed for a single country at different points in time. In fact, one of the criticisms of the index is that it compares countries with very different historical traditions, social customs, and mores.[1] Although this difficulty is not eliminated by considering a single country at different points in time (since these customs change over time), the index arguably provides a better basis for comparison and, as will be shown, uncovers interesting insights.

The Humana Index is calculated from responses to 40 questions related to human rights. The first six questions are rights or freedoms concerning the freedom of movement and the flow of information. These questions ask if there is "freedom to": travel in one's own country, travel outside the country, peacefully associate and assemble, teach ideas and receive information, monitor human rights violations, and publish and be educated in one's native language. The next 12 questions are concerned with the extent of the state's use of various forms of coercion. These questions ask if there is "freedom from": serfdom, slavery or child labor; extra-judicial killings or disappearances; torture or coercion by the state; compulsory work permits or conscription of labor; capital punishment by the state; indefinite detention without charge; court sentences of corporal punishment; compulsory membership of state organizations and parties; compulsory religion or state ideology in schools; deliberate state policies to control artistic works; political censorship of the press; and censorship of mail or telephone tapping. The next ten questions in this index attempt to capture the rights or freedoms of political opposition as well as the extent to which various rights are available to women and minorities. These questions ask if there are "freedoms for or rights to": peaceful political opposition, multi-party elections by secret and universal ballot, political and legal equality for women, social and economic equality for women, social and economic equality for minorities, independent newspapers, independent book publishing, independent radio and television networks, independent courts, and independent trade unions.

The next seven questions examine the extent to which basic juridical rights are respected. These questions ask if there are "legal rights": from deprivation of nationality, of innocence until proven guilty, to free legal aid and council of one's own choice, from secret civilian trials, to be brought promptly before a judge or court, from police searches of the home without a warrant, and from arbitrary seizure of personal property. Finally, the last five questions examine the extent to which one may exercise personal freedoms that may run counter to the values of society as a whole. These questions ask if there are "personal rights": to inter-racial, inter-religious, or civil marriage; to equality of the sexes during marriage and for divorce proceedings; to practice any religion; to use contraceptive pills or devices; and to practice homosexuality between consenting adults.

Some of these questions are not utilized in the application of this index to Iraq. There are some rights or freedoms that are not considered in the calculation of the index because there is too little information for a comparison through time. Eight such rights are excluded for this reason, including the freedom to monitor human rights violations; freedom from court sentences of corporal punishment; freedom for independent radio and television; legal rights to free legal aid and counsel; legal rights from police searches without a warrant and from arbitrary seizure; the personal right to practice homosexuality with consenting adults; and the freedom to use contraceptive pills or devices. Still, partial information about these excluded rights is given when available. Likewise, since they were addressed earlier, the rights concerning the position of women are excluded from this index. These are the rights to political and legal equality for women; the rights to social and economic equality for women; and the personal rights to equality of the sexes during marriage and in divorce proceedings. As noted, the freedom to use contraceptives, clearly a freedom that concerns women, is excluded because of the problems of comparison over time. In total 11 rights or freedoms are excluded from the calculation of the Humana Index as it applies to Iraq.

Not all the noted freedoms or rights are, arguably, equally important. It might, for example, be reasoned that freedom from capital punishment is more pressing than rights to independent trade unions or that freedom from torture is more important than protections against arbitrary seizure. For this reason the Humana Index gives greater weight to some questions than others. The following rights, corresponding to questions 7 to 13 in the index, are thus given three times the weight of other rights: the "freedom from" serfdom, slavery, or child labor; extra-judicial killings or disappearances; torture or coercion by the state; compulsory work or conscription of labor; capital punishment by the state; indefinite detention without charge; and court sentences of corporal punishment. Of course, this weighting system reflects personal value judgments about which rights are more or less important, but as the judgments that underlie the weighting system appear to be sensible, Humana's weighting preferences are used.

Four possible scores are available for each question, the maximum being 3 and the minimum zero. The scores received for questions 7 to 13 in the index will be multiplied by three to reflect the greater weight attached to the rights that correspond to these questions; the maximum score that a single one of these weighted questions is able to receive is therefore 9 (3×3). Since there are six weighted questions (one weighted question will be excluded from the index because of lack of information) the maximum points that are available from the weighted questions is 54 (9×6). The 23 remaining questions each receive a maximum of 3 points; the maximum points available from these non-weighted questions is thus 69 (3×23). The maximum total score that is attainable is 123. The Humana Index is computed by dividing the total score received by the maximum score that is attainable.

The 29 questions are examined below at three different points in Iraq's political history: under the monarchy in 1947–8, under the Qassem government in 1958–60, and under the Ba'th in the first part of the 1980s. These periods have been chosen because they represent difficult periods for the respective regime. The period 1947–8 was a time of agitation against the Portsmouth Agreement with Britain. Similarly, the period 1958–60, under the Qassem government, represented a time when that regime was under attack from its nationalist and conservative opponents. Finally, in the early to middle 1980s under the Ba'th, Iraq was engaged in a costly and unpopular war with Iran and the regime was forced to implement drastic cutbacks in its development plan and social spending. One advantage of choosing these periods is that information about rights and freedoms is more available in these than in other periods. Presented below are the questions and the scores given corresponding to the relevant period. A brief discussion is given below each question explaining these scores.

Iraq under the monarchy 1947–8	Iraq under Qassem 1958–60	Iraq under the Ba'th early/middle 1980s

Freedom to:
1. Travel in own country

2	3	1

At the time of the monarchy, the Rights and Duties of Cultivators Law No. 28 of 1933 prohibited the migration of farmhands who were indebted to their landlord. Since most farmhands were perpetually in debt to their landlords, this law was intended to ensure a plentiful supply of labor to the tribal sheikhs (landlords). It proved practically impossible to enforce the law, however, and between 1947 and 1957, over 200,000 people migrated to Baghdad alone.[2] While no evidence of internal travel restriction under the Qassem government was found, the war with Iran limited movement in the border regions and Kurdish areas in the 1980s and checkpoints were erected to intercept army deserters.

2. Travel outside the country
3   3   0

No restrictions are known to have existed at the time of the monarchy or Qassem. Under the Ba'th government, travel, except in official state or business capacities, was restricted before the onset of the Iran-Iraq war in 1980 and altogether banned in 1982.

3. Peacefully associate and assemble
1   1   0

Under the monarchy as well as Qassem there was a modest tolerance for peaceful assembly, but demonstrations often turned violent and the government retaliated by arresting opposition leaders.[3] Except for those that it staged itself, demonstrations were brutally suppressed under the Ba'th, as in the noted protests in the Shia holy cities.

4. Teach ideas and receive information
1   1   0

A modest amount of freedom to teach and receive information was available under both the monarchy and Qassem, including teachers' freedom to vaguely or indirectly criticize the government,[4] which was impossible to do later under the Ba'th.

5. Monitor human rights violations
NA   NA   0

No knowledge about the extent to which human rights violations were (or could be) monitored under the monarchy and Qassem is available. Nevertheless, it appears that human rights violations could at least be publicly exposed in court, as when the accused Communists in 1948 and later some defendants in the Mehdawi court complained of torture.[5] In contrast, public statements about human rights under the Baath were almost totally absent; inquiries by human rights organizations were met with either denials or no response from the Iraqi government.[6]

6. Publish and educate in native language
3   3   2

   Publishing and education in ethnic language has been long tolerated by successive Iraqi governments, but the output of these publications, like other forms of press and education, was very tightly controlled from the late 1970s onwards.

Freedom from:
7. Serfdom, slavery and child labor
1   2   3
The conditions of Iraq's peasant population at the time of the monarchy have correctly been described as that of serfdom;[7] child labor was prevalent especially in rural areas. Under Qassem, land reform improved the lot of the rural peasants (although there was a decline in agricultural output immediately after the reform);[8] child labor started to decline in this period. By the early 1980s, serfdom was eliminated and child labor was greatly reduced.

8. Extra-judicial killings or disappearances
1   1   0
Instances of extra-judicial killings occurred under the monarchy, as in, for example, the suppression of the Assyrian rebellion and quelling of various tribal uprisings in the 1930s. No disappearances are known to have taken place under the monarchy. While no instances of extra-judicial killings or disappearances conducted as a policy of the state are known to have occurred under Qassem, deaths often resulted from political rivalries, as in the Nationalist–Communist clashes in Mosul in 1959 and the campaign of assassination waged by the nationalists that, according to the ICP first secretary, accounted for the deaths of 286 "communists and democrats" from 1958 to 1961.[9] In contrast to the earlier periods when they were rare and unorganized, extra-judicial killings and mass disappearances were carried out as instruments of state policy in the 1980s.

9. Torture or coercion by state
0   0   0
Successive Iraqi governments have used torture, including for ordinary (non-political) offenses.[10]

10. Compulsory work or conscription of labor
2   3   1
Under the monarchy, the rural areas of southern Iraq were not subject to the same laws that governed the rest of the country but to their own "tribal" laws. As a result, tribal sheikhs could compel their farmhands to perform labor without pay on specific projects. Such conscription of labor was constrained by custom, however. This dual legal system was abolished in 1958 by the Qassam government. Compulsory conscription of labor was enforced during the war with Iran: workers were forced to work during holidays and for longer hours and labor was conscripted into the army for indefinite periods of time; refusal of military service was punishable by death.

11. Capital punishment by the state

0   0   0

Successive Iraqi governments have used capital punishment.

12. Indefinite detention without charge

1   1   0

Under the monarchy, Article 79 of the Criminal Procedure Act allowed for the arrest of persons who "it is believed may disturb the peace," and to hold the persons in detention for indefinite periods of time.[11] This law permitted the government to arrest prospective opponents at politically turbulent times. Generally, however, persons arrested in such a way were either quickly brought to trial or released. The same tactic was used by the Qassem government. Under the Ba'th, however, people are often held without trial for years, sometimes because of infractions committed by family members.

13. Court sentences of corporal punishment

NA   NA   0

It is not known whether Iraqi law has formal provisions for corporal punishment, although torture, which may be regarded as a form of corporal punishment, has been used by successive Iraqi governments.

14. Compulsory membership of state organizations and parties

3   3   1

Prior to the Ba'th government, membership in state organizations and parties was largely voluntary. With the Ba'th takeover of power, Ba'th party membership was encouraged in some professions (such as medicine and law) and required for military officers. Promotion in government employment was often related to Ba'th membership.[12]

15. Compulsory religion or state ideology in schools

2   2   1

Under the monarchy schoolchildren were subjected to a modest amount of nationalist propaganda in schools as part of an attempt at nation building.[13] Likewise, under Qassem, the defense of the generally popular 14th of July revolution became an added item of ideology. By the late 1970s and early 1980s, however, official propaganda had developed into a cult of personality centered around Saddam Hussain; the adulation of the leader in songs and poetry, the 17th of July revolution and its achievements, and membership in Ba'th youth organizations were required.

16. Deliberate state policies to control artistic works

3   3   0

There is some evidence that the state attempted to control artistic output during the monarchy and under Qassem: writers and intellectuals whose works were hostile to government often faced loss of employment or even arrest. Yet there was no organized campaign to control artistic works. By the late 1970s, however, all artistic output was under the direct control of the state.

17. Political censorship of the press

1   1   0

See the section entitled *The mass media*.

18. Censorship of mail or telephone tapping

2   2   0

Although the activities of dissidents during the monarchy and Qassem periods were scrutinized, there is no evidence of widespread mail and telephone monitoring, in contrast to the situation under the Ba'th, when these were extensive.

Freedom for or rights to:
19. Peaceful political opposition

1   2   0

Under the monarchy, the ICP (which neither called for the violent overthrow of the monarchy nor participated in armed action against the state) was banned, while other opposition parties were allowed to exist until 1954. Under Qassem, peaceful political opposition was tolerated, but only briefly legalized. During the Ba'th's rule no political pluralism was tolerated. Thus, although in a coalition with the ruling Ba'th since the early 1970s, the ICP was not allowed to directly criticize the government. Subsequent to the dissolution of this coalition, no party was allowed to censure the Ba'th, even indirectly.

20. Multi-party elections by secret and universal ballot

1   0   0

Multi-party elections were held under the monarchy, but the range of political parties that were allowed to participate was restricted and the indirect voting system resulted in a parliament that was unrepresentative of the Iraqi public at large. No elections were held during the Qassem period. Elections to the national assembly held during the rule of the Ba'th were a sham: the candidates for the assembly were chosen by the regime, and the legislature had no legal right to vote down RCC resolutions, which were binding.[14]

21. Political and legal equality for women
See Chapter 6.

22. Social and economic equality for women
See Chapter 6.

23. Social and economic equality for ethnic minorities
1   2   0
Successive Iraqi governments have granted legal equality for ethnic minorities. However, the majority Shia population, despite their formal equality, formed a disproportionate number of the poor and, as we have seen, was under-represented in government. While the Qassem regime, and later the Ba'th, enacted policies that improved the lot of the poor, and hence the Shia indirectly, the Ba'th's repression of the Kurds resulted in more than Kurdish 100,000 deaths. That is, the killings of minorities occurred in spite of the legal equality and narrowing social and economic disparities.

24. Independent newspapers
2   2   0
See the section entitled *The mass media.*

25. Independent book publishing
2   2   0
A modest amount of freedom to publish was available at the time of the monarchy and Qassem regime. By the late 1970s, however, no independent book publishing was allowed in Iraq.

26. Independent radio and television networks
NA   NA   0
Iraq has never had independent television networks, and it is not known whether independent radio existed in the past. In any case, by the late 1970s, radio and television were tightly controlled by government.

27. All courts enjoy total independence
2   0   0
During the monarchy, courts had a modest degree of autonomy, and political opponents were tried in ordinary (criminal) courts. By contrast, special, highly politicized, courts such as the Mehdawi court under Qassem and Revolutionary courts under the Ba'th were set up to try political opponents of the respective regime; rulings from these courts were not subject to appeal, but there was a possibility of clemency.

28. Independent trade unions
1   2   0
Beginning in 1944–45, state recognition was given to 16 independent trade unions for the first time in Iraq. Unions were, however, quickly suppressed within a few years, when it became clear that they would

strike in support of their demands. Trade unions also suffered in the Qassem era, but for different reasons: the regime wanted to reduce the ICP's domination of trade associations, and so indirectly backed independent or pro-government candidates. Nevertheless, free elections for these associations were frequently held, and the Qassem government did not always get its way in who controlled these unions.[15] The Ba'th created state-sponsored, party-controlled unions and de-legalized all others. Trade unions thus became an appendage of the state.[16]

Legal rights:
29. From deprivation of nationality
0   3   0
Iraqi law under the monarchy provided for the withdrawal of nationality, and indeed there are some known cases in which this was done to political opponents of the regime.[17] Withdrawal of citizenship is not known to have been practiced by the Qassem government, but was resurrected by the Ba'th government: in 1980, the Ba'th government deported some 50,000 Iraqis of Iranian origin.

30. Innocent until proven guilty
0   0   0
In principle, this is upheld by successive Iraqi governments. In practice, however, persons were often tortured even before they appeared in court.

31. Free legal aid and counsel of own choice
NA   NA   0
No information on free legal counsel is available for the monarchy or Qassem periods. Free counsel was available during the rule of the Ba'th, but was often irrelevant, especially in special (revolutionary) courts where the role of the attorney was sometimes limited to asking for clemency.

32. From civilian trials in secret
3   3   0
This principle was generally abided by under the monarchy and Qassem regimes where (civilian) political opponents were tried in criminal courts. During the Ba'th's tenure, however, special courts were often convened in secret.

33. To be brought promptly before a judge or court
0   0   0
Successive Iraqi governments have violated this principle. Prisoners were often detained for months before they were brought to trial. This took extreme form under the Ba'th where some political prisoners were detained for years without trial.

34. From police searches of home without a warrant
NA   NA   0
No information about this is available.

35. From arbitrary seizure of personal property
NA   NA   0
No information is available on seizure of property under the monarchy
and Qassem administration. It did occur under the Ba'th, however.

Personal rights:
36. To inter-racial, inter-religious, or civil marriage
0   0   0
Social pressures rather than government policy are the binding constraint
in inter-religious marriages. Persons are legally entitled to marry across
religions and sects, but the personal costs to people that do so are usually
high, including social ostracism and sometimes death, often by a family
member. Generally speaking, it is easier for a Muslim man to marry a
non-Muslim woman than the reverse.

37. Equality of sexes during marriage and for divorce proceeding
See Chapter 6.

38. To practice any religion
3   3   3
The freedom to practice any religion has been respected by successive
Iraqi governments.

39. To use contraceptive pills or devices
NA   NA   3
The contraceptive pill was not available for use at the time of the
monarchy or Qassem, as it became available for general use only in the
1960s; and no information concerning the availability or use of other
contraceptive devices is available for these periods. Under the Ba'th,
however, contraceptive devices, including pills, were generally available,
although parents were encouraged to have large families.

40. To practice homosexuality between consenting adults
NA   NA   NA
No information is available on this question.

Notes

1 Human development theory and Iraq's development story

1 Keith Griffin and John Knight, 'Human Development: The Case for Renewed Emphasis', in Wilber and Jameson (eds.), *The Political Economy of Development and Underdevelopment*, 5th edition, McGraw-Hill, 1992, pp. 576–609, p. 576. See also Amartya Sen, 'Development: Which Way Now?', pp. 5–26 in same volume.

2 See Amartya Sen, 'Development Thinking at the Beginning of the XXI Century', in Louis Emmerij (ed.), *Economic and Social Development in the XXI Century*, Inter-American Development Bank, Washington DC, 1997, pp. 531–51.

3 Albert O Hirschman, *The Strategy of Economic Development*, Yale University Press, New Haven, 1958; Ragnar Nurkse, *Problems of Capital Formation in Underdeveloped Countries*, Oxford University Press, New York, 1953; and W.W. Rostow, *The Stages of Economic Growth: A Non-Communist Manifesto*, 2nd ed., Cambridge University Press, New York, 1971. See also Paul Rosenstein-Rodan, 'Problems of Industrialisation of Eastern and South-Eastern Europe,' *Economic Journal*, Vol. 53, June/September 1943, pp. 202–11 for a similarly growth-centred outlook.

4 Amartya Sen, 'Development Thinking at the Beginning of the XXI Century', p. 535.

5 See for example Alberto Alesina and Dani Rodrik, 'Distributive Politics and Economic Growth', *The Quarterly Journal of Economics*, Vol. 109, No. 2, May 1994, pp. 465–90, who show how inequality can retard economic growth.

6 Amartya Sen, 'Development Thinking at the Beginning of the XXI Century', p. 537.

7 Amartya Sen, 'Development Thinking at the Beginning of the XXI Century'. See also Gary Becker, Human Capital: *Human Capital: A Theoretical and Empirical Analysis, with Special Reference to Education*, Chicago, University of Chicago Press, 3rd ed., 1993.

8 Keith Griffin and John Knight, 'Human Development: The Case for Renewed Emphasis', p. 577.

9 Amartya Sen, 'Development: Which Way Now?'

10 Amartya Sen, *Commodities and Capabilities*, North Holland Press, Amsterdam, 1985, p. 17.

11 Amartya Sen, 'Development as Capability Expansion', in *Human Development and the International Development Strategy for the 1990s*, Keith Griffin and John Knight (eds.), Macmillan, London 1990, pp. 41–58.

12 Quoted by Mahbub ul-Haq, *Reflections on Human Development*, Oxford University Press, London 1995, p. 13.

13 Amartya Sen, 'Development Thinking at the Beginning of the XXI Century', 1997, pp. 540–2.

14 Amartya Sen, 'Development: Which Way Now?', p. 15.
15 Keith Griffin and John Knight, 'Human Development: The Case for Renewed Emphasis', in *Human Development and the International Development Strategy*, p. 9–40.
16 Amartya Sen, 'Development as Capability Expansion', in *Human Development and the International Development Strategy*, pp. 48–9.
17 Amartya Sen, 'Development as Capability Expansion', in *Human Development and the International Development Strategy*, p. 53.
18 For an exploration of this thesis as regards East Asian societies, see Fareed Zakaria, 'Culture Is Destiny: A Conversation with Lee Kuan Yew', *Foreign Affairs*, Vol. 73, 1994. As concerns Iraq, a similar theme is struck in Saddam Hussain's address to the General Federation of Iraqi Women in Saddam Hussein, *Social and Foreign Affairs in Iraq*, Khalid Kishtainy (trans.), London, Croom Helm, 1979.
19 Frances Hasso, 'Empowering Governmentalities rather than Women: The *Arab Human Development Report 2005* and Western Development Logics, *International Journal of Middle Eastern Studies*, Vol. 41, No. 1, 2009, pp. 63–82.
20 Sharath Srinavasan, 'No Democracy without Justice: Political Freedom in Amartya Sen's 'Capability Approach,' *The Journal of Human Development*, Vol. 8, No. 3, 2007.
21 Severine Deneulin, 'Promoting Human Freedoms under Conditions of Inequalities: a procedural framework', *The Journal of Human Development*, Vol. 6, No. 1, 2005. See also Indraneel Dasgupta's excellent review of Sen's *Development as Freedom* in *Economica*, Vol. 73, pp. 157–8.
22 Amartya Sen, 'Development as Capability Expansion', 1990, p. 49.
23 Amartya Sen, 'Development as Capability Expansion', 1990, pp. 49–50.
24 Amartya Sen, *Commodities and Capabilities*, 1985, pp. 40–41.
25 Amartya Sen, 'Development as Capability Expansion', 1990.
26 Abbas Alnasrawi, *The Economy of Iraq: Oil, Wars, Destruction of Development and Prospects, 1950-2010*, Greenwood Press, London, 1994; Abbas Alnasrawi, *Iraq's Burdens: Oil, Sanctions and Underdevelopment*, Greenwood Press, London, 2002.
27 Hanna Batatu, The *Old Social Classes and Revolutionary Movements of Iraq: A Study of Iraq's Old Landed and Commercial Classes and of its Communists, Ba'thists and Free Officers*, Princeton University Press, Princeton NJ, 1978.
28 Marion Farouk Sluglett and Peter Sluglett, *Iraq since 1958*, I. B. Tauris, London, 2003.
29 Amartya Sen, 'Development as Capability Expansion', p. 49.
30 Amartya Sen, 'Description as Choice', in *Choice, Welfare and Measurement*, Blackwell Publishers, Oxford, 1982, pp. 432–449.
31 Mahbub ul-Haq, *Reflections on Human Development*, Oxford University Press, London. p.21.
32 George Psacharopoulos, 'Returns to Education: A Further International Update and Implications', *The Journal of Human Resources*, Vol. 20, No. 4, 1985, Table 8. Also see John B. Knight and Richard H. Sabot, *Education, Productivity and Inequality: The East African Natural Experiment*, Oxford University Press, Oxford, 1990.
33 Keith Griffin and Terry McKinley, *Implementing a Human Development Strategy*, St. Martin's Press, New York, 1994, pp. 4–6.
34 Charles Tripp, *A History of Iraq*, Cambridge University Press, Cambridge UK, 2002.
35 Edith Penrose and E. F. Penrose, *Iraq: International Relations and National Development*, Boulder CO, Westview Press, 1978.

36 For a thorough and critical look at the natural resource curse see Andrew Rosser, 'The Political Economy of the Resource Curse: A Literature Survey', Working Paper 268, Institute of Development Studies, University of Sussex, April 2006.

37 Jeffrey Sachs, 'How to Handle the Macroeconomics of Oil Wealth', in *Escaping the Resource Curse*, Macartan Humphreys, Jeffrey Sachs and Joseph Stiglitz (eds.), Colombia University Press, New York, 2007, pp. 173–93.

38 The original formulation of the rentier state hypothesis is attributed to Hossein Mahdavy. See his 'The Patterns and Problems of Economic Development in Rentier States: the Case of Iran', in M.A. Cook, ed., *Studies in the Economic History of the Middle* East, London: Oxford University Press, 1970, 428–67.

39 Hazem Beblawi, 'The Rentier State in the Arab World', in *The Rentier State*, H. Beblawi and G. Luciani, (eds.), London: Croom Helm, 1987, 85–98.

40 Lisa Anderson, 'The State in the Middle East and North Africa', *Comparative Politics*, Vol. 20, No. 1, October 1987.

41 Giacomo Luciani, 'Allocation vs. Production States: A Theoretical Framework', in *The Arab State*, G. Luciani, ed., Berkeley and London: University of California Press, 1990, 65–84.

42 Quintan Wiktorowicz, 'The Limits of Democracy in the Middle East: The Case of Jordan', *The Middle East Journal*, Vol. 53, No. 4, 1999.

43 Samir al-Khalil, *Republic of Fear: The Politics of Modern Iraq*, University of California Press, Berkeley, 1989.

44 See Donald Richards, 'The Predatory State in Comparative Perspective', Unpublished Working Paper, Economics Department, Indiana State University, 2006, in reference to Latin America.

45 Jakob De Haan and Clemens Siermann, 'New evidence on the relationship between democracy and economic growth', *Public Choice*, Vol. 86, No. 1–2, pp. 175–98, 1996.

46 Samuel Huntington, *Political Order in Changing Societies*, Yale University Press, New Haven, CT, 1968.

47 Amartya Sen, *Development as Freedom*, Chapter 6.

48 See, for example, John F. Helliwell, 'Empirial Linkages Between Democracy and Economic Growth', National Bureau of Economic Research, Working Paper No. W4066, May 1992; Jakob De Haan and Clemens Siermann, 'New evidence'; and Amartya Sen, *Development as Freedom*, Chapter 6.

49 Amartya Sen, *Development as Freedom*, Chapter 6.

50 Ahmed Mushfiq Mobarak, 'Determinants of Volatility and Implications for Economic Development', Research Program on Political and Economic Change, University of Colorado, Boulder, Working Paper PEC2004-0001, January 2004.

51 Jean Dreze and Amartya Sen, *Hunger and Public Action*, Clarendon Press, Oxford, 1989. See also Amartya Sen, *Development as Freedom*.

52 Amartya Sen, *Development as Freedom*, p. 181.

53 For an exploration of this argument as regards East Asian societies, see Fareed Zakaria, 'Culture Is Destiny: A Conversation with Lee Kuan Yew', *Foreign Affairs*, Vol. 73, 1994. For an examination of the same general thesis see Saddam Hussein's address to the General Federation of Iraqi Women in Saddam Hussein, *Social and Foreign Affairs in Iraq*, Khalid Kishtainy (trans.), London, Croom Helm, 1979. See also, Amartya Sen, *Development as Freedom*, Chapters 6 and 10.

54 Amartya Sen, *Development as Freedom*, Chapters 6 and 10.

55 Friedrich Nietzsche, *Beyond Good and Evil*, Penguin Books, New York, 1990.

56 See Amnesty International, 'Guantánamo Bay – a human rights scandal', undated, <http://www.amnestyusa.org/war-on-terror/guantanamo-bay–a-human-rights-scandal/page.do?id=1108202> accessed 3-03-09.

57 UNDP, *Arab Human Development Report 2003*, National Press, Amman, 2003, p. 19.
58 Isam al-Khafaji, *Tormented Births: Passages to Modernity in Europe and the Middle East*, I. B. Tauris Publishers, London, 2004.
59 Charles Tripp, *A History of Iraq*.
60 Edith Penrose and E. F. Penrose, *Iraq: International Relations and National Development*.

2   Social, political, and economic evolution of Iraq, 1920–1990

1 See Peter Sluglett, *Britain in Iraq 1914-1932*, Ithaca Press, London, 1976, pp. 103–14.
2 Ibid., p. 80.
3 Ibid., p. 37.
4 Calculated from Table 7-4 in Hanna Batatu, *The Old Social Classes and Revolutionary Movements of Iraq*, Princeton University Press, Princeton NJ, 1978, p. 180; and Appendix 2 in Majid Khadduri, *Independent Iraq 1932-58*, Oxford University Press, London, 1960, p. 371.
5 Hanna Batatu, *The Old Social Classes*, p. 322.
6 Ibid., p. 323.
7 See A. Shikara, 'Faisal's Ambitions of Leadership in the Fertile Crescent: Aspirations and Constraints', in *The Integration of Modern Iraq*, Abbas Kelidar (ed.), Croom Helm, London, 1979, pp. 32–45.
8 Peter Sluglett, *Britain in Iraq*, p. 43.
9 David Pool, 'From Elite to Class: The Transformation of Iraqi Political Leadership', in *The Integration of Modern Iraq*, Abbas Kelidar (ed.), Croom Helm, London, 1979, p. 65.
10 No estimate of the religious/sectarian or ethnic makeup of the country at its inception in the 1920s is available. These figures are taken from Abdul Karim al-Uzri, *The Problematic of Government in Iraq*, (in Arabic), London, 1991, p. 273, and have the disadvantage in that they are estimates based on the regional distribution of the population of the 1947 census. Nevertheless, they are consistent with other estimates of the ethnic/religious breakdown of the Iraqi population such as that of Gabriel Baer, *Population and Society in the Middle East*, Praeger Press, New York, 1966, p. 105.
11 For brief but informative discussions of some of the differences between the two sects see Peter Sluglett and Marion Farouk Sluglett, 'Some Reflections on the Sunni/Shi'i Question in Iraq', *British Society for Middle East Studies,* Vol. 5, No. 2, 1978, pp. 78–89, and Abbas Kelidar, 'The Shii Imami Community and Politics in the Arab East', *Middle Eastern Studies*, Vol. 19, No. 1, January 1983, pp. 3–16.
12 Hanna Batatu, *The Old Social Classes*, p. 45.
13 Roger Owen, *The Middle East in the World Economy 1800-1914*, Tauris and Co. Publishers, New York, 1993, p. 275.
14 Ibid., p. 276.
15 Hanna Batatu, *The Old Social Classes*, p. 29.
16 Ibid., pp. 224–243.
17 Roger Owen, *The Middle East in the World Economy*, p. 183.
18 Hanna Batatu, *The Old Social Classes*, p. 74.
19 Saleh Haider, 'Land Problems of Iraq' (unpublished thesis), University of London, 1942, pp. 556–660, printed with omissions in Charles Issawi (ed.), *The Economic History of the Middle East 1800-1914*, University of Chicago, Chicago, 1966, pp. 164–78.

20 Roger Owen, *The Middle East in the World Economy*, p. 280.
21 Hanna Batatu, *The Old Social Classes*, pp. 74–78.
22 Peter Sluglett, *Britain in Iraq*, p. 231.
23 Hanna Batatu, *The Old Social Classes*, p. 96.
24 Peter Sluglett, *Britain in Iraq*, p. 240.
25 Ibid., p. 247.
26 Hanna Batatu, *The Old Social Classes*, p. 105.
27 Ibid., pp. 96–97.
28 Ibid., p. 91.
29 Majid Khadduri, *Independent Iraq 1932-58*, p. 51.
30 Samir al-Khalil, *Republic of Fear: The Politics of Modern Iraq*, University of California Press, Berkeley, 1989, p. 160.
31 Mohammad Tarbush, *The Role of the Military in Politics: A Case Study of Iraq to 1941*, Kegan Paul, London, 1982, p. 94.
32 Hanna Batatu, *The Old Social Classes*, p. 30.
33 Peter Sluglett, *Britain in Iraq*, p. 181.
34 For a thorough exploration of the 'Assyrian Uprising' see R. S. Stafford, *The Tragedy of the Assyrians*, Allen and Unwin, London, 1935.
35 Majid Khadduri, *Independent Iraq*, pp. 176–177.
36 Samir al-Khalil, *The Republic of Fear*, p. 159.
37 Roger Owen and Sevket Pamuk, *A History of Middle East Economies in the Twentieth Century*, Harvard University Press, Cambridge, 1998, p. 54.
38 Hanna Batatu, *The Old Social Classes*, p. 30.
39 Gerald de Gaury, *Three Kings in Baghdad: 1921–1958*, Hutchinson, London, 1961, p. 146.
40 Hanna Batatu, *The Old Social Classes*, p. 103.
41 Ibid., p. 109.
42 Ibid., p. 35.
43 M. S. Hasan, 'Growth and Structure of Iraq's Population, 1867-1947', *Bulletin of the Oxford University Institute of Statistics*, XX, 1958, pp. 339–53.
44 Hanna Batatu, *The Old Social Classes*, p. 108.
45 Ibid., pp. 614–627.
46 N. F. Safwa, *Iraq in the Memoirs of Foreign Diplomats* (in Arabic), Beirut, 1969, p. 227.
47 See Hanna Batatu, *The Old Social Classes*, p. 548.
48 Ibid., pp. 537–71.
49 Samir al-Khalil, *Republic of Fear*, p. 227.
50 Michel Aflaq, *For the Sake of the Baath*, (in Arabic), Beirut, al-Talai Press, p. 29.
51 Hanna Batatu, *The Old Social Classes*, pp. 722–48.
52 Theobald, Robin and Jawad, Sa'ad, 'Problems of Rural Development in an Oil Rich Economy: Iraq 1958-75', in *Iraq: The Contemporary State*, Tim Niblock (ed.), Croom Helm, London, 1982, p. 199.
53 Hanna Batatu, *The Old Social Classes*, p. 841.
54 Ibid., p. 839.
55 Ibid., p. 826.
56 Ibid., pp. 866–89.
57 Ibid., p. 988.
58 Marion Farouk Sluglett and Peter Sluglett, *Iraq Since 1958*, Routledge and Kegan, New York, 1986, p. 86.
59 Hanna Batatu, *The Old Social Classes*, p. 991.
60 Peter Sluglett and Marion Farouk-Sluglett, *Iraq Since 1958*, p. 95.
61 Edith Penrose, 'Industrial Policy and Performance in Iraq', in *The Integration of Modern Iraq*, p. 151.

62 Peter Sluglett and Marion Farouk-Sluglett, *Iraq Since 1958*, p. 138.
63 Rony Gabbay, *Communism and Agrarian Reform in Iraq*, Croom Helm, London, 1978, p. 178.
64 Samir al-Khalil, *The Republic of Fear*, pp. 234–5.
65 Peter Sluglett and Marion Farouk-Sluglett, *Iraq Since 1958*, p. 79. Also see Peter Sluglett, 'The Kurds', in *Saddam's Iraq: Revolution or Reaction*, Zed Books, London, 1986, pp. 177–88.
66 Peter Sluglett, 'The Kurds', in *Saddam's Iraq*, p. 191.
67 Sa'ad Jawad, 'Recent Developments in the Kurdish Issue', in *Iraq: The Contemporary State*, Tim Niblock (ed.), Croom Helm, London, 1982, p. 56.
68 U. Zaher, 'The Opposition', In *Saddam's Iraq*, p. 171.
69 Peter Sluglett and Marion Farouk-Sluglett, *Iraq Since 1958*, p. 206.
70 Ibid., pp. 160–4.
71 Phebe Marr, *The Modern History Of Iraq*, Westview Press, Boulder, 1985, p. 27.
72 Peter Sluglett and Marion Farouk-Sluglett, *Iraq Since 1958*, p. 175.
73 Ibid., p. 198.
74 Majid Khadduri, *Socialist Iraq*, The Middle East Institute, Washington DC, 1978, pp. 67–9.
75 Hanna Batatu, 'Iraq's Underground Shia Movements: Characteristics, Causes and Prospects', *Middle East Journal*, 35, 1981, pp. 578–94.
76 For an interesting discussion of this phenomenon see Zuhair al-Jaza'iri, 'Ba'thist Ideology and Practice', in *Iraq Since the Gulf War: Prospects for Democracy*, Zed Books, London, 1994, pp. 32–47.
77 Compare, for example, Arab Ba'th Socialist Party, *The 1968 Revolution in Iraq: Experience and Prospects*, The Political Report of the Eighth Congress of the Arab Ba'th Socialist Party in Iraq January 1974, Ithaca Press, London, 1979,with later Ba'thist pronouncements in Marion Farouk Sluglett and Peter Sluglett, 'Iraqi Ba'thism: Nationalism, Socialism and National Socialism', in *Saddam's Iraq*, pp. 104–5.
78 Marion Farouk-Sluglett, 'Socialist Iraq 1963-1978 – Towards a Reappraisal', *Orient*, Vol. 23, No. 2, 1982, pp. 206–18.
79 Marion Farouk Sluglett and Peter Sluglett, *Iraq Since 1958*, p. 209.
80 For a thorough discussion of this thesis see Thom Workman, *The Social Origins of the Iran-Iraq War*, Lynne Rienner Publishers, London, 1994.
81 See Samir al-Khalil, *The Republic of Fear*, pp. 270–6.
82 For a discussion of the economic impact of the Iran-Iraq war see Abbas Alnasrawi, 'Economic Devastation, Underdevelopment and Outlook', in *Iraq Since the Gulf War*, pp. 72–96.
83 Samir al-Khalil, *The Republic of Fear*, p. 34.
84 Jabr Muhsin, 'The Gulf War', In *Saddam's Iraq*, p. 241.
85 Joseph Sassoon, *Economic Policy in Iraq 1932-1950*, Frank Cass, London, 1987, p. 181.
86 The value of the ID was set equal to the value of the £ sterling in the period from independence in 1932 until the 14th of July revolution in 1958 took Iraq out of the "sterling area".
87 Joseph Sassoon, *Economic Policy in Iraq 1932–1950*, Frank Cass, London, 1987, pp. 57–65.
88 Ibid, p. 146.
89 International Bank for Reconstruction and Development (IBRD), *The Economic Development of Iraq*, Washington DC, 1952, p. 17.
90 Doreen Warriner, *Land Reform and Development in the Middle East: A Study of Egypt, Syria and Iraq*, Royal Institute of International Affairs, London, pp. 141–2.

91 Joseph Sassoon, *Economic Policy*, p. 4.
92 Central Statistical Organization, *National Income in Iraq: Selected Studies*, Shafik Press, Baghdad, 1970, pp. 9–10.
93 Abbas Alnasrawi, *The Economy of Iraq*, Greenwood Press, London, 1994, p. 31.
94 Roger Owen, *The Middle East in the World Economy*, p. 273.
95 M. S. Hasan, 'Growth and Structure', pp. 344–5.
96 Fadhil al-Ansari, *The Population Issue: The Case of Iraq*, (in Arabic), Ministry of Culture Press, Damascus, 1980, p. 139.
97 Joseph Sassoon, *Economic Policy*, p. 170.
98 Calculated from OPEC, *Annual Statistical Bulletin 1994*, p. 47.
99 These were the Iraq Petroleum Company (IPC), the Basra Petroleum Company (BPC), and the Mosul Oil Company (MOC), all of which were foreign owned.
100 Abbas Alnasrawi, *The Economy of Iraq*, p. 2. For a detailed history of oil agreements see S. M. Longrigg, *Oil in the Middle East*, Royal Institute of International Affairs, Oxford, 1961.
101 Roger Owen and Pamuk, Sevket, *A History of Middle East Economies in the Twentieth Century*, Harvard University Press, Cambridge, 1998, p. 54.
102 Abbas Alnasrawi, *The Economy of Iraq*, p. 3.
103 Ibid., p. 11.
104 Central Statistical Organization, *National Income in Iraq*, p. 17.
105 Joseph Sassoon, *Economic Policy*, p. 235.
106 Abbas Alnasrawi, *The Economy of Iraq*, p. 20.
107 Joseph Sassoon, *Economic Policy*, p. 259.
108 Principal Bureau of Statistics, *Statistical Abstract 1939*, p. 120.
109 Central Bureau of Statistics, *Statistical Abstract 1960*, Zahra' Press, Baghdad, 1961, p. 336.
110 International Labour Office (ILO), *Year Book of Labour Statistics: Retrospective Edition on Population Censuses 1945-89*, Geneva, 1990, p. 61.
111 Hanna Batatu, *The Old Social Classes*, pp. 472–3.
112 Ibid., p. 471.
113 IBRD, *The Economic Development of Iraq*, p. 1.
114 Central Statistical Organization, *National Income in Iraq*, pp. 9–10.
115 Joseph Sassoon, *Economic Policy*, p. 4.
116 Directorate General of Census, *Abstract of the General Census of 1957*; pp. 14 and 24.
117 World Bank, *World Development Report (WDR) 1982*, Oxford University Press, New York, 1982, p. 155.
118 World Bank, *WDR 1982*, p. 151.

3 Economic growth, consumption, income distribution, and capital formation

1 Mahbub ul-Haq, *Reflections on Human Development*, Oxford University Press, London.
2 See Bassam Yousif, 'Non-renewable resource depletion and reinvestment: issues and evidence for an oil-exporting country', *Environment and Development Economics*, Vol. 14, pp. 211–26, 2009. Because of the lack of data, a complete study of the capital balance was not feasible.
3 Jeffrey Sachs, 'How to Handle the Macroeconomics of Oil Wealth', in *Escaping the Resource Curse*, Macartan Humphreys, Jeffrey Sachs and Joseph Stiglitz (eds.), Colombia University Press, New York, 2007, pp. 173–93.
4 K. Haseeb, *The National Income of Iraq 1953-61*, Oxford University Press, London, 1964, pp. 13–15. One ID exchanged officially for one £ sterling or

US$2.80 until 1970. The rate was then increased slightly to 2.96 and 2.97 in 1971 and 1972 respectively and further to 3.39 in 1973, where it remained until 1981. In 1982 the ID was devalued to 3.21, a rate of exchange which remained in effect throughout the 1980s. However, these official exchange rates varied markedly from market rates especially during the 1980s. IMF, *International Financial Statistics Yearbook 1985*, pp. 356–7 and IMF, *International Financial Statistics Yearbook 1995*, New York, 1995, pp. 448–9.

5 K. Haseeb, *The National Income of Iraq*, pp. 29–32.
6 Calculated from UN, *Yearbook of National Accounts Statistics 1971*, Vol. 1, New York, 1973, p. 487.
7 Calculated from UN, *Yearbook of National Accounts Statistics 1971*, p. 487 and (for population estimates) IMF, *International Financial Statistics Yearbook 1986*, New York, 1987, p. 400.
8 Calculated from IMF, *International Financial Statistics Yearbook 1986*, p. 400. As no estimates of the GDP deflator are available for the years before 1965, it is not possible to compute a real rate of growth for earlier periods using the same data.
9 Abbas Alnasrawi, *The Economy of Iraq*, Ch. 3.
10 The computation of real values of these macroeconomic aggregates requires individual price indexes, which are unavailable for this period. These values were therefore calculated using the consumer price index, which is assumed to be a reasonable proxy for the relevant price indexes.
11 See UN, *National Accounts Statistics: Analysis of Main Aggregates 1988-989*, New York, 1991, pp. 133 and 139 for studies whose conclusions are based on prior data: Abbas Alnasrawi, *The Economy of Iraq*, Chapters 4 and 5.
12 Note for example the discrepancy in the estimates of the GDP deflator for the 1980s between UN, *National Accounts Statistics: Analysis of Main Aggregates 1988-989*, New York, 1991, p. 240, which suggests that the deflator more than doubled between 1980 and 1989 and UN, National Accounts Aggregate Database, available at http://unstats.un.org, accessed 07-12-09, which indicates a far more modest rise in the deflator of roughly 50 percent for the same period.
13 Broadly similar trends emerge when these macroeconomic aggregates are evaluated in the domestic currency.
14 Calculated from IMF, *International Financial Statistics Yearbook 1985*, pp. 358–9.
15 Organization of Petroleum Exporting Countries (OPEC), *Annual Statistical Bulletin 1994*, Vienna, 1995, p. 122.
16 OPEC, *Annual Statistical Bulletin 1994*, p. 47.
17 According to Paul Stevens, 'Iraqi Oil Policy: 1961-76', in *Iraq: The Contemporary State*, Tim Niblock (ed.), Croom Helm, London, 1982.
18 OPEC, *Annual Statistical Bulletin 1994*, p. 47.
19 OPEC, *Annual Statistical Bulletin 1994*, p. 122.
20 For a detailed discussion of the Iraqi economy during the Iran-Iraq War see Abbas Alnasrawi, *The Economy of Iraq*, Chapter 5. For a graphical illustration of the collapse in oil exports after 1980, see Chapter 2, Figure 2.1.
21 OPEC, *Annual Statistical Bulletin 1994*, p. 47.
22 Calculated from UN, *National Accounts Statistics: Main Aggregates and Detailed Tables 1990*, p. 911.
23 Calculated from CSO, *Annual Abstract of Statistics 1978*, Baghdad, undated, p. 256.
24 Abbas Alnasrawi, *The Economy of Iraq*, Chapter 7.
25 Email correspondence with Humam al-Shamaa, an economist and consultant to the Iraqi government, April 2009.
26 Abbas Alnasrawi, *The Economy of Iraq*, p. 93.

27 Email correspondence with Humam al-Shamaa, April 2009.
28 See Abbas Alnasrawi, *The Economy of Iraq*, and Bassam Yousif, *Development and Political Violence*.
29 UN, *National Accounts Statistics: Analysis of Main Aggregates 1988–1989*, New York, 1991, pp. 133 and 139.
30 Calculated from CSO, *Annual Abstract of Statistics 1978*, undated, p. 256.
31 Ahmed M. Jiyad, 'The Development of Iraq's Foreign Debt: From Liquidity to Unsustainability', in Kamil A. Mehdi (ed.), *Iraq's Economic Predicament*, Reading, Ithaca Press, 2002, pp. 85–137, pp. 87 and 101.
32 Abbas Alnasrawi, *The Economy of Iraq*, chapter 5.
33 Isam al-Khafaji, 'The Parasitic Base of the Ba'thist Regime', in Committee Against the Repression of Democratic Rights in Iraq (CARDRI) (ed.), *Saddam's Iraq: Revolution or Reaction*, Zed Books, London, 1986, pp. 73–88, p. 84.
34 See consumer price index reported in IMF, *International Financial Statistics Yearbook 1995*, pp. 450–1. Consumer price data are available only for 1978 and prior years.
35 CSO, *Annual Abstract of Statistics 1989*, Baghdad, undated, p. 197.
36 Ismail Aubaid Hummadi, Economic Growth, p. 167.
37 In terms of the ratio of the income of the bottom 40 percent to the top 20 percent in 1971, the distribution of income in Iraq was more egalitarian than Brazil's in 1989 (7:67.5 percent), Mexico's in 1984 (11.9:55.9 percent), and Malaysia's in 1989 (12.9:53.7 percent); it was comparable to the United Kingdom's in 1988 (14.6:44.3 percent) but slightly less equal than the South Korea's in 1988 (19.7:42.2 percent), and India's in 1989–90 (21.3:41.3 percent). World Bank, *World Development Report 1994*, Oxford University Press, New York, 1994, pp. 220–1.
38 Isam al-Khafaji, 'The Parasitic Base of the Ba'thist Regime', in *Saddam's Iraq: Revolution or Reaction*, Zed Books, London, 1986, pp. 73–88. For a list of these businessmen see Isam al-Khafaji, *Tormented Births*, pp. 286–90.
39 See Kiren Aziz Chaudhry, 'Consuming Interests: Market Failure and the Social Foundations of Iraqi Etatisme', in Kamil A. Mahdi (ed.) *Iraq's Economic Predicament*, Ithaca Press, Reading UK, 2002, pp. 233–65.
40 Abbas Alnasrawi, *The Economy of Iraq*, pp. 96–9. See also Kiren Chaudhry, 'Economic Liberalization and the Lineages of the Rentier State', *Comparative Politics*, Vol. 27., No. 1, October 1994, pp. 1–25.
41 Even during the market-orientated economy of the monarchy, the state's contribution to gross fixed capital formation was 50% between 1953 and 1958. Isam al-Khafaji, 'The Parasitic Base of the Ba'thist Regime', p. 74.
42 Calculated from UN, *National Accounts Statistics: Main Aggregates and Detailed Tables 1990*, p. 913.
43 Calculated from UN, *National Accounts Statistics: Main Aggregates and Detailed Tables 1990*, p. 913.
44 Abbas Alnasrawi, *The Economy of Iraq*, p. 71.
45 Abbas Alnasrawi, *The Economy of Iraq*, p. 92.
46 In 1971, before the oil price explosion of the early 1970s, crude oil extraction accounted for 99.0 percent of the value added generated in the mining and quarrying sector; this increased to 99.6 percent in 1975, after the rise in crude oil prices. Calculated from Central Statistical Organization, *Annual Abstract of Statistics 1976*, Baghdad, undated, p. 178. The mining and petroleum sectors are thus effectively one and the same.
47 Calculated from UN, *National Accounts Statistics: Main Aggregates and Detailed Tables 1990*, p. 913.
48 UN, National Accounts Aggregate Database, available at http://unstats.un.org, accessed 07-12-09.

49   See Joe Stork 'Oil and the Penetration of Capitalism in Iraq', in *Oil and Class Struggle*, Petter Nore and Terisa Turner (eds.), Zed Press, London, 1980, for an exploration of this view; and Abbas Alnasrawi, *The Economy of Iraq*, p. 164.
50   Joe Stork 'Oil and the Penetration of Capitalism in Iraq'.
51   Alice Amsden, *Asia's Next Giant: South Korea and Late Industrialization*, Oxford University Press, 1989; Dani Rodrik, 'Getting Interventions Right: How South Korea and Taiwan Grew Rich,' *Economic Policy*, Vol. 20, pp. 78–91, April 1995.
52   Edith and E. F. Penrose, *Iraq: International Relations and National Development*.
53   Isam al-Khafaji, *Tormented Births: Passages to Modernity in Europe and the Middle East*, p. 266.
54   Edith and E. F. Penrose, *Iraq: International Relations and National Development*.
55   Calculated from UN, *National Accounts Statistics: Main Aggregates and Detailed Tables 1990*, p. 912.
56   In nominal terms, the mining sector grew by more than 500 percent in 1970–1975, substantially higher than the growth of any of the other sectors. Calculated from UN, *National Accounts Statistics: Main Aggregates and Detailed Tables 1984*, New York, 1986, p. 750.
57   Calculated from UN, *National Accounts Statistics: Main Aggregates and Detailed Tables 1990*, p. 912.
58   Calculated from UN, *National Accounts Statistics: Main Aggregates and Detailed Tables 1984*, p. 750.
59   The relatively good performance of agriculture in the latter period is discussed in greater detail in Chapter 5.
60   Abbas Alnasrawi, *The Economy of Iraq*, pp. 95–6.
61   See in this regard Bassam Yousif and Eric Davis, 'Iraq: Understanding Autocracy, Oil and Conflict in a Historical and Socio-Political Context,' in *Democracy in the Arab World: Explaining the Deficit*, Ibrahim al-Badawi and Samir Makdisi (eds.), Routledge, 2011, pp. 227–253.
62   See Abbas Alnasrawi, *The Economy of Iraq*, pp. 127–49, for his assessment of Iraq's development experience and pp. 89-91 for a discussion of the politicization of planning.

4   Education

1   Keith Griffin and John Knight, 'Human Development: The Case for Renewed Emphasis', In *Human Development and the International Development Strategy*, pp. 10–11.
2   George Psacharopoulos, 'Returns to Education: A Further International Update and Implications', *The Journal of Human Resources*, Vol. 20, No. 4, 1985, Table 8. Also see John B. Knight and Richard H. Sabot, *Education, Productivity and Inequality: The East African Natural Experiment*, Oxford University Press, Oxford, 1990.
3   Although these censuses have different definitions of literacy, literacy rates are recomputed so they can be compared. The 1947, 1957, and 1965 censuses consider the 5-years-old and above population, while the 1977 and 1987 censuses consider the 10-years-old and above population in the calculation of literacy rates. The divergence in definitions is reconciled as data (incomplete for 1957) about the educational status of persons in the 5–9 years old age group are available for 1957 and 1965, which permits the recalculation of literacy rates for persons 10 years and older. The literacy rates of the 5–9 years old

population cohort and that of the population as a whole are found to be broadly similar for 1957 and 1965. Consequently, the literacy rates of the 5 years and older and 10 years and older populations are no different for 1957 and 1965. For a detailed explanation see Bassam Yousif, *Development and Political Violence in Iraq, 1950-1990*, Ph.D. Dissertation, University of California: Riverside, 2001, pp. 126–8.

4 Abdul A. al-Rubaiy and Khawla F. al-Zubaidy, 'Knowledge Within Reach: Iraq's Response to the Illiteracy Dilemma', *Educational Research Quarterly*, Vol. 12, No. 4, 1990, p. 57.

5 Ibid., p. 59

6 See Alya Sousa, 'The Eradication of Illiteracy in Iraq', in *Iraq: The Contemporary State*, Tim Niblock (ed.), Croom Helm, London, 1982, pp. 100–08.

7 Ibid. p. 107.

8 Ibid.

9 Alan Richards and John Waterbury, *A Political Economy of the Middle East: State, Class, and Economic Development*, Westview Press, Boulder, 1990, pp. 114–16.

10 The gross enrollment rate is derived from the total number of pupils attending school divided by the population of the relevant age group, the 6 to 11 years of age or 7 to 12 years of age population for example. This statistic may thus include adults who attend primary school. By contrast, net enrollments are calculated by dividing the number of pupils attending school who belong to the relevant age group by the population of that age group. Enrollment rates for the 6 to 11 years old and 7 to 12 years old populations are of course not strictly comparable. Nevertheless, data on enrollment rates are available from 1960 onwards for the 6 to 11 years old population, and these provide sufficient points for comparison.

11 The reasons for the sudden decline in 1965 are not known.

12 No data for the 12 to 17 years old population are available before 1970; data before 1970 are available only for the 13 to 18 years old population.

13 UNESCO, *Statistical Yearbook 1984*, 3-178.

14 Ibid.; and UNESCO, *Statistical Yearbook 1990*, 3-175.

15 Edith Penrose and E. F. Penrose, *Iraq: International Relations and National Development*, Ernest Benn, London, 1978, pp. 249-50, for example, claim that the expansion in educational enrollment immediately after the 1958 revolution resulted in a decline in educational standards.

16 UNESCO, *Basic Facts and Figures 1960*, Paris, 1961, p. 32.

17 UNESCO, *Statistical Yearbook 1965*, p. 167.

18 UNESCO, *Statistical Yearbook 1985*, III-175.

19 Liora Lukitz, *Iraq: the Search for National Identity*, Frank Cass, London, 1995, p. 111. See also Victor Clark, *Compulsory Education in Iraq*, UNESCO Press, Paris, 1951, pp. 25–7.

20 It ought to be mentioned, however, that these conditions are not unique to Iraq, but are found throughout the developing world. See R. P. Dore, *The Diploma Disease, Qualification and Development*, Allen and Unwin, London, 1976.

21 The rate is calculated by dividing the number of students who failed by the number who took the examination.

22 Suggested in a conversation with Douglas Mitchell, Professor of Education, University of California Riverside.

23 I am indebted to Karen Pfeifer for this observation. June 2008.

24 General Federation of Iraqi Women, *The Working Program of the Iraqi Republic to Improve the Woman's Status*, Baghdad, 1980, p. 23.

25 Central Statistical Organization, *Numbers and Indicators: Educational and Social Services*, (in Arabic), Baghdad, Undated, pp. 7 and 9.

26 UNESCO, *Statistical Yearbook 1978-79*, Paris, 1980, p. 689.
27 UNESCO, *Statistical Yearbook 1990*, 4-62.
28 Alya Sousa, 'The Eradication of Illiteracy', p. 105.
29 Central Statistical Organization, *Numbers and Indicators: Educational and Social Services* (in Arabic), Baghdad, Undated, pp. 7–8.
30 UNESCO, Statistical Yearbook 1988, 3-47; and UNESCO, *Statistical Yearbook 1994*, 3-48.
31 Central Statistical Organization, *Numbers and Indicators: Educational and Social Services*, pp. 9–10.
32 UNESCO, Statistical Yearbook 1988, 3-47; and UNESCO, Statistical Yearbook 1994, 3-48.
33 In 1970 and 1971, for example, the female repeater rate was 22 percent and 25 percent respectively, while the general (male and female) rate was 25 percent and 30 percent respectively. See UNESCO, *Statistical Yearbook 1976*, Paris, 1977, p. 271.
34 UNESCO, *Statistical Yearbook 1977*, p. 158.
35 Calculated from Central Statistical Organization, *Annual Abstract of Statistics 1987*, Baghdad, undated, pp. 46 and 48.
36 UNESCO, *Statistical Yearbook 1977*, p. 158.
37 Ibid.
38 These themes are explored in greater detail in Chapter 6.
39 As Table 4.11 indicates, 91 percent of the 7 to 14 years old economically active female population was engaged in agriculture in 1977, but only 51 percent in 1987, and while 74 percent of the 15 to 19 years old economically active female population was engaged in agriculture in 1977, only 34 percent were in 1987.
40 Calculated from Bureau of Statistics, *Statistical Abstract for the Financial Years 1927/28 to 1937/38*, pp. 53, 55 and 58.
41 Central Bureau of Statistics, *Statistical Abstract 1960*, pp. 76, 77 and 80.
42 See Keith Griffin and Terry McKinley, *Implementing a Human Development Strategy*, St.Martin's Press, New York, 1994, pp. 39–45.
43 The proportions may not total 100 percent because it is not clear in which level some expenditures ought to be recorded. Also, these statistics do not include the considerable expense of Iraq's adult literacy campaign, since the campaign was paid from the development rather than ordinary budget. The inclusion of the costs of the campaign, which began in 1978 and continued throughout the early 1980s, would undoubtedly swell the estimate of the portion of expenditures devoted to primary education for 1980.
44 UNDP, *Human Development Report 1994*, Oxford University Press, New York, 1994, p. 140.
45 UNDP, *Human Development Report 1994*, Oxford University Press, p. 141.
46 See J. S. Birks and C. Sinclair, 'The Challenge of Human Resources Development in Iraq', In *Iraq: the Contemporary State*, Tim Niblock (ed.), Croom Helm, London, 1982, pp. 241–55.
47 These statistics are taken from Abbas Salih Mehdi and Olive Robinson, 'Economic Development and the Labour Market in Iraq', *International Journal of Manpower*, Vol. 4, No. 2, 1983, pp. 1–40.
48 Abbas Alnasrawi, *The Economy of Iraq*, p. 94.
49 Ministry of Planning, *Man: The Objective of Revolution*, Baghdad, 1978, p. 87.
50 See Chapter 7, Section 2.
51 In respect to the Middle East, this argument about control of content of adult literacy programs is made by Alan Richards and John Waterbury, *A Political Economy of the Middle East: State, Class, and Economic Development*, Westview Press, Boulder, 1998, Chapter 5.
52 See Saddam Hussein's speech to the General Federation of Iraqi Youth in

February 1976 entitled 'Let us Win the Youth to Safeguard our Future', in Saddam Hussein, *Social and Foreign Affairs in Iraq*, Khalid Kishtainy (trans.), Croom Helm, London, 1979, pp. 53–62.

53 For a similarly skeptical view of the independence of the state from society, see Kiren Aziz Chaudhry, 'Consuming Interests: Market Failure and the Social Foundations of Iraqi Etatisme', in Kamil A. Mahdi (ed.) *Iraq's Economic Predicament*, Ithaca Press, Reading UK, 2002, pp. 233–65.

5 Housing, basic services, nutrition, and health

1 See, for example, T. Paul Schultz and Ayset Tansil, 'Wage and labor supply effects of illness in Cote d'Ivoire and Ghana: Instrumental variable estimates for days disabled', *Journal of Development Economics*, Vol. 53, 1997, pp. 251–285, in which the authors show that wage rates are higher for men whose health standing makes them less likely to miss work.

2 These are measles, diphtheria, whooping cough, polio, tuberculosis, and tetanus.

3 See Keith Griffin and Terry McKinley, *Implementing a Human Development Strategy*, pp. 47–8.

4 Ibid, p.45.

5 While here the focus is the misallocation of health resources in developing countries, evidence suggests similar misalignment in spending in rich countries as well. Even though the US, for example, spends a greater proportion of its GDP on health than any other country, its distorted spending results in an overall performance ranking of 37 out of 191 countries. See World Health Organization (WHO), *World Health Report 2000*, Geneva, 2000, <http://www.who.int/whr/2000/en/whr00_en.pdf>, accessed 7-07-05.

6 Given the constraints of available data, the households that reside in mud-homes, tents, huts, and *sarifas* (huts made of reed and mat, covered with mud) are considered to be inadequately housed. However, it is possible that the living conditions in some mud-homes or tents are better than those in some brick homes. Nonetheless, the general rule follows that living conditions in the former tend to be poor.

7 Hanna Batatu, *The Old Social Classes and Revolutionary Movements of Iraq*, Princeton University Press, Princeton NJ, 1978, p. 134.

8 Calculated from Central Statistical Organization, *The General Census of 1977*, p. 14.

9 Calculated from Central Statistical Organization, *Annual Abstract of Statistics 1971*, Baghdad, Undated, p. 51.

10 United Nations Economic and Social Commission for Western Asia (UNESCWA), *Statistical Abstract of the ESCWA Region 1983-1992*, Amman, 1994, p. 94.

11 UN, *Compendium of Social Statistics and Indicators 1988*, New York, 1991, p. 396.

12 Central Statistical Organization, *Annual Abstract of Statistics 1993*, Baghdad, 1994, p. 401.

13 Ibid.

14 Fluctuations from one year to another in agricultural production are common, and this leads to difficulties when the productions of individual years are compared. Consequently, the average levels of output for the periods noted have been calculated.

15 Kamil Mahdi, 'Iraq's Agrarian System: Issues of Policy and Performance', in Kamil A. Mahdi (ed.) *Iraq's Economic predicament*, Ithaca Press, Reading UK,

2002, p. 323.

16 Roger Owen and Sevket Pamuk, *A History of Middle East Economies in the Twentieth Century*, Harvard University Press, Cambridge, 1999, pp. 164–5.

17 Kamil Mahdi, 'Iraq's Agrarian System: Issues of Policy and Performance', pp. 331–2.

18 IMF, *International Financial Statistics Yearbook 1999*, p. 522.

19 Karen Pfeifer, 'Parameters of Economic Reform in North Africa', *Review of African Political Economy*, Vol. 26, No. 82, 1999, pp. 441–54.

20 Calculated from Central Statistical Organization, *Annual Abstract of Statistics 1978*, Baghdad, undated, p. 177; UNESCWA, *Statistical Abstract of the ESCWA Region 1978-87*, pp. 140–1; and UN, *National Accounts Statistics: Main Aggregates and Detailed Tables 1984*, New York, 1986, p. 750.

21 Adding net imports to total domestic output yields total domestic supply, which is then divided by estimates of the total population to yield per capita availability.

22 Hanna Batatu, *The Old Social Classes*, pp. 469–75.

23 The disparity between the two sets of data is likely the result of different data sources or methods for calculating infant mortality. For example, the direct method of estimating infant mortality is based on registration of births or collected data of birth histories, while the indirect method uses the number of children born compared to the number that have died. Each method has advantages and drawbacks, and none is accurate in every situation. Still, the two estimates, albeit substantially different, nonetheless illustrate the same long-term trend. The more complete World Bank estimates are used here in order to facilitate comparisons. For a comparison of infant mortality rates (using a variety of sources and methods) for Iraq, between the late 1980s and early 1990s, see Abbas F. Al-Saadi, 'Infant Mortality and the Economic Embargo in Iraq', *Population Bulletin of UNESCWA*, No. 44. For an illustration of how these methods could yield divergent estimates of mortality, see Jacob, Adetunji, 'Infant Mortality Rates in Africa: Does Method of Estimation Matter?', Harvard Center for Population and Development Studies, <http://www.hsph.harvard.edu/hcpds/wpweb/95_03.pdfa>, accessed 7-18-05.

24 See Alan Richards and John Waterbury, *A Political Economy of the Middle East*, 1998, Chapter 5.

25 Ibid.

26 UNECWA, *Statistical Abstract of the ECWA Region*, 1982, p. 122.

27 Calculated from ibid, and UN, *National Accounts Statistics: Analysis of Main Aggregates 1986*, New York, 1989, p. 396.

28 The real value of health expenditure is derived by deflating health expenditure by the price index for medical and health services.

29 Central Statistical Organization, *Annual Abstract of Statistics 1988*, Baghdad, undated, pp. 46 and 49.

30 See UNICEF, *The State of the World's Children 1988*, New York, Oxford University Press, 1988, p. 68; and UNICEF, *The State of the World's Children 1991*, p. 106.

31 Abbas F. Al-Saadi, 'Infant Mortality and the Economic Embargo in Iraq', *Population Bulletin of UNESCWA*, No. 44, 1996, pp. 45–6.

32 Ibid, p. 54.

33 Haris Gazdar and Athar Hussain, 'Crisis and Response: A Study of the Impact of Economic Sanctions in Iraq', in Kamil A. Mahdi (ed.) *Iraq's Economic Predicament*, Ithaca Press, Reading UK, 2002, pp. 30–83, p. 73.

34 See Giovanni Cornia, 'Country Experience with Adjustment', in Giovanni Cornia, Richard Jolly and Frances Stewart (eds.), *Adjustment with a Human Face*, Vol. 1, Clarendon Press, New York, 1987, pp. 105–27.

35 Giovanni Cornia, 'Investing in Human Resources: Health, Nutrition and Development in the 1990s'. In Keith Griffin and John Knight (eds.), *Human Development and the International Development Strategy for the 1990s*, Macmillan, London, 1990, pp. 175–6.
36 Giovanni Cornia, 'Country Experience', p. 109.
37 Ibid, pp. 123–4.
38 Hanna Batatu, *The Old Social Classes*.

6 The position of women

1 See Amatrya Sen, *Development as Freedom*, Chapter 8.
2 All figures, except those for Iraq, are taken from Amatrya Sen, *Development as Freedom*, pp. 104–5. Estimates for Iraq are calculated from Central Statistical Organization, *Annual Abstract of Statistics 1998–1999*, Baghdad, undated, p. 47.
3 See, for example, Ray Strachey, *The Cause: A Short History of the Woman's Movement in Great Britain*, Virago Press, London, 1978.
4 Tarik M. Yousef, 'Development, Growth and Policy Reform in the Middle East and North Africa', *Journal of Economic Perspectives*, Vol. 18, No. 3, Summer 2004, pp. 91–115.
5 World Bank, *Gender and Development in the Middle East and North Africa: Women in the Public Sphere*, Washington DC, 2004.
6 See, for example, Bernard Lewis, *What Went Wrong? Western Impact and Middle Eastern Response*, Oxford University Press, Oxford UK, 2002.
7 See, for instance, Bernard Lewis, *What Went Wrong?*, Chapter 3.
8 Nawal El Saadawi, *The Hidden Face of Eve*, Sherif Hetata (trans.), Zed Books, London, 1980, p. 184; and Judith E. Tucker, 'The Arab Family in History: "Otherness" and the Study of the Family', in *Arab Women*, Judith Tucker (ed.), Indiana University Press, Indianapolis IN, 1984, p. 203.
9 Gabriel Baer, *Population and Society in the Arab East*, Hanna Szoke (trans.), Praeger, New York, 1964.
10 Madelain Farah, 'Marriage and Sexuality in Islam: A Translation of al-Ghazali's Book on the Etiquette of Marriage from the Ihya', University of Utah, Salt Lake City, 1984, pp. 106–13, *Women in Islam and the Middle East*, Ruth Roded (ed.), Tauris, London, 1990, p. 159.
11 Doreen Ingram, *The Awakened: Women in Iraq*, Beirut, 1983, p. 50.
12 Gabriel Baer, *Population and Society*, pp. 37–8.
13 Ibid., p. 36.
14 Ibid., p. 45.
15 Noel Coulson and Doreen Hinchcliffe, 'Women and Law Reform in Contemporary Islam', in *Women in the Muslim World*, Lois Beck and Nikki Keddie (eds.), Harvard University Press, Cambridge, 1978, p. 45.
16 Ihsan al-Hassan, *The Effects of Industrialization on the Social Status of Iraqi Woman*, General Federation of Iraqi Women, Baghdad, Iraq, 1980, pp. 10–11.
17 Doreen Ingram, *The Awakened*, 1983, p. 52.
18 Noel Coulson and Doreen Hinchcliffe, 'Women and Law Reform', p. 46.
19 Doreen Ingram, *The Awakened*, p. 52.
20 Gabriel Baer, *Population and Society*, p. 39.
21 Ibid., p. 40.
22 Ruth Roded (ed.), *Women in Islam and the Middle East: A Reader*, Introduction, Tauris Publishers, London, 1999, pp. 1–23.
23 See John C. Caldwell, *The Theory of Fertility Decline*, Academic Press, London, 1982, pp. 206–8 and pp. 353–6.

24 Ibid., pp. 208–11.
25 Deniz Kandiyoti, 'End of Empire; Islam, Nationalism and Women in Turkey', in *Women Islam and the State*, Deniz Kandiyoti (ed.), Temple University Press, Philadelphia PA, 1991, pp. 22–47, p. 39.
26 See Jacqueline Ismael, 'Social Policy and Social Change: The Case of Iraq', *Arab Studies Quarterly*, Vol. 2, No. 3, 1980, pp. 235–47; Suad Joseph, 'Elite Strategies for State Building: Women, Family, Religion and the State', in *Women Islam and the State*, pp. 176–22; and Suad Joseph, 'The Mobilization of Iraqi Women into the Wage Labor Force', *Studies in Third World Societies*, No. 16, Boswell Printing, Williamsburg, 1982, pp. 69–90.
27 Deniz Kandiyoti, 'Introduction', in *Women Islam and the State*.
28 Ibid.
29 Sherifa Zuhur, 'Women and Empowerment in the Arab World', *Arab Studies Quarterly*, Vol. 25, No. 4, Fall 2003, pp. 17–38, p. 19.
30 See, for example, M. Ghoussoub, 'Feminism – or the Eternal Masculine – in the Arab World', *New Left Review*, January/February 1987, pp. 3–13.
31 For a discussion of the data, see Chapter 4.
32 A. A. al-Rubaiy and K. F. al-Zubaidy, 'Knowledge Within Reach: Iraq's response to the Illiteracy Dilemma', *Educational Research Quarterly*, Vol. 12, No. 4, 1990, pp. 53–61, p. 57.
33 Christopher Lucas, 'Arab Illiteracy and the Mass Literacy Campaign in Iraq', *Comparative Education Review*, Vol. 25, No. 1, February 1981, pp. 74–84, p. 82.
34 For definitions and a discussion of the data see Chapter 4.
35 See Amatrya Sen, *Development as Freedom*, pp. 193–5.
36 Unfortunately, no data are available after the 1978/9 academic year.
37 Calculated from Central Statistical Organization, *Annual Abstract of Statistics 1978*, pp. 226 and 229.
38 Calculated from Central Statistical Organization, *Annual Abstract of Statistics 1989*, pp. 251 and 254.
39 See Alan Richards and John Waterbury, *A Political Economy of the Middle East*, 1998, Chapter 4.
40 The rate of economic activity is obtained by dividing the 7 years and older population that is engaged in work (paid or unpaid) by the total 7 years and above population.
41 Alan Richards and John Waterbury, *A Political Economy of the Middle East*, 1998, pp. 83–4.
42 Fawzia al-Attia, 'Social and Cultural Change and their Effects on Women's Participation in National Development in the Arab Gulf Region', (in Arabic), In *Man and Society in the Arab Gulf*, Vol. 1, Basrah University Centre for Arab Gulf Studies, Baghdad, 1979, p. 131.
43 Calculated from table 2/18 in Central Statistical Organization, *Annual Abstract of Statistics 1989*, Baghdad, 1990, p. 107.
44 Central Statistical Organization, *The General Census of 1977*, p. 127.
45 Central Statistical Organization, *Annual Abstract of Statistics 1989*, p. 45.
46 Central Statistical Organization, *The General Census of 1977*, p. 126.
47 Central Statistical Organization, *Annual Abstract of Statistics 1989*, p. 45.
48 Central Statistical Organization, *The General Census of 1977*, p. 126.
49 Central Statistical Organization, *Annual Abstract of Statistics 1989*, p. 45.
50 See Rebecca Miles, 'Employment and Unemployment in Jordan: The Importance of the Gender System', *World Development*, Vol. 30, No. 3, 2002, pp. 413–26.
51 Calculated from Central Statistical Organization, *Numbers and Indicators: Population and Work Force* (in Arabic), Baghdad, Undated, p. 16.

52 Ibid.
53 Calculated from Central Statistical Organization, *Annual Abstract of Statistics 1973*, Baghdad, Undated, pp. 416–417.
54 Calculated from Central Statistical Organization, *Numbers and Indicators: Population*, p. 16.
55 Alan Richards and John Waterbury, *A Political Economy of the Middle East*, 1998, p. 138.
56 Tarik M. Yousef, 'Development, Growth and Policy Reform in the Middle East', p. 103.
57 Suad Joseph, 'The Mobilization of Iraqi Women into the Wage Labor Force', pp. 76–7.
58 Ibid. p. 69.
59 Keith Griffin, *Alternative Strategies for Economic Development*, Macmillan, London, 1989, p. 39.
60 Sana al-Khayyat, *Honour and Shame: Women in Modern Iraq*, Saqi Books, London, 1990.
61 Janeen Baxter, 'Gender Equality and Participation in Housework: A Cross-National Perspective', *Journal of Comparative Family Studies*, Vol. 28, Autumn 1997, pp. 220–47.
62 J. N. D. Anderson, 'A Law of Personal Status for Iraq', *International and Comparative Law Quarterly*, Vol. 9, Part 4, 1960, pp. 542–63, p. 543.
63 Ibid., p. 553.
64 Gabriel Baer, *Population and Society*, p. 55.
65 J. N. D. Anderson, 'A Law of Personal Status', p. 558.
66 Ibid., p. 555.
67 Ibid., p. 559.
68 Ibid., p. 558.
69 Ibid., p. 563.
70 See Amal Rassam, 'Revolution Within the Revolution? Women and the State in Iraq', in *Iraq: The Contemporary State*, Tim Niblock (ed.), Croom Helm, London, 1982, pp. 93–6.
71 Jamal J. Nasir, *The Status of Women Under Islamic Law and Modern Islamic Legislation*, Graham and Trotman, London, 1994, p. 145.
72 See Jamal J. Nasir, *The Status of Women Under Islamic Law*, for a comparison of these laws with those of other Arab countries.
73 Suha Omar, 'Women: Honour, Shame and Dictatorship', in *Iraq Since the Gulf War: Prospects for Democracy*, Fran Hazelton (ed.), Zed Books, London, 1994, pp. 60–71, p. 66. For more on Saddam Hussein's viewpoint on the rights of women, see his *Social and Foreign Affairs in Iraq*, Khalid Kishtainy (trans.), London, Croom Helm, 1979, pp. 35-41.
74 Hanna Batatu, 'Iraq's Underground Shia Movements: Characteristics, Causes and Prospects', *The Middle East Journal*, Vol. 35, 1981, p. 593.
75 Amal Rassam, 'Revolution Within', p. 97.
76 Suad Joseph, 'The Mobilization of Iraqi Women into the Wage Labor Force'.
77 Samir al-Khalil, *The Republic of Fear: The Politics of Modern Iraq*, Berkeley CA, University of California Press, 1989.
78 For a brief but informative explanation of how the high level of illiteracy was impeding the development programs in Iraq, see Abbas Salih Mehdi and Olive Robinson, 'Economic Development and the Labour Market in Iraq', *International Journal of Manpower*, Vol. 4, No. 2, p. 26.
79 Abdul A. al-Rubaiy and Khawla F. al-Zubaidy, 'Knowledge Within Reach: Iraq's Response to the Illiteracy Dilemma', *Educational Research Quarterly*, Vol. 12, No. 4, 1990, p. 59.
80 Amal Rassam, 'Revolution Within', p. 96.

81 Samir al-Khalil, *The Republic of Fear*, p. 92.
82 Arab Ba'th Socialist Party, *The 1968 Revolution in Iraq: Experience and Prospects*, The Political Report of the Eighth Congress of the Arab Ba'th Socialist Party in Iraq January 1974, London, Ithaca Press, 1979 p. 115.
83 Saddam Hussain, *Social and Foreign Affairs*, p. 16.
84 Ibid.
85 Deborah Cobbett, 'Women in Iraq', in *Saddam's Iraq: Revolution or Reaction*, London, Zed Books, pp. 120–37, p. 126; and Suha Omar, 'Women', p. 65.
86 Christine Moss Helms, *Iraq: The Eastern Flank of the Arab World*, Washington DC, The Brookings Institution, 1984, p. 99.
87 This was Revolutionary Command Council Decision 1110. See Suha Omar, 'Women', p. 64.

7 Human rights and political freedoms

1 UNDP, *Human Development Report 2000*, Oxford University Press, New York, 2000, pp. 20–1.
2 See Majid Khadduri, *Socialist Iraq*, The Middle East Institute, Washington DC, 1978, Appendix A, pp. 183–98.
3 This figure is an average for the period June 1947 to September 1948. The subsequent clampdown on Communist activity meant that the paper did not appear for some months after January 1948. See Hanna Batatu, *The Old Social Classes*, p. 607.
4 For an excellent exploration of the intellectual currents in Iraq in the 10 years that preceded the 1958 revolution and immediately thereafter see Abdul-Salaam Yousif, 'The Struggle for Cultural Hegemony During The Iraqi Revolution', in *The Iraqi Revolution of 1958*, Robert A. Fernea and Roger Louis (eds.), Tauris Publishers, London, 1991.
5 Samir al-Khalil, *Republic of Fear: The Politics of Modern Iraq*, University of California Press, Berkeley, 1989, p. 85.
6 U. Zaher, 'The Opposition', In *Saddam's Iraq: Revolution or Reaction*, Zed Books, London, 1986, p. 164.
7 See Hanna Batatu, *The Old Social Classes*, p. 859.
8 Ibid, p. 1110.
9 Article 19, *Freedom of Information and Expression in Iraq*, London, 1987, p. 28.
10 Central Statistical Organization, *Annual Abstract of Statistics 1989*, Baghdad, undated, p. 366.
11 See Majid Kadduri, *Independent Iraq 1932-58*, Oxford University Press, London, 1960.
12 Hanna Batatu, *The Old Social Classes*, p. 744.
13 Ibid., p. 1198.
14 Ibid., p. 690.
15 Ibid., pp. 742–3.
16 Samir al-Khalil, *The Republic of Fear*, p. 227.
17 Central Statistical Organization, *Numbers and Indicators: Population and Workforce* (in Arabic), Baghdad, undated, p. 4.
18 See Majid Khadduri, *Republican Iraq*, pp. 137–47.
19 Samir al-Khalil, *The Republic of Fear*, p. 224.
20 Hanna Batatu, *The Old Social Classes*, p. 1078.
21 Christine Moss Helms, *Iraq: Eastern Flank of the Arab World*, Washington DC, 1984, p. 87.
22 Data are obtained from a variety of sources that are not always in agreement so

an attempt has been made to draw the most plausible inferences from the data.

23 See Amnesty International, <http://www.amnestyusa.org/abolish/abret2.html>, accessed 10-12-05

24 Uriel Dann, *Iraq Under Qassem*, Praeger, New York, 1969, p. 87.

25 U. Zaher, 'The Opposition', in *Saddam's Iraq*, p. 143.

26 A. Abbas, 'The Iraqi armed Forces, Past and Present', in *Saddam's Iraq: Revolution or Reaction*, Zed Books, London, 1986, p. 214.

27 Amnesty International, *The Death Penalty*, Amnesty International Publications, London 1979, p. 172.

28 See Amnesty International, *The Death Penalty*, addenda and update section; and Marion Farouk Sluglett and Peter Sluglett, *Iraq Since 1958*, Routledge and Kegan, New York, 1986, p. 186.

29 Mohamed Zainy, *The Iraqi Economy Under the Regime of Saddam Hussein*, (in Arabic), al-Rafid, London, 1996, p. 445.

30 Human Rights Watch, *Human Rights in Iraq*, Yale University Press, London, 1990, p. 23.

31 Human Rights Watch, *Human Rights in Iraq*, Yale University Press, London, 1990, p. 27.

32 See Isam al-Khafaji, al-Khafaji, Isam, 'State Terror and the Degradation of Politics in Iraq', *Middle East Report*, Vol. 22, No. 3, May-June 1992, pp. 15–22.

33 Charles Tripp, *A History of Iraq*, p. 237.

34 Stephen Longrigg, *Iraq, 1900 to 1950*, Oxford University Press, London, 1953, p. 242.

35 The same Bakr Sidqi was largely behind the army's bloody suppression of the Assyrians in northern Iraq where perhaps 3,000 Assyrians were killed under the blown up pretext of rebellion. See R. S. Stafford, *The Tragedy of the Assyrians*, Allen and Unwin, London, 1935.

36 A. Abbas, 'The Iraqi Armed Forces, Past and Present', in *Saddam's Iraq*, p. 213. It is doubtful that these sentences were ever carried out, especially as it has been noted elsewhere that the "Communist soldiers who had been rounded up in 1937" were freed by the Rashid Ali government in 1941, in response to Communist support for the government's anti-British position. See Hanna Batatu, *The Old Social Classes*, p. 455.

37 Majid Khadduri, *Independent Iraq*, pp. 237–8.

38 The leaders were Yusuf Salman Yusuf , also known as Fahd, the legendary leader of the party, Zaki Basim, and Mohammed Al-Shabibi. See Hanna Batatu, *The Old Social Classes*, pp. 537–71.

39 U. Zaher, 'The Opposition', In *Saddam's Iraq*, p. 147.

40 Uriel Dann, *Iraq Under Qassem*, p. 47.

41 Thus on 20 September 1959, the former head of the political police, the former interior minister, and two other officials of the old regime were executed. See Uriel Dann, *Iraq Under Qassem*, Praeger, New York, 1969, p.249.

42 According to the ICP, in the three days following the coup, 5000 Communists were killed either in open confrontation with the new regime or in the countrywide search for Communists that began soon after the fighting stopped. See U. Zaher, 'The Opposition', in *Saddam's Iraq*, p. 32.

43 Hanna Batatu, *The Old Social Classes*, p. 989.

44 A subsequent Iraq Government investigation into the atrocities committed by the Ba'th uncovered that, among other things, the Ba'thist National Guard Special Investigations Bureau alone had killed 104 persons. It is therefore exceedingly unlikely that the total number of Communists and other leftists deprived of life was as low as the official Ba'th figures suggest. See Republic of Iraq, *Al-Munharifun* (The Deviationists) (in Arabic), Baghdad, 1964.

45 Public Broadcasting Corporation (PBS) Frontline, *The Survival of Saddam*, January 2000, <http://www.pbs.org/wgbh/pages/frontline/shows/saddam>, accessed 10-22-05.
46 Charles Tripp, *A History of Iraq*, p. 171.
47 Hanna Batatu, *The Old Social Classes*, p. 989.
48 Marion Farouk Sluglett and Peter Sluglett, *Iraq Since 1958*, p. 86.
49 Samir al-Khalil, *The Republic of Fear*, p. 56.
50 Hanna Batatu, *The Old Social Classes*, pp. 1093–1110.
51 Ibid.
52 Majid Khadduri, *Socialist Iraq*, pp. 67–9; and Hanna Batatu, *The Old Social Classes*, p. 1093.
53 Amnesty International, *The Death Penalty*, p. 173.
54 Human Rights Watch, *Human Rights in Iraq*, p. 49. Marion Farouk Sluglett and Peter Sluglett, *Iraq Since 1958*, p. 186, gives the number of executed Communist soldiers as 12.
55 Marion Farouk Sluglett and Peter Sluglett, *Iraq Since 1958*, p. 209
56 Samir al-Khalil, *The Republic of Fear*, p. 70.
57 Amnesty International, *When the State Kills*, pp. 152–3.
58 One report from a mother who was burying her executed son, in the Shia holy city of Najaf, in the middle of 1982 may indicate the extent of this undercounting. She was told by the person conducting the burial that 300 people who bore the marks of torture had been buried there in the last week. It is always very difficult to measure the accuracy of such reports, but the content of the mother's testimony is not inconsistent with accounts of this type. Furthermore, the 300 tortured persons who had been buried could not have been confused with casualties of the ongoing war with Iran since the attendant makes the distinction between torture victims and war "martyrs", as the war dead were called. See 'Interview with an Iraqi Mother, Ba'th Terror–Two Personal Accounts', In *Saddam's Iraq*, p. 113.
59 Hanna Batatu, *The Old Social Classes*, pp. 1099–1100.
60 The word *anfal* literally means "the spoils [of war]". The term appears in the Holy Quran and is the title of the eighth *sura*.
61 For a detailed discussion of the *Anfal* campaign see Human Rights Watch, *Iraq's Crime of Genocide*, Yale University Press, New Haven, 1995. For government reports that meticulously document the regime's actions see Human Rights Watch, *Bureaucracy of Repression: The Iraqi Government in Its own Words*, Yale University Press, 1994.
62 Human Rights Watch, *Iraq's Crime of Genocide*, p. 230.
63 Law 666 of 7 May 1980 withdrew Iraqi citizenship from "every Iraqi of foreign extraction, if it is apparent that he is not in support of the nation, the people, and the [Arab] nationalist aims of the [Ba'thist 17th of July] revolution." The critical phrase "of foreign extraction" was applied liberally to include those persons who were themselves Iraqi, or even those whose fathers' were Iraqi, but had foreign (usually Iranian) grandfathers. See Abdul Karim al-Uzri, Abdul Karim al-Uzri, *The Problematic of Government in Iraq*, (in Arabic), London, 1991, p. 281.
64 Samir al-Khalil, *The Republic of Fear*.
65 Abdul Karim al-Uzri, *The Problematic of Government in Iraq*, p. 106.
66 Phebe Marr, 'The Political Elite in Iraq', in *Political Elites in The Middle East*, George Lenczowski (ed.), American Enterprise Institute, Washington DC, 1975, p. 133.
67 See Abdul Karim al-Uzri, *The Problematic of Government in Iraq*, p. 106.
68 See Hanna Batatu's chapter 'The Shaikhs, Aghas, and Peasants', in *The Old Social Classes*, pp. 63–152.

69 Hanna Batatu, *The Old Social Classes*, p. 748.
70 Ibid., pp.1078–9.
71 Hanna Batatu, 'Iraq Underground Shia Movements: Characteristics, Causes and Prospects', *The Middle East Journal*, Vol. 35, 1981.
72 Calculated from Central Statistical Organization, *Annual Abstract of Statistics 1983*, Baghdad, undated, p. 49.
73 Marion Farouk Sluglett and Peter Sluglett, *Iraq Since 1958*, p. 135.
74 Amatzia Baram, 'Neo-Tribalism in Iraq: Saddam Hussein's Tribal Policies', *International Journal of Middle Eastern Studies*, Vol. 29, No. 1, February 1997, pp. 1–31.
75 See Amatzia Baram, *Culture, History and Ideology in the formation of Ba'thist Iraq, 1968-89*, St. Martin's Press, New York, 1991.
76 See PBS Frontline, '*The Survival of Saddam.*, <http://www.pbs.org/wgbh/pages/frontline/shows/saddam/> accessed 12-11-09.
77 See Samir al-Khalil, *Republic of Fear*, pp. 120–124, for a discussion of this point.
78 Thom Workman, *The Social Origins of the Iran-Iraq War*, Lynne Rienner Publishers, London, 1994.
79 Charles Humana, *World Human Rights Guide*, Facts on File Publications, New York, 1986.
80 An earlier form of this Humana Index study appears in Bassam Yousif and Eric Davis, 'Iraq: Understanding Autocracy, Oil and Conflict in a Historical and Socio-Political Context', in *Democracy in the Arab World: Explaining the Deficit*, Ibrahim al-Badawi and Samir Makdisi (eds.), Routledge, 2010. As this is an updated and revised survey, it contains more comprehensive explanations of scores of the rights and freedoms of the index (in the Appendix) and, consequently, the results differ slightly from the original study.
81 For text of this document see Charles Humana, *World Human Rights Guide*, pp. 325–27.
82 Principal Bureau of Statistics, *Statistical Abstract 1939*, Baghdad, 1939, p. 65. These figures do not include those who were executed for taking part in the numerous tribal uprisings of the time.
83 Central Bureau of Statistics, *Statistical Abstract 1961*, Baghdad, 1962, p. 238.
84 Amnesty International, *When the State Kills*, p. 152.
85 Charles Humana, *World Human Rights Guide*, p. 132.
86 Thom Workman, *The Social Origins of the Iran-Iraq War*, p. 157.
87 Charles Tripp, *A History of Iraq*, pp. 235–6.

8 Conclusion

1 An important theme in Hanna Batatu, *The Old Social* Classes, and more recently Eric Davis, *Memories of State: Politics, History and Collective Identity in Modern Iraq*, University of California Press, Berkeley and Los Angeles CA, 2005 (especially Chapter 3) is that substantial public support for equalizing development has existed in Iraq since the 1930s.
2 See Sami Zubaida, 'Democracy, Iraq and the middle east', *Open Democracy*, 2005. http://www.opendemocracy.net/democracy-opening/iraq_3042.jsp. Accessed 11-22-10. See also, Bassam Yousif, 'The Political Economy of Sectarianism in Iraq, *International Journal of Contemporary Iraqi Studies*, 2011, Vol. 4, No. 3, pp. 357–367, for a discussion of how socioeconomic factors have combined to elevate sectarianism in Iraq.

Appendix: The Humana Index

1 Charles Humana, *World Human Rights Guide*, Facts on File Publications, New York, 1986, p. 2.
2 See Hanna Batatu, *The Old Social Classes*, p. 133.
3 For example, the police opened fire on striking oil workers in what came to be known as the massacre of Gawarpaghi in 1946 and in the Wathba of 1948. Ibid., p. 623.
4 Personal conversations with persons who were students and teachers at the time of the monarchy and under the Qassen regime.
5 See See Hanna Batatu, *The Old Social Classes*, p. 537 and Uriel Dann, *Iraq under Qassem*, p. 248.
6 See Human Rights Watch, *Human Rights in Iraq*, pp. 118–21; and Charles Humana, *World Human Rights Guide*, p. 132.
7 See Hanna Batatu, *The Old Social Classes*, pp. 63–152.
8 Ibid., p. 841.
9 See Hanna Batatu, *The Old Social Classes*, p. 954.
10 See Amnesty International, *Torture in the Eighties*, London, 1984, p. 231; and Amnesty International, *When the State Kills*, p. 153.
11 See Fran Hazelton, Iraq to 1963, In *Saddam's Iraq*, p. 21.
12 See Human Rights Watch, *Human Rights in Iraq*.
13 See Sati al-Husri', *My Memoirs in Iraq*, (in Arabic), Volume 1, Al-Talia' Press, Beirut, 1967.
14 See Human Rights Watch, *Human Rights in Iraq*, pp. 22–3.
15 See Hanna Batatu, *The Old Social Classes*, pp. 604–27 and 943–65.
16 See Marion-Farouk Sluglett, and Peter Sluglett, *Iraq Since 1958*, p. 139.
17 Hanna Batatu, *The Old Social Classes*, p. 444.

References

Abbas, A., 'The Iraqi Armed Forces, Past and Present', in *Saddam's Iraq: Revolution or Reaction*, Zed Books, London, 1986, pp. 203–226.

Adetunji, Jacob, 'Infant Mortality Rates in Africa: Does Method of Estimation Matter?', Harvard Center for Population and Development Studies, <http://www.hsph.harvard.edu/hcpds/wpweb/95_03.pdfa>, accessed 7-18-05.

Aflaq, Michel, *For the Sake of the Baath*, (in Arabic), al-Talai Press, Beirut, 1959.

al-Ansari, Fadhil, *The Population Issue: The Case of Iraq* (in Arabic), Ministry of Culture Press, Damascus, 1980.

Alesina, Alberto and Dani Rodrik, 'Distributive Politics and Economic Growth', *The Quarterly Journal of Economics*, Vol. 109, No. 2, May 1994, pp. 465–490.

Alnasrawi, Abbas, 'Economic Devastation, Underdevelopment and Outlook', in *Iraq Since the Gulf War: Prospects for Democracy*, Fran Hazelton (ed.), Zed Books, London, 1994, pp. 72–96.

Alnasrawi, Abbas, *The Economy of Iraq: Oil, Wars, Destruction of Development and Prospects, 1950-2010*, Greenwood Press, London, 1994.

Alnasrawi, Abbas, *Iraq's Burdens: Oil, Sanctions and Underdevelopment*, Greenwood Press, London, 2002.

Amnesty International, *The Death Penalty*, Amnesty International Publications, London, 1979.

Amnesty International, *Report and Recommendations of an Amnesty International Mission to The Government of the Republic of Iraq 22 – 28 January 1983*, Amnesty International Publications, London, 1983.

Amnesty International, *Torture in the Eighties*, London, 1984.

Amnesty International, *When the state Kills*, Amnesty International Publications, London, 1989.

Amnesty International, *Iraq Disappearances: Unsolved Cases Since the early 1980s*, London, October 1997.

Amnesty International, 'Guantánamo Bay – a human rights scandal', undated, <http://www.amnestyusa.org/war-on-terror/guantanamo-bay—a-human-rights-scandal/page.do?id=1108202>, accessed 3-03-09.

Amnesty International, <http://www.amnestyusa.org/abolish/abret2.html>, accessed 10-12-05

Amsden, Alice, *Asia's Next Giant: South Korea and Late Industrialization*, Oxford University Press, 1989.

Anderson, J. N. D., 'A Law of Personal Status for Iraq', *International and Comparative Law Quarterly*, Vol. 9, Part 4, 1960, pp. 542–63, p. 543.

Anderson, Lisa, 'The State in the Middle East and North Africa', *Comparative Politics*, Vol. 20, No. 1, October 1987.

Arab Ba'th Socialist Party, *The 1968 Revolution in Iraq: Experience and Prospects*, The Political Report of the Eighth Congress of the Arab Ba'th Socialist Party in Iraq, January 1974, Ithaca Press, London, 1979.

Article 19, *Freedom of Information and Expression in Iraq*, London, 1987.

al-Attia, Fawzia, 'Social and Cultural Change and their Effects on Women's Participation in National Development in the Arab Gulf Region' (in Arabic), in *Man and Society in the Arab Gulf*, Vol. 1, Basrah University Centre for Arab Gulf Studies, Baghdad, 1979.

Baer, Gabriel, *Population and Society in the Middle East*, Praeger Press, New York, 1966.

Baram, Amatzia, *Culture, History and Ideology in the Formation of Ba'thist Iraq, 1968-89*, St. Martin's Press, New York, 1991.

Baram, Amatzia, 'Neo-Tribalism in Iraq: Saddam Hussein's Tribal Policies', *International Journal of Middle Eastern Studies*, Vol. 29, No. 1, February 1997, pp. 1–31.

Batatu, Hanna, The *Old Social Classes and Revolutionary Movements of Iraq: A Study of Iraq's Old Landed and Commercial Classes and of its Communists, Ba'thists and Free Officers*, Princeton University Press, Princeton NJ, 1978.

Batatu, Hanna, 'Iraq's Underground Shia Movements: Characteristics, Causes and Prospects', *Middle East Journal*, Vol. 35, No. 4, 1981, pp. 578–94.

Baxter, Janeen, 'Gender Equality and Participation in Housework: A Cross-National Perspective', *Journal of Comparative Family Studies*, Vol. 28, Autumn 1997, pp. 220–244.

Beblawi, Hazem, 'The Rentier State in the Arab World', in *The Rentier State*, H. Beblawi and G. Luciani, (eds.), Croom Helm, London, 1987, pp. 85–98.

Becker, Gary, *Human Capital: A Theoretical and Empirical Analysis, with Special Reference to Education*, Chicago, University of Chicago Press, 3rd ed., 1993.

Birks, J. S. and Sinclair, C., 'The Challenge of Human Resources Development in Iraq', in *Iraq: the Contemporary State*, Tim Niblock (ed.), Croom Helm, London, 1982, pp. 241–255.

Bureau of Statistics, *Statistical Abstract for the Financial Years 1927/28 to 1937/38*, Government Press, Baghdad, 1939.

Caldwell, John C., *The Theory of Fertility Decline*, Academic Press, London, 1982.

Central Bureau of Statistics, *Statistical Abstract 1960*, Zahra Press, Baghdad, 1961.

Central Bureau of Statistics, *Statistical Abstract 1961*, Baghdad, 1962.

Central Bureau of Statistics, *Statistical Abstract 1962*, Baghdad, 1963.

Central Statistical Organization, *General Population Census of 1965*, Baghdad, 1973.

Central Statistical Organization, *Statistical Abstract 1967*, Government Press, Baghdad, 1968.

Central Statistical Organization, *National Income in Iraq: Selected Studies*, Shafik Press, Baghdad, 1970.

Central Statistical Organization, *Annual Abstract of Statistics 1970*, Baghdad, undated.

Central Statistical Organization, *Annual Abstract of Statistics 1971*, Baghdad, undated.

Central Statistical Organization, *Annual Abstract of Statistics 1972*, Baghdad, undated.

Central Statistical Organization, *Annual Abstract of Statistics 1973*, Baghdad, undated.

Central Statistical Organization, *Annual Abstract of Statistics 1974*, Baghdad, undated.

Central Statistical Organization, *Annual Abstract of Statistics 1975*, Baghdad, undated.

Central Statistical Organization, *Annual Abstract of Statistics 1976*, Baghdad, undated.

Central Statistical Organization, *Annual Abstract of Statistics 1978*, Baghdad, undated.

Central Statistical Organization, *Annual Abstract of Statistics 1980*, Baghdad, undated.

Central Statistical Organization, *Annual Abstract of Statistics 1982*, Baghdad, undated.

Central Statistical Organization, *Annual Abstract of Statistics 1983*, Baghdad, undated.

Central Statistical Organization, *Annual Abstract of Statistics 1985*, Baghdad, undated.

Central Statistical Organization, *Annual Abstract of Statistics 1987*, Baghdad, undated.

Central Statistical Organization, *Annual Abstract of Statistics 1988*, Baghdad, undated.

Central Statistical Organization, *Annual Abstract of Statistics 1989*, Baghdad, 1990.

Central Statistical Organization, *Annual Abstract of Statistics 1990*, Baghdad, 1991.

Central Statistics Organization, *Annual Abstract of Statistics 1991*, Baghdad, 1992.

Central Statistical Organization, *Annual Abstract of Statistics 1993*, Baghdad, 1994.

Central Statistical Organization, *Annual Abstract of Statistics 1998–1999*, Baghdad, undated.

Central Statistical Organization, *Numbers and Indicators: Educational and Social Services* (in Arabic), Baghdad, undated.

Central Statistical Organization, *Numbers and Indicators: Population and Work Force* (in Arabic), Baghdad, undated.

Central Statistical Organization, *The General Census of the 1977* (in Arabic), Baghdad, undated.

Chaudhry, Kiren Aziz, 'Consuming Interests: Market Failure and the Social Foundations of Iraqi Etatisme', in Kamil A. Mahdi (ed.) *Iraq's Economic Predicament*, Ithaca Press, Reading UK, 2002, pp. 233–265.

Chaudhry, Kiren Aziz, 'Economic Liberalization and the Lineages of the Rentier State', *Comparative Politics*, Vol. 27., No. 1, October 1994, pp. 1–25.

Clark, Victor, *Compulsory Education in Iraq*, UNESCO Press, Paris, 1951.

Cobbett, Deborah 'Women in Iraq', in *Saddam's Iraq: Revolution or Reaction*, Zed Books, London, 1986, pp. 120–137.

Cornia, Giovanni, 'Country Experience with Adjustment', in Giovanni Cornia, Richard Jolly and Frances Stewart (eds.), *Adjustment with a Human Face*, Vol. 1, Clarendon Press, New York, 1987, pp. 105–127.

Cornia, Giovanni, 'Investing in Human Resources: Health, Nutrition and Development in the 1990s', in Keith Griffin and John Knight (eds.), *Human Development and the International Development Strategy for the 1990s*, Macmillan, London, 1990, pp. 159–188.

Coulson, Noel, and Hinchcliffe, Doreen, 'Women and Law Reform in Contemporary Islam', in *Women in the Muslim World*, Lois Beck and Nikki Keddie (eds.), Harvard University Press, Cambridge, 1978.

Dann, Uriel, *Iraq Under Qassem*, Praeger, New York, 1969.

Davis, Eric, *Memories of State: Politics, History and Collective Identity in Modern Iraq*, University of California Press, Berkeley and Los Angeles CA, 2005.

Dasgupta, Indraneel, Review of Sen's *Development as Freedom* in *Economica*, Vol. 73, pp. 157–8.

Deneulin, Severine, 'Promoting Human Freedoms under Conditions of Inequalities: a procedural framework', *The Journal of Human Development*, Vol. 6, No. 1, 2005, pp. 75–92.

Directorate General of Census, *Abstract of the General Census of 1957* (in Arabic), Volume 2, Baghdad, 1964.

Dore, R. P., *The Diploma Disease, Qualification and Development*, Allen and Unwin, London, 1976.

194   *References*

Dreze, Jean and Amartya Sen, *Hunger and Public Action*, Clarendon Press, Oxford, 1989.

FAO, *FAO Trade Yearbook 1979*, Rome, 1980.

FAO, *FAO Trade Yearbook 1988*, Rome, 1990.

Farah, Madelain, 'Marriage and Sexuality in Islam: A Translation of al-Ghazali's Book on the Etiquette of Marriage from the Ihya', University of Utah, Salt Lake City, 1984, pp. 106–113, in *Women in Islam and the Middle East*, Ruth Roded (ed.), Tauris, London, 1990.

Gabbay, Rony, *Communism and Agrarian Reform in Iraq*, Croom Helm, London, 1978.

de Gaury, Gerald, *Three Kings in Baghdad: 1921-1958*, Hutchinson, London, 1961.

Gazdar, Haris and Athar Hussain, 'Crisis and Response: A Study of the Impact of Economic Sanctions in Iraq', in Kamil A. Mahdi (ed.) *Iraq's Economic Predicament*, Ithaca Press, Reading UK, 2002, pp. 30–83.

General Federation of Iraqi Women: *A Practical Translation to the Objectives of the Revolution in Work and Creativity*, Baghdad, 1980.

Ghoussoub, M., 'Feminism – or the Eternal Masculine – in the Arab World', *New Left Review*, No. 161, January/February 1987, pp. 3-13.

Griffin, Keith and John Knight, 'Human Development: The Case for Renewed Emphasis', in Keith Griffin and John Knight (eds.), *Human Development and the International Development Strategy for the 1990s*, Macmillan, London 1990, pp. 9–40; reprinted as 'Human Development: The Case for Renewed Emphasis', in Wilber and Jameson (eds.), *The Political Economy of Development and Underdevelopment*, 5th edition, McGraw Hill, 1992, pp. 576–609.

Griffin, Keith and Terry McKinley, *Implementing a Human Development Strategy*, St. Martin's Press, New York, 1994.

Griffin, Keith, *Alternative Strategies for Economic Development*, Macmillan, London, 1989.

de Haan, Jakob and Clemens Siermann, 'New evidence on the relationship between democracy and economic growth', *Public Choice*, Vol. 86, No. 1–2, 1996, pp. 175–98.

Helliwell, John F., 'Empirial Linkages Between Democracy and Economic Growth', National Bureau of Economic Research, Working Paper No. W4066, May 1992.

Huntington, Samuel, *Political Order in Changing Societies*, Yale University Press, New Haven CT, 1968.

ul-Haq, Mahbub, *Reflections on Human Development*, Oxford University Press, London, 1995.

Haider, Saleh, *Land Problems of Iraq* (unpublished thesis), University of London, 1942, pp. 556–660, printed with omissions in Charles Issawi, The *Economic History of the Middle East 1800-1914*, University of Chicago, Chicago 1966, pp. 164–178.

Hasan, M. S., 'Growth and Structure of Iraq's Population, 1867-1947', *Bulletin of the Oxford University Institute of Statistics*, XX, 1958, pp. 339–53.

al-Hassan, Ihsan, *The Effects of Industrialization on the Social Status of Iraqi Woman*, General Federation of Iraqi Women, Baghdad, Iraq, 1980.

Haseeb, K., *The National Income of Iraq 1953-61*, Oxford University Press, London, 1964.

Hasso, Frances, 'Empowering Governmentalities rather than Women: The *Arab Human Development Report 2005* and Western Development Logics', *International Journal of Middle Eastern Studies*, Vol. 41, No. 1, 2009, pp. 63–82.

Helms, Christine Moss, *Iraq: The Eastern Flank of the Arab World*, The Brookings Institution, Washington DC, 1984.

Hirschman, Albert O., *The Strategy of Economic Development*, Yale University Press, New Haven, 1958.

Hummadi, Ismail Aubaid, *Economic Growth and Structural Changes in the Iraqi Economy with Emphasis on Agriculture: 1953-1975*, Ph.D. Dissertation, University of Colorado: Boulder, 1978.

Human Rights Watch, *Human Rights in Iraq*, Yale University Press, London, 1990.

Human Rights Watch, *Bureaucracy of Repression: The Iraqi Government in its own Words*, Yale University Press, London, 1994.

Human Rights Watch, *Iraq's Crime of Genocide*, Yale University Press, New Haven, 1995.

Humana, Charles, *World Human Rights Guide*, Facts on File Publications, New York, 1986.

Hussein, Saddam, *Saddam Hussein on Current Events in Iraq*, Khalid Kishtainy (trans.), Longman, London, 1977.

Hussein, Saddam, *Social and Foreign Affairs in Iraq*, Khalid Kishtainy (trans.), Croom Helm, London, 1979.

Ingram, Doreen, *The Awakened: Women in Iraq*, Beirut, 1983.

'Interview with an Iraqi Mother, Ba'th Terror – Two Personal Accounts', in *Saddam's Iraq: Revolution or Reaction*, Zed Books, London, 1986, pp. 108–114.

IBRD, *The Economic Development of Iraq*, Washington DC, 1952.

ILO, *Year Book of Labour Statistics: Retrospective Edition on Population Censuses 1945-89*, Geneva, 1990.

IMF, *International Financial Statistics Yearbook 1985*, New York, 1986.

IMF, *International Financial Statistics Yearbook 1986*, New York, 1987.

IMF, *International Financial Statistics Yearbook 1999*, New York, 2000.

Ismael, Jacqueline, 'Social Policy and Social Change: The Case of Iraq', *Arab Studies Quarterly*, Vol. 2, No. 3, 1980, pp. 235–247.

Issa, Shaker M.,'The Distribution of Income in Iraq, 1971', in *The Integration of Modern Iraq*, Abbas Kelidar (ed.), Croom Helm, London, 1979, pp. 123–134.

Jawad, Sa'ad, 'The Kurdish Problem in Iraq', in *The Integration of Modern Iraq*, A. Kelidar (ed.), Croom Helm, London, 1979, pp. 171–181.

Jawad, Sa'ad, 'Recent Developments in the Kurdish Issue', in *Iraq: The Contemporary State*, Tim Niblock (ed.), Croom Helm, London, 1982, pp. 47–61.

al-Jaza'iri, Zuhair, 'Ba'thist Ideology and Practice', in *Iraq Since the Gulf War: Prospects for Democracy*, Fran Hazelton (ed.), Zed Books, London, 1994, pp. 32–51.

Jiyad, Ahmed M., 'The Development of Iraq's Foreign Debt: From Liquidity to Unsustainability', *Iraq's Economic Predicament*, in Kamil A Mehdi (ed.), Ithaca Press, Reading, NY, 2002, pp. 85–137.

Joseph, Suad, 'The Mobilization of Iraqi Women into the Wage Labor Force', *Studies in Third World Societies*, No. 16, Boswell Printing, Williamsburg, 1982, pp. 69–90.

Joseph, Suad, 'Elite Strategies for State Building: Women, Family, Religion and the State', in *Women Islam and the State*, Deniz Kandiyoti (ed.), Temple University Press, Philadelphia PA, 1991, pp. 176–22.

Kandiyoti, Deniz, 'End of Empire; Islam, Nationalism and Women in Turkey', in *Women, Islam and the State*, Deniz Kandiyoti (ed.), Temple University Press, Philadelphia PA, 1991, pp. 22–47.

Khadduri, Majid, *Independent Iraq, 1932-58*, Oxford University Press, London, 1960.

Khadduri, Majid, *Republican Iraq*, Oxford University Press, New York, 1969.

Khadduri, Majid, *Socialist Iraq*, The Middle East Institute, Washington DC, 1978.

al-Khafaji, Isam, 'The Parasitic Base of the Ba'thist Regime', in *Saddam's Iraq: Revolution or Reaction*, Zed Books, London, 1986, pp. 73–84.

al-Khafaji, Isam, *Tormented Births: Passages to Modernity in Europe and the Middle East*, I. B. Tauris Publishers, London, 2004.

al-Khafaji, Isam, 'State Terror and the Degradation of Politics in Iraq', *Middle East Report*, Vol. 22, No. 3, May-June 1992, pp. 15–22.

al-Khalil, Samir, *Republic of Fear: The Politics of Modern Iraq*, University of California Press, Berkeley, 1989.

al-Khayyat, Sana, *Honour and Shame: Women in Modern Iraq*, Saqi Books, London, 1990.

Kelidar, Abbas, 'The Shii Imami Community and Politics in the Arab East', *Middle Eastern Studies*, Vol. 19, No. 1, January 1983, pp. 3–16.

Knight, John B. and Richard H. Sabot, *Education, Productivity and Inequality: The East African Natural Experiment*, Oxford University Press, Oxford, 1990.

Lewis, Bernard, *What Went Wrong? Western Impact and Middle Eastern Response*, Oxford University Press, Oxford, 2002.

Longrigg, S. M., *Iraq, 1900 to 1950*, Oxford University Press, London, 1953.

Longrigg, S. M., *Oil in the Middle East*, Royal Institute of International Affairs, Oxford, 1961.

Lucas, Christopher, 'Mass Mobilization for Illiteracy Eradication in Iraq', *Convergence*, Vol. 15, No. 3, 1982, pp. 19–27.

Luciani, Giacomo, 'Allocation vs. Production States: A Theoretical Framework', in *The Arab State*, G. Luciani, ed., Berkeley and London: University of California Press, 1990, 65–84.

Lukitz, Liora, *Iraq: The Search for National Identity*, Frank Cass, London, 1995.

Mahdavy, Hossein, 'The Patterns and Problems of Economic Development in Rentier States: the Case of Iran', in M.A. Cook, ed., *Studies in the Economic History of the Middle East*, London: Oxford University Press, 1970, 428–467.

Marr, Phebe, 'The Political Elite in Iraq', in *Political Elites in The Middle East*, George Lenczowski (ed.), American Enterprise Institute, Washington DC, 1975, pp. 109–149.

Marr, Phebe, *The Modern History Of Iraq*, Westview Press, Boulder Co, 1985.

Mahdi, Kamil, 'Iraq's Agrarian System: Issues of Policy and Performance', *Iraq's Economic predicament*, in Kamil A. Mahdi (ed.) Ithaca Press, Reading, 2002, pp. 321–341.

Mehdi, Abbas Salih and Robinson, Olive, 'Economic Development and the Labour Market in Iraq', *International Journal of Manpower*, Vol. 4, No. 2, 1983, pp. 1–40.

Miles, Rebecca, 'Employment and Unemployment in Jordan: The Importance of the Gender System', *World Development*, Vol. 30, No. 3, 2002, pp. 413–26.

Ministry of Planning, *Man: The Objective of Revolution*, Baghdad, 1978.

Mobarak, Ahmed Mushfiq, 'Determinants of Volatility and Implications for Economic Development', Research Program on Political and Economic Change, University of Colorado, Boulder, Working Paper PEC2004-0001, January 2004.

Muhsin, Jabr, 'The Gulf War', in *Saddam's Iraq: Revolution or Reaction*, Zed Books, London, 1986, pp. 227–243.

Nasir, Jamal J., *The Status of Women Under Islamic Law and Modern Islamic Legislation*, Graham and Trotman, London, 1994.

Nietzsche, Friedrich, *Beyond Good and Evil*, Penguin Books, New York, 1990.

Nurkse, Ragnar, *Problems of Capital Formation in Underdeveloped Countries*, Oxford University Press, New York, 1953.

Omar, Suha, 'Women: Honour, Shame and Dictatorship', in *Iraq Since the Gulf War: Prospects for Democracy*, Fran Hazelton (ed.), Zed Books, London, 1994, pp. 60–71.

OPEC, *Annual Statistical Bulletin 1994*, Vienna, 1995.

OPEC, *Annual Statistical Bulletin 1998*, Vienna, 1999.

Owen, Roger, *The Middle East in the World Economy 1800-1914*, Tauris, New York, 1993.

Owen, Roger and Sevket Pamuk, *A History of Middle East Economies in the Twentieth Century*, Harvard University Press, Cambridge, 1998.

Pellet, Peter, 'Sanctions, Food, Nutrition and Health in Iraq', in *Iraq Under Siege: The Deadly Impact of sanctions and War*, Anthony Arnove (ed.), South End Press, Cambridge, MA, 2000.

Penrose, Edith, 'Industrial Policy and Performance in Iraq', in *The Integration of Modern Iraq*, Abbas Kelidar (ed.), Croom Helm, London, 1979, pp. 150–169.

Penrose, Edith and E. F. Penrose, *Iraq: International Relations and National Development*, Boulder CO, Westview Press, 1978.

Pfeifer, Karen, 'Parameters of Economic Reform in North Africa', *Review of African Political Economy*, Vol. 26, No. 82, 1999, pp. 441–454.

Pool, David, 'From Elite to Class: The Transformation of Iraqi Political Leadership', in *The Integration of Modern Iraq*, Abbas Kelidar (ed.), Croom Helm, London, 1979, pp. 63–87.

Principal Bureau of Statistics, *Statistical Abstract 1939*, Baghdad, 1939.

Principal Bureau of Statistics, *Statistical Abstract 1956*, Baghdad, 1957.

Psacharopoulos, George, 'Returns to Education: A Further International Update and Implications', *The Journal of Human Resources*, Vol. 20, No. 4, 1985, pp. 583–604.

PBS Frontline, *The Survival of Saddam*, January 2000, <http://www.pbs.org/wgbh/pages/frontline/shows/saddam>, accessed 10-22-05.

al-Qaysi, Abdul Wahab, *The Impact of Modernization on Iraqi Society During the Ottoman Era*, (PhD. Dissertation), University of Michigan, 1958.

Rassam, Amal, 'Revolution Within the Revolution? Women and the State in Iraq', in *Iraq: The Contemporary State*, Tim Niblock (ed.), Croom Helm, London, 1982, pp. 88–99.

Republic of Iraq, *Al-Munharifun* ('The Deviationists') (in Arabic), Baghdad, 1964.

Richards, Alan and Waterbury, John, *A Political Economy of the Middle East: State, Class, and Economic Development*, Westview Press, Boulder Co, 1990.

Richards, Alan, and John Waterbury, *A Political Economy of the Middle East: State, Class, and Economic Development*, Westview Press, Boulder Co, 1998.

Richards, Donald, 'The Predatory State in Comparative Perspective', Unpublished Working Paper, Economics Department, Indiana State University, 2006.

Roded, Ruth (ed.), *Women in Islam and the Middle East: A Reader*, Introduction, Tauris Publishers, London, 1999.

Rodrik, Dani, 'Getting Interventions Right: How South Korea and Taiwan Grew Rich', *Economic Policy*, Vol. 20, pp. 78–91, April 1995.

Rosenstein-Rodan, Paul, 'Problems of Industrialisation of Eastern and South-Eastern Europe', *Economic Journal*, Vol. 53, June/September 1943, pp. 202–11.

Rosser, Andrew, 'The Political Economy of the Resource Curse: A Literature Survey', Working Paper 268, Institute of Development Studies, University of Sussex, April 2006.

Rostow, W.W., *The Stages of Economic Growth: A Non-Communist Manifesto*, 2nd ed., Cambridge University Press, New York, 1971.

al-Rubaiy, Abdul A. and al-Zubaidy, Khawla F., 'Knowledge Within Reach: Iraq's Response to the Illiteracy Dilemma', *Educational Research Quarterly*, Vol. 12, No. 4, 1990, pp. 53–61.

El Saadawi, Nawal, *The Hidden Face of Eve*, Sherif Hetata (trans.), Zed Books, London, 1980.

al-Saadi, Abbas F., 'Infant Mortality and the Economic Embargo in Iraq', *Population Bulletin of UNESCWA*, No. 44, 1996, pp. 45–66.

Sachs, Jeffrey, 'How to Handle the Macroeconomics of Oil Wealth', in *Escaping the Resource Curse*, Macartan Humphreys, Jeffrey Sachs and Joseph Stiglitz (eds.), Colombia University Press, New York, 2007, pp. 173–93.

Safwa, N. F., *Iraq in the Memoirs of Foreign Diplomats* (in Arabic), Beirut, 1969.

Sassoon, Joseph, *Economic Policy in Iraq 1932-1950*, Frank Cass, London, 1987.

Sen, Amartya, 'Description as Choice', in *Choice, Welfare and Measurement*, Blackwell Publishers, Oxford, 1982.

Sen, Amartya, *Commodities and Capabilities*, North Holland Press, Amsterdam, 1985.

Sen, Amartya, 'Development: Which Way Now?', *The Political Economy of Development and Underdevelopment*, 5th edition, McGraw Hill, 1992, pp. 5–26.

Sen, Amartya, 'Development as Capability Expansion', in *Human Development and the International Development Strategy for the 1990s*, Keith Griffin and John Knight (eds.), Macmillan, London 1990, pp. 41–58.

Sen, Amartya, 'Development Thinking at the Beginning of the XXI Century', in Louis Emmerij (ed.), *Economic and Social Development in the XXI Century*, Inter-American Development Bank, Washington DC, 1997, pp. 531–551.

Sen, Amartya, *Development as Freedom*, Knopf, New York, 1999.

Shikara A., 'Faisal's Ambitions of Leadership in the Fertile Crescent: Aspirations and Constraints', in *The Integration of Modern Iraq*, Abbas Kelidar (ed.), Croom Helm, London, 1979, pp. 32–45.

Schultz, T. Paul and Ayset Tansil, 'Wage and labor supply effects of illness in Cote d'Ivoire and Ghana: Instrumental variable estimates for days disabled', *Journal of Development Economics*, Vol. 53, 1997, pp. 251–285.

Sluglett, Marion Farouk, 'Socialist Iraq 1963-1978 – Towards a Reappraisal', *Orient*, Vol. 23, No. 2, 1982, pp. 206–218.

Sluglett, Marion Farouk and Peter Sluglett, 'Some Reflections on the Sunni/Shi'i Question in Iraq', *British Society for Middle East Studies*, Vol. 5, No. 2, 1978, pp. 78–89.

Sluglett, Marion Farouk and Peter Sluglett, 'Iraqi Ba'thism: Nationalism, Socialism and National Socialism', in *Saddam's Iraq: Revolution or Reaction*, Zed Books, London, 1986, pp. 89–107.

Sluglett, Marion Farouk and Peter Sluglett, *Iraq since 1958*, I. B. Tauris, London, 2003.

Sluglett, Peter, *Britain in Iraq 1914-1932*, Ithaca Press, London, 1976.

Sluglett, Peter, 'The Kurds', in *Saddam's Iraq: Revolution or Reaction,* Zed Books, London, 1986, pp. 177–202.

Sousa, Alya, 'The Eradication of Illiteracy in Iraq', in *Iraq: The Contemporary State*, Tim Niblock (ed.), Croom Helm, London, 1982, pp. 100-108.

Srinavasan, Sharath, 'No Democracy without Justice: Political Freedom in Amartya Sen's Capability Approach', *The Journal of Human Development*, Vol. 8, No. 3, 2007, pp. 457–480.

Stafford, R. S., *The Tragedy of the Assyrians*, Allen and Unwin, London, 1935.

Stevens, Paul, 'Iraqi Oil Policy: 1961-76', in *Iraq: The Contemporary State*, Tim Niblock (ed.), Croom Helm, London, 1982, pp. 168–190.

Stork, Joe, 'Oil and the Penetration of Capitalism in Iraq', in *Oil and Class Struggle*, Petter Nore and Terisa Turner (eds.), Zed Press, London, 1980, pp. 172–198.

Strachey, Ray, *The Cause: A Short History of the Woman's Movement in Great Britain*, Virago Press, London, 1978.

Theobald, Robin and Sa'ad Jawad, 'Problems of Rural Development in an Oil Rich Economy: Iraq 1958-75', in *Iraq: The Contemporary State*, Tim Niblock (ed.), Croom Helm, London, 1982, pp. 191–218.

Tarbush, Mohammad, *The Role of the Military in Politics: A Case Study of Iraq to 1941*, Kegan Paul, London, 1982.

Todaro, Michael P., *Economic Development in the Third World*, Longman, New York, 1985.

Tucker, Judith E., 'The Arab Family in History: "Otherness" and the Study of the

Family', in *Arab Women*, Judith Tucker (ed.), Indiana University Press, Indianapolis, 1984.

Tripp, Charles, *A History of Iraq*, Cambridge University Press, Cambridge UK, 2002.

UN, *Compendium of Social Statistics 1977*, New York, 1977.

UN, *Compendium of Social Statistics and Indicators 1988*, New York, 1991.

UN, *Demographic Yearbook Special Issue: Population Ageing and the Situation of the Elderly*, New York, 1993.

UN, *Yearbook of National Accounts Statistics 1971*, Vol. 1, New York, 1973.

UN, *Yearbook of National Accounts Statistics 1975*, New York, 1976.

UN, *Yearbook of National Accounts Statistics 1979*, New York, 1980.

UN, *National Accounts Statistics: Analysis of Main Aggregates 1985*, New York, 1988.

UN, *National Accounts Statistics: Analysis of Main Aggregates 1987*, New York, 1990.

UN, *National Accounts Statistics: Main Aggregates and Detailed Tables 1984*, New York, 1986.

UN, *National Accounts Statistics: Analysis of Main Aggregates 1988-89*, New York, 1991.

UN, *National Accounts Statistics: Main Aggregates and Detailed Tables 1990*, New York, 1992.

UN, National Accounts Aggregate Database, available at http://unstats.un.org, accessed 07-12-09.

UNDP, *Human Development Report 1991*, Oxford University Press, New York, 1991.

UNDP, *Human Development Report 1994*, Oxford University Press, New York, 1994.

UNDP, *Human Development Report 2000*, Oxford University Press, New York, 2000.

UNDP, *Arab Human Development Report 2003*, National Press, Amman, 2003.

UNESCO, *Basic Facts and Figures 1954*, Paris, 1955.

UNESCO, *Basic Facts and Figures 1958*, Paris, 1959.

UNESCO, *Basic Facts and Figures 1960*, Paris, 1961.

UNESCO, *Statistical Yearbook 1965*, Paris, 1966.

UNESCO, *Statistical Yearbook 1970*, Paris, 1971.

UNESCO, *Statistical Yearbook 1974*, Paris, 1975.

UNESCO, *Statistical Yearbook 1975*, Paris, 1976.

UNESCO, *Statistical Yearbook 1976*, Paris, 1977.

UNESCO, *Statistical Yearbook 1977*, Paris, 1978.

UNESCO, *Statistical Yearbook 1978-9*, Paris, 1980.

UNESCO, *Statistical Yearbook 1982*, Paris, 1982.

UNESCO, *Statistical Yearbook 1984*, Paris, 1985.

UNESCO, *Statistical Yearbook 1985*, Paris, 1985.

UNESCO, *Statistical Yearbook 1986*, Paris, 1986.

UNESCO, *Statistical Yearbook 1988*, Paris, 1988.

UNESCO, *Statistical Yearbook 1990*, Paris, 1990.

UNESCO, *Statistical Yearbook 1992*, Paris, 1992

UNESCO, *Statistical Yearbook 1994*, Paris, 1995.

UNECWA, *Statistical Abstract of the ECWA Region 1970-79*, 4th issue, Beirut, 1981.

UNECWA, *Statistical Abstract of the ECWA Region 1971-80*, 5th edition, Baghdad, 1982.

UNECWA, *Survey of the Economic and Social Developments in the ECWA Region 1983*, Baghdad, 1983.

UNESCWA, *Statistical Abstract of the ESCWA Region 1978-87*, 12th edition, Baghdad, 1989.

UNESCWA, *Unified Arab Statistical Abstract 1980-1988*, Baghdad, 1990.

UNESCWA, *Survey of the Economic and Social Developments in the ESCWA Region*, Amman, 1992.

UNESCWA, *Statistical Abstract of the ESCWA Region 1983-1992*, 14th edition, Amman, 1994.

UNICEF, *The State of the World's Children 1985*, Oxford University Press, New York, 1985.

UNICEF, *The State of the World's Children 1988*, Oxford University Press, New York, 1988.

UNICEF, *The State of the World's Children 1991*, Oxford University Press, New York, 1991.

UNICEF, *The State of the World's Children 1993*, Oxford University Press, New York, 1993.

al-Uzri, Abdul Karim, *The Problematic of Government in Iraq* (in Arabic), London, 1991.

Wiktorowicz, Quintan, 'The Limits of Democracy in the Middle East: The Case of Jordan', *The Middle East Journal*, Vol. 53, No. 4, 1999, pp. 606–620.

Warriner, Doreen, *Land Reform and Development in the Middle East: A Study of Egypt, Syria and Iraq*, Royal Institute of International Affairs, London, 1961.

World Bank, *World Development Report 1978*, Oxford University Press, New York, 1978.

World Bank, *World Development Report 1979,* Oxford University Press, New York, 1979.

World Bank, *World Development Report 1982*, Oxford University Press, New York, 1982.

World Bank, *World Development Report 1984*, Oxford University Press, New York, 1984.

World Bank, *World Development Report 1987,* Oxford University Press, New York, 1987.

World Bank, *World Development Report 1990*, Oxford University Press, New York, 1990.

World Bank, *World Development Report 1992*, Oxford University Press, New York, 1992.

World Bank, *World Development Report 1994*, Oxford University Press, New York, 1994.

World Bank, *Gender and Development in the Middle East and North Africa: Women in the Public Sphere*, Washington DC, 2004.

WHO, *World Health Report 2000*, Geneva, 2000, <http://www.who.int/whr/2000/en/whr00_en.pdf>, accessed 7-07-05.

Workman, Thom, *The Social Origins of the Iran-Iraq War*, Lynne Rienner Publishers, London, 1994.

Yousef, Tarik, M., 'Development, Growth and Policy Reform in the Middle East and North Africa', *Journal of Economic Perspectives*, Vol. 18, No. 3, Summer 2004, pp. 91–115.

Yousif, Abdul-Salaam, 'The Struggle for Cultural Hegemony During The Iraqi Revolution', in *The Iraqi Revolution of 1958*, Robert A. Fernea and Roger Louis (eds.), Tauris Publishers, London 1991, pp. 172–196.

Yousif, Bassam, 'Development and Political Violence in Iraq, 1950-1990', PhD dissertation, UC Riverside, 2001.

Yousif, Bassam, 'Non-renewable resource depletion and reinvestment: issues and evidence for an oil-exporting country', *Environment and Development Economics*, Vol. 14, No 2, April 2009, pp. 211–226.

Yousif, Bassam, 'The Political Economy of Sectarianism in Iraq, *International Journal of Contemporary Iraqi Studies*, Vol. 4, No. 3, 2011, pp. 357–367.

Yousif, Bassam, and Eric Davis, 'Iraq: Understanding Autocracy, Oil and Conflict in a Historical and Socio-Political Context', with Eric Davis, in *Democracy in the Arab World: Explaining the Deficit*, Ibrahim al-Badawi and Samir Makdisi (eds.), Routledge, 2011, pp. 227–253.

Zaher, U., 'The Opposition', in *Saddam's Iraq: Revolution or Reaction,* Zed Books, London, 1986, pp. 138–176.

Zaher, U., 'Political Developments in Iraq 1963-1980', in *Saddam's Iraq: Revolution or Reaction,* Zed Books, London, 1986, pp. 30–53.

Zainy, Mohamed, *The Iraqi Economy Under the Regime of Saddam Hussein*, (in Arabic), al-Rafid, London, 1996.

Zakaria, Fareed, 'Culture Is Destiny: A Conversation with Lee Kuan Yew', *Foreign Affairs*, Vol. 73, 1994, pp. 109–126.

Zubaida, Sami, 'Democracy, Iraq and the middle east', *Open Democracy*, 2005. <http://www.opendemocracy.net/democracy-opening/iraq_3042.jsp>, accessed 11-22-10.

Zuhur, Sherifa, 'Women and Empowerment in the Arab World', *Arab Studies Quarterly*, Vol. 25, No. 4, Fall 2003, pp. 17–38.

Index

Added to the page reference 't' denotes a table

For Product Safety Concerns and Information please contact our EU
representative GPSR@taylorandfrancis.com
Taylor & Francis Verlag GmbH, Kaufingerstraße 24, 80331 München, Germany

www.ingramcontent.com/pod-product-compliance
Ingram Content Group UK Ltd.
Pitfield, Milton Keynes, MK11 3LW, UK
UKHW020956180425
457613UK00019B/707